European Union E-Commerce Law

A project of

Stanford-Vienna Transatlantic Technology Law Forum
(A joint venture of Stanford Law School and
the University of Vienna School of Law)

Forum on Contemporary Europe/Freeman Spogli Institute for
International Studies, Stanford University

Stanford Center for E-Commerce

European Union E-Commerce Law
Consolidated Legislation

Edited by
Siegfried Fina

Stanford Law Books
An imprint of Stanford University Press
Stanford, California

© 2008 MANZ'sche Verlags- und Universitätsbuchhandlung GmbH, Wien.

Published in the USA by
Stanford University Press
Stanford, California

ISBN 978-0-8047-6035-5

Library of Congress Cataloging-in-Publication Data
    European Union e-commerce law : consolidated legislation / edited by Siegfried Fina.
        p. cm.
    "A project of Stanford-Vienna Transatlantic Technology Law Forum (a joint venture of Stanford Law School and the University of Vienna School of Law), Forum on Contemporary Europe/Freeman Spogli Institute for International Studies, Stanford University, [and] Stanford Center for E-Commerce."
    ISBN 978-0-8047-6035-5 (pbk. : alk. paper)
    1. Electronic commerce—Law and legislation—European Union countries. I. Fina, Siegfried. II. Stanford-Vienna Transatlantic Technology Law Forum. III. Forum on Contemporary Europe. IV. Stanford Center for E-Commerce.
KJE959.5.C65E97   2008
343.2409'944—dc22   2008016287

Published simultaneously in Austria by
MANZ'sche Verlags- und Universitätsbuchhandlung
Johannesgasse 23
1010 Vienna, Austria
www.manz.at

Printed in the United States of America on acid-free, archival-quality paper

Preface

This volume focuses on the legal framework of the European Union for online business activities in Europe. The purpose of this project was to collect the most relevant EU legislation pertaining to online business activities in Europe and to publish it in consolidated form. The legal texts of this collection were printed as published in the Official Journal of the European Union and reflect the relevant EU law as of February 1, 2008. The collection is structured by subject areas. This will make it easier to find the relevant legislation for each topic.

Although this collection covers the most relevant EU legislation for e-commerce activities, at least from the editor's perspective, more specific EU legislation in this field can be found on the EU Information Technology Law webpage of the Stanford-Vienna Transatlantic Technology Law Forum at http://www.law.stanford.edu/program/centers/ttlf/law/eu/it/.

This collection is a joint project of the Stanford-Vienna Transatlantic Technology Law Forum (a joint venture of Stanford Law School and the University of Vienna School of Law), the Stanford Center for E-Commerce, and Stanford University's Forum on Contemporary Europe at the Freeman Spogli Institute for International Studies, in cooperation with the Danube University Krems Department of European Integration and Business Law and the Lower Austria Research Institute of European and International Technology Law. In addition, this is also a transatlantic collaborative project of Manz Publishing Company, which distributes this volume in Europe (except UK), and Stanford University Press, which distributes this volume in the U. S. and some other English speaking countries.

Lastly, I would like to thank Alinda Berisha and Ulrike Haider-Moser, who supported the electronic editing of the consolidated legal texts and the proofreading.

Stanford/Vienna, June 2008   *Siegfried Fina*

Contents

Number

E-Commerce
1   E-Commerce Directive (Directive 2000/31/EC)

Consumer Protection
2   Distance Selling Directive (Directive 97/7/EC)
3   Distance Selling Directive for Financial Services (Directive 2002/65/EC)

E-Signatures
4   E-Signature Directive (Directive 1999/93/EC)

Copyright
5   Information Society Copyright Directive (Directive 2001/29/EC)
6   Database Directive (Directive 96/9/EC)
7   Software Copyright Directive (Directive 91/250/EC)

Conditional Access
8   Conditional Access Directive (Directive 98/84/EC)

E-Money
9   E-Money Directive (Directive 2000/46/EC)

Domain Names
10   2002 ".eu" Domain Name Regulation (Regulation (EC) 733/2002)
11   2004 ".eu" Domain Name Regulation (Regulation (EC) 874/2004)

Privacy/Data Protection
12   Directive on Privacy and Electronic Communications (Directive 2002/58/EC)
13   Data Retention Directive (Directive 2006/24/EC)
14   Data Protection Directive (Directive 95/46/EC)
15   2001 Standard Contractual Clauses for the Transfer of Personal Data to Non-EU Member States (Commission Decision 2001/497/EC)
16   2002 Standard Contractual Clauses for the Transfer of Personal Data to Processors Established in Non-EU Member States (Commission Decision 2002/16/EC)

V

Contents

Applicable Contract Law

17 Convention on the Law Applicable to Contractual Obligations
(Rome Convention)

Jurisdiction

18 Jurisdiction and Enforcement Regulation (Regulation (EC) 44/2001)

1

E-Commerce Directive
Directive 2000/31/EC of the European Parliament and of the Council of 8 June 2000 on certain legal aspects of information society services, in particular electronic commerce, in the Internal Market (Directive on electronic commerce)

OJ L 178, 17. 7. 2000, p. 1

THE EUROPEAN PARLIAMENT AND THE COUNCIL OF THE EUROPEAN UNION,

Having regard to the Treaty establishing the European Community, and in particular Articles 47(2), 55 and 95 thereof,

Having regard to the proposal from the Commission[1]),

Having regard to the opinion of the Economic and Social Committee[2]),

Acting in accordance with the procedure laid down in Article 251 of the Treaty[3]),

Whereas:

(1) The European Union is seeking to forge ever closer links between the States and peoples of Europe, to ensure economic and social progress; in accordance with Article 14(2) of the Treaty, the internal market comprises an area without internal frontiers in which the free movements of goods, services and the freedom of establishment are ensured; the development of information society services within the area without internal frontiers is vital to eliminating the barriers which divide the European peoples.

(2) The development of electronic commerce within the information society offers significant employment opportunities in the Community, particularly in small and medium-sized enterprises, and will stimulate economic growth and investment in innovation by European companies, and can also enhance the competitiveness of European industry, provided that everyone has access to the Internet.

(3) Community law and the characteristics of the Community legal order are a vital asset to enable European citizens and operators to take full advantage, without consideration of borders, of the opportunities afforded by electronic commerce; this Directive therefore has the purpose of ensuring a high level of Community legal integration in order to establish a real area without internal borders for information society services.

---

[1]) OJ C 30, 5. 2. 1999, p. 4.
[2]) OJ C 169, 16. 6. 1999, p. 36.
[3]) Opinion of the European Parliament of 6 May 1999 (OJ C 279, 1. 10. 1999, p. 389), Council common position of 28 February 2000 (OJ C 128, 8. 5. 2000, p. 32) and Decision of the European Parliament of 4 May 2000 (not yet published in the Official Journal).

1

(4) It is important to ensure that electronic commerce could fully benefit from the internal market and therefore that, as with Council Directive 89/552/EEC of 3 October 1989 on the coordination of certain provisions laid down by law, regulation or administrative action in Member States concerning the pursuit of television broadcasting activities[4]), a high level of Community integration is achieved.

(5) The development of information society services within the Community is hampered by a number of legal obstacles to the proper functioning of the internal market which make less attractive the exercise of the freedom of establishment and the freedom to provide services; these obstacles arise from divergences in legislation and from the legal uncertainty as to which national rules apply to such services; in the absence of coordination and adjustment of legislation in the relevant areas, obstacles might be justified in the light of the case-law of the Court of Justice of the European Communities; legal uncertainty exists with regard to the extent to which Member States may control services originating from another Member State.

(6) In the light of Community objectives, of Articles 43 and 49 of the Treaty and of secondary Community law, these obstacles should be eliminated by coordinating certain national laws and by clarifying certain legal concepts at Community level to the extent necessary for the proper functioning of the internal market; by dealing only with certain specific matters which give rise to problems for the internal market, this Directive is fully consistent with the need to respect the principle of subsidiarity as set out in Article 5 of the Treaty.

(7) In order to ensure legal certainty and consumer confidence, this Directive must lay down a clear and general framework to cover certain legal aspects of electronic commerce in the internal market.

(8) The objective of this Directive is to create a legal framework to ensure the free movement of information society services between Member States and not to harmonise the field of criminal law as such.

(9) The free movement of information society services can in many cases be a specific reflection in Community law of a more general principle, namely freedom of expression as enshrined in Article 10(1) of the Convention for the Protection of Human Rights and Fundamental Freedoms, which has been ratified by all the Member States; for this reason, directives covering the supply of information society services must ensure that this activity may be engaged in freely in the light of that Article, subject only to the restrictions laid down in paragraph 2 of that Article and in Article 46(1) of the Treaty; this Directive is not intended to affect national fundamental rules and principles relating to freedom of expression.

(10) In accordance with the principle of proportionality, the measures provided for in this Directive are strictly limited to the minimum needed to achieve the objective of the proper functioning of the internal market; where action at Community level is necessary, and in order to guarantee an area which is truly without internal frontiers as far as electronic commerce is concerned, the Directive must ensure a high level of protection of objectives

---

[4]) OJ L 298, 17. 10. 1989, p. 23. Directive as amended by Directive 97/36/EC of the European Parliament and of the Council (OJ L 202, 30. 7. 1997, p. 60).

of general interest, in particular the protection of minors and human dignity, consumer protection and the protection of public health; according to Article 152 of the Treaty, the protection of public health is an essential component of other Community policies.

(11) This Directive is without prejudice to the level of protection for, in particular, public health and consumer interests, as established by Community acts; amongst others, Council Directive 93/13/EEC of 5 April 1993 on unfair terms in consumer contracts[5]) and Directive 97/7/EC of the European Parliament and of the Council of 20 May 1997 on the protection of consumers in respect of distance contracts[6]) form a vital element for protecting consumers in contractual matters; those Directives also apply in their entirety to information society services; that same Community acquis, which is fully applicable to information society services, also embraces in particular Council Directive 84/450/EEC of 10 September 1984 concerning misleading and comparative advertising[7]), Council Directive 87/102/EEC of 22 December 1986 for the approximation of the laws, regulations and administrative provisions of the Member States concerning consumer credit[8]), Council Directive 93/22/EEC of 10 May 1993 on investment services in the securities field[9]), Council Direc-

tive 90/314/EEC of 13 June 1990 on package travel, package holidays and package tours[10]), Directive 98/6/EC of the European Parliament and of the Council of 16 February 1998 on consumer production in the indication of prices of products offered to consumers[11]), Council Directive 92/59/EEC of 29 June 1992 on general product safety[12]), Directive 94/47/EC of the European Parliament and of the Council of 26 October 1994 on the protection of purchasers in respect of certain aspects on contracts relating to the purchase of the right to use immovable properties on a timeshare basis[13]), Directive 98/27/EC of the European Parliament and of the Council of 19 May 1998 on injunctions for the protection of consumers' interests[14]), Council Directive 85/374/EEC of 25 July 1985 on the approximation of the laws, regulations and administrative provisions concerning liability for defective products[15]), Directive 1999/44/EC of the European Parliament and of the Council of 25 May 1999 on certain aspects of the sale of consumer goods and associated guarantees[16]), the future Directive of the European Parliament and of the Council concerning the distance marketing of consumer financial services and Council Directive 92/28/EEC of 31 March 1992 on the advertising of

---

[5]) OJ L 95, 21. 4. 1993, p. 29.

[6]) OJ L 144, 4. 6. 1999, p. 19.

[7]) OJ L 250, 19. 9. 1984, p. 17. Directive as amended by Directive 97/55/EC of the European Parliament and of the Council (OJ L 290, 23. 10. 1997, p. 18).

[8]) OJ L 42, 12. 2. 1987, p. 48. Directive as last amended by Directive 98/7/EC of the European Parliament and of the Council (OJ L 101, 1. 4. 1998, p. 17).

[9]) OJ L 141, 11. 6. 1993, p. 27. Directive as last amended by Directive 97/9/EC of the

European Parliament and of the Council (OJ L 84, 26. 3. 1997, p. 22).

[10]) OJ L 158, 23. 6. 1990, p. 59.

[11]) OJ L 80, 18. 3. 1998, p. 27.

[12]) OJ L 228, 11. 8. 1992, p. 24.

[13]) OJ L 280, 29. 10. 1994, p. 83.

[14]) OJ L 166, 11. 6. 1998, p. 51. Directive as amended by Directive 1999/44/EC (OJ L 171, 7. 7. 1999, p. 12).

[15]) OJ L 210, 7. 8. 1985, p. 29. Directive as amended by Directive 1999/34/EC (OJ L 141, 4. 6. 1999, p. 20).

[16]) OJ L 171, 7. 7. 1999, p. 12.

1

medicinal products[17]); this Directive should be without prejudice to Directive 98/43/EC of the European Parliament and of the Council of 6 July 1998 on the approximation of the laws, regulations and administrative provisions of the Member States relating to the advertising and sponsorship of tobacco products[18]) adopted within the framework of the internal market, or to directives on the protection of public health; this Directive complements information requirements established by the abovementioned Directives and in particular Directive 97/7/EC.

(12) It is necessary to exclude certain activities from the scope of this Directive, on the grounds that the freedom to provide services in these fields cannot, at this stage, be guaranteed under the Treaty or existing secondary legislation; excluding these activities does not preclude any instruments which might prove necessary for the proper functioning of the internal market; taxation, particularly value added tax imposed on a large number of the services covered by this Directive, must be excluded form the scope of this Directive.

(13) This Directive does not aim to establish rules on fiscal obligations nor does it pre-empt the drawing up of Community instruments concerning fiscal aspects of electronic commerce.

(14) The protection of individuals with regard to the processing of personal data is solely governed by Directive 95/46/EC of the European Parliament and of the Council of 24 October 1995 on the protection of individuals with regard to the processing of personal data and on the free movement of such data[19]) and Directive 97/66/EC of the European Parliament and of the Council of 15 December 1997 concerning the processing of personal data and the protection of privacy in the telecommunications sector[20]) which are fully applicable to information society services; these Directives already establish a Community legal framework in the field of personal data and therefore it is not necessary to cover this issue in this Directive in order to ensure the smooth functioning of the internal market, in particular the free movement of personal data between Member States; the implementation and application of this Directive should be made in full compliance with the principles relating to the protection of personal data, in particular as regards unsolicited commercial communication and the liability of intermediaries; this Directive cannot prevent the anonymous use of open networks such as the Internet.

(15) The confidentiality of communications is guaranteed by Article 5 Directive 97/66/EC; in accordance with that Directive, Member States must prohibit any kind of interception or surveillance of such communications by others than the senders and receivers, except when legally authorised.

(16) The exclusion of gambling activities from the scope of application of this Directive covers only games of chance, lotteries and betting transactions, which involve wagering a stake with monetary value; this does not cover promotional competitions or games where the purpose is to encourage the sale of goods or services and where payments, if they arise, serve

---

[17]) OJ L 113, 30. 4. 1992, p. 13.
[18]) OJ L 213, 30. 7. 1998, p. 9.

[19]) OJ L 281, 23. 11. 1995, p. 31.
[20]) OJ L 24, 30. 1. 1998, p. 1.

only to acquire the promoted goods or services.

(17) The definition of information society services already exists in Community law in Directive 98/34/EC of the European Parliament and of the Council of 22 June 1998 laying down a procedure for the provision of information in the field of technical standards and regulations and of rules on information society services[21]) and in Directive 98/84/EC of the European Parliament and of the Council of 20 November 1998 on the legal protection of services based on, or consisting of, conditional access[22]); this definition covers any service normally provided for remuneration, at a distance, by means of electronic equipment for the processing (including digital compression) and storage of data, and at the individual request of a recipient of a service; those services referred to in the indicative list in Annex V to Directive 98/34/EC which do not imply data processing and storage are not covered by this definition.

(18) Information society services span a wide range of economic activities which take place on-line; these activities can, in particular, consist of selling goods on-line; activities such as the delivery of goods as such or the provision of services off-line are not covered; information society services are not solely restricted to services giving rise to on-line contracting but also, in so far as they represent an economic activity, extend to services which are not remunerated by those who receive them, such as those offering on-line information or commercial communications, or those providing tools allowing for search, access and retrieval of data; information society services also include services consisting of the transmission of information via a communication network, in providing access to a communication network or in hosting information provided by a recipient of the service; television broadcasting within the meaning of Directive EEC/ 89/552 and radio broadcasting are not information society services because they are not provided at individual request; by contrast, services which are transmitted point to point, such as video-on-demand or the provision of commercial communications by electronic mail are information society services; the use of electronic mail or equivalent individual communications for instance by natural persons acting outside their trade, business or profession including their use for the conclusion of contracts between such persons is not an information society service; the contractual relationship between an employee and his employer is not an information society service; activities which by their very nature cannot be carried out at a distance and by electronic means, such as the statutory auditing of company accounts or medical advice requiring the physical examination of a patient are not information society services.

(19) The place at which a service provider is established should be determined in conformity with the case-law of the Court of Justice according to which the concept of establishment involves the actual pursuit of an economic activity through a fixed establishment for an indefinite period; this requirement is also fulfilled where a company is constituted for a given period; the place of establishment of a company providing services via an Internet

---

[21]) OJ L 204, 21. 7. 1998, p. 37. Directive as amended by Directive 98/48/EC (OJ L 217, 5. 8. 1998, p. 18).

[22]) OJ L 320, 28. 11. 1998, p. 54.

1

website is not the place at which the technology supporting its website is located or the place at which its website is accessible but the place where it pursues its economic activity; in cases where a provider has several places of establishment it is important to determine from which place of establishment the service concerned is provided; in cases where it is difficult to determine from which of several places of establishment a given service is provided, this is the place where the provider has the centre of his activities relating to this particular service.

(20) The definition of "recipient of a service" covers all types of usage of information society services, both by persons who provide information on open networks such as the Internet and by persons who seek information on the Internet for private or professional reasons.

(21) The scope of the coordinated field is without prejudice to future Community harmonisation relating to information society services and to future legislation adopted at national level in accordance with Community law; the coordinated field covers only requirements relating to on-line activities such as on-line information, on-line advertising, on-line shopping, on-line contracting and does not concern Member States' legal requirements relating to goods such as safety standards, labelling obligations, or liability for goods, or Member States' requirements relating to the delivery or the transport of goods, including the distribution of medicinal products; the coordinated field does not cover the exercise of rights of pre-emption by public authorities concerning certain goods such as works of art.

(22) Information society services should be supervised at the source of the activity, in order to ensure an effective protection of public interest objectives; to that end, it is necessary to ensure that the competent authority provides such protection not only for the citizens of its own country but for all Community citizens; in order to improve mutual trust between Member States, it is essential to state clearly this responsibility on the part of the Member State where the services originate; moreover, in order to effectively guarantee freedom to provide services and legal certainty for suppliers and recipients of services, such information society services should in principle be subject to the law of the Member State in which the service provider is established.

(23) This Directive neither aims to establish additional rules on private international law relating to conflicts of law nor does it deal with the jurisdiction of Courts; provisions of the applicable law designated by rules of private international law must not restrict the freedom to provide information society services as established in this Directive.

(24) In the context of this Directive, notwithstanding the rule on the control at source of information society services, it is legitimate under the conditions established in this Directive for Member States to take measures to restrict the free movement of information society services.

(25) National courts, including civil courts, dealing with private law disputes can take measures to derogate from the freedom to provide information society services in conformity with conditions established in this Directive.

(26) Member States, in conformity with conditions established in this Directive, may apply their national rules on criminal law and criminal proceedings with a view to taking all investi-

gative and other measures necessary for the detection and prosecution of criminal offences, without there being a need to notify such measures to the Commission.

(27) This Directive, together with the future Directive of the European Parliament and of the Council concerning the distance marketing of consumer financial services, contributes to the creating of a legal framework for the on-line provision of financial services; this Directive does not pre-empt future initiatives in the area of financial services in particular with regard to the harmonisation of rules of conduct in this field; the possibility for Member States, established in this Directive, under certain circumstances of restricting the freedom to provide information society services in order to protect consumers also covers measures in the area of financial services in particular measures aiming at protecting investors.

(28) The Member States' obligation not to subject access to the activity of an information society service provider to prior authorisation does not concern postal services covered by Directive 97/67/EC of the European Parliament and of the Council of 15 December 1997 on common rules for the development of the internal market of Community postal services and the improvement of quality of service[23]) consisting of the physical delivery of a printed electronic mail message and does not affect voluntary accreditation systems, in particular for providers of electronic signature certification service.

(29) Commercial communications are essential for the financing of information society services and for de-

veloping a wide variety of new, charge-free services; in the interests of consumer protection and fair trading, commercial communications, including discounts, promotional offers and promotional competitions or games, must meet a number of transparency requirements; these requirements are without prejudice to Directive 97/7/EC; this Directive should not affect existing Directives on commercial communications, in particular Directive 98/43/EC.

(30) The sending of unsolicited commercial communications by electronic mail may be undesirable for consumers and information society service providers and may disrupt the smooth functioning of interactive networks; the question of consent by recipient of certain forms of unsolicited commercial communications is not addressed by this Directive, but has already been addressed, in particular, by Directive 97/7/EC and by Directive 97/66/EC; in Member States which authorise unsolicited commercial communications by electronic mail, the setting up of appropriate industry filtering initiatives should be encouraged and facilitated; in addition it is necessary that in any event unsolicited commercial communities are clearly identifiable as such in order to improve transparency and to facilitate the functioning of such industry initiatives; unsolicited commercial communications by electronic mail should not result in additional communication costs for the recipient.

(31) Member States which allow the sending of unsolicited commercial communications by electronic mail without prior consent of the recipient by service providers established in their territory have to ensure that the service providers consult regularly and respect the opt-out registers in which natural persons not wishing to receive such

---

[23]) OJ L 15, 21. 1. 1998, p. 14.

commercial communications can register themselves.

(32) In order to remove barriers to the development of cross-border services within the Community which members of the regulated professions might offer on the Internet, it is necessary that compliance be guaranteed at Community level with professional rules aiming, in particular, to protect consumers or public health; codes of conduct at Community level would be the best means of determining the rules on professional ethics applicable to commercial communication; the drawing-up or, where appropriate, the adaptation of such rules should be encouraged without prejudice to the autonomy of professional bodies and associations.

(33) This Directive complements Community law and national law relating to regulated professions maintaining a coherent set of applicable rules in this field.

(34) Each Member State is to amend its legislation containing requirements, and in particular requirements as to form, which are likely to curb the use of contracts by electronic means; the examination of the legislation requiring such adjustment should be systematic and should cover all the necessary stages and acts of the contractual process, including the filing of the contract; the result of this amendment should be to make contracts concluded electronically workable; the legal effect of electronic signatures is dealt with by Directive 1999/93/EC of the European Parliament and of the Council of 13 December 1999 on a Community framework for electronic signatures[24]); the acknowledgement of receipt by a service provider may take the form of the on-line provision of the service paid for.

(35) This Directive does not affect Member States' possibility of maintaining or establishing general or specific legal requirements for contracts which can be fulfilled by electronic means, in particular requirements concerning secure electronic signatures.

(36) Member States may maintain restrictions for the use of electronic contracts with regard to contracts requiring by law the involvement of courts, public authorities, or professions exercising public authority; this possibility also covers contracts which require the involvement of courts, public authorities, or professions exercising public authority in order to have an effect with regard to third parties as well as contracts requiring by law certification or attestation by a notary.

(37) Member States' obligation to remove obstacles to the use of electronic contracts concerns only obstacles resulting from legal requirements and not practical obstacles resulting from the impossibility of using electronic means in certain cases.

(38) Member States' obligation to remove obstacles to the use of electronic contracts is to be implemented in conformity with legal requirements for contracts enshrined in Community law.

(39) The exceptions to the provisions concerning the contracts concluded exclusively by electronic mail or by equivalent individual communications provided for by this Directive, in relation to information to be provided and the placing of orders, should not enable, as a result, the by-passing of those provisions by providers of information society services.

---

[24]) OJ L 13, 19. 1. 2000, p. 12.

1

(40) Both existing and emerging disparities in Member States' legislation and case-law concerning liability of service providers acting as intermediaries prevent the smooth functioning of the internal market, in particular by impairing the development of cross-border services and producing distortions of competition; service providers have a duty to act, under certain circumstances, with a view to preventing or stopping illegal activities; this Directive should constitute the appropriate basis for the development of rapid and reliable procedures for removing and disabling access to illegal information; such mechanisms could be developed on the basis of voluntary agreements between all parties concerned and should be encouraged by Member States; it is in the interest of all parties involved in the provision of information society services to adopt and implement such procedures; the provisions of this Directive relating to liability should not preclude the development and effective operation, by the different interested parties, of technical systems of protection and identification and of technical surveillance instruments made possible by digital technology within the limits laid down by Directives 95/46/EC and 97/66/EC.

(41) This Directive strikes a balance between the different interests at stake and establishes principles upon which industry agreements and standards can be based.

(42) The exemptions from liability established in this Directive cover only cases where the activity of the information society service provider is limited to the technical process of operating and giving access to a communication network over which information made available by third parties is transmitted or temporarily stored, for the sole pur-

pose of making the transmission more efficient; this activity is of a mere technical, automatic and passive nature, which implies that the information society service provider has neither knowledge of nor control over the information which is transmitted or stored.

(43) A service provider can benefit from the exemptions for 'mere conduit' and for 'caching' when he is in no way involved with the information transmitted; this requires among other things that he does not modify the information that he transmits; this requirement does not cover manipulations of a technical nature which take place in the course of the transmission as they do not alter the integrity of the information contained in the transmission.

(44) A service provider who deliberately collaborates with one of the recipients of his service in order to undertake illegal acts goes beyond the activities of 'mere conduit' or 'caching' and as a result cannot benefit from the liability exemptions established for these activities.

(45) The limitations of the liability of intermediary service providers established in this Directive do not affect the possibility of injunctions of different kinds; such injunctions can in particular consist of orders by courts or administrative authorities requiring the termination or prevention of any infringement, including the removal of illegal information or the disabling of access to it.

(46) In order to benefit from a limitation of liability, the provider of an information society service, consisting of the storage of information, upon obtaining actual knowledge or awareness of illegal activities has to act expeditiously to remove or to disable access to

the information concerned; the removal or disabling of access has to be undertaken in the observance of the principle of freedom of expression and of procedures established for this purpose at national level; this Directive does not affect Member States' possibility of establishing specific requirements which must be fulfilled expeditiously prior to the removal or disabling of information.

(47) Member States are prevented from imposing a monitoring obligation on service providers only with respect to obligations of a general nature; this does not concern monitoring obligations in a specific case and, in particular, does not affect orders by national authorities in accordance with national legislation.

(48) This Directive does not affect the possibility for Member States of requiring service providers, who host information provided by recipients of their service, to apply duties of care, which can reasonably be expected from them and which are specified by national law, in order to detect and prevent certain types of illegal activities.

(49) Member States and the Commission are to encourage the drawing-up of codes of conduct; this is not to impair the voluntary nature of such codes and the possibility for interested parties of deciding freely whether to adhere to such codes.

(50) It is important that the proposed directive on the harmonisation of certain aspects of copyright and related rights in the information society and this Directive come into force within a similar time scale with a view to establishing a clear framework of rules relevant to the issue of liability of intermediaries for copyright and relating rights infringements at Community level.

(51) Each Member State should be required, where necessary, to amend any legislation which is liable to hamper the use of schemes for the out-of-court settlement of disputes through electronic channels; the result of this amendment must be to make the functioning of such schemes genuinely and effectively possible in law and in practice, even across borders.

(52) The effective exercise of the freedoms of the internal market makes it necessary to guarantee victims effective access to means of settling disputes; damage which may arise in connection with information society services is characterised both by its rapidity and by its geographical extent; in view of this specific character and the need to ensure that national authorities do not endanger the mutual confidence which they should have in one another, this Directive requests Member States to ensure that appropriate court actions are available; Member States should examine the need to provide access to judicial procedures by appropriate electronic means.

(53) Directive 98/27/EC, which is applicable to information society services, provides a mechanism relating to actions for an injunction aimed at the protection of the collective interests of consumers; this mechanism will contribute to the free movement of information society services by ensuring a high level of consumer protection.

(54) The sanctions provided for under this Directive are without prejudice to any other sanction or remedy provided under national law; Member States are not obliged to provide criminal sanctions for infringement of national provisions adopted pursuant to this Directive.

(55) This Directive does not affect the law applicable to contractual obli-

gations relating to consumer contracts; accordingly, this Directive cannot have the result of depriving the consumer of the protection afforded to him by the mandatory rules relating to contractual obligations of the law of the Member State in which he has his habitual residence.

(56) As regards the derogation contained in this Directive regarding contractual obligations concerning contracts concluded by consumers, those obligations should be interpreted as including information on the essential elements of the content of the contract, including consumer rights, which have a determining influence on the decision to contract.

(57) The Court of Justice has consistently held that a Member State retains the right to take measures against a service provider that is established in another Member State but directs all or most of his activity to the territory of the first Member State if the choice of establishment was made with a view to evading the legislation that would have applied to the provider had he been established on the territory of the first Member State.

(58) This Directive should not apply to services supplied by service providers established in a third country; in view of the global dimension of electronic commerce, it is, however, appropriate to ensure that the Community rules are consistent with international rules; this Directive is without prejudice to the results of discussions within international organisations (amongst others WTO, OECD, Uncitral) on legal issues.

(59) Despite the global nature of electronic communications, coordination of national regulatory measures at European Union level is necessary in order to avoid fragmentation of the internal market, and for the establishment of an appropriate European regulatory framework; such coordination should also contribute to the establishment of a common and strong negotiating position in international forums.

(60) In order to allow the unhampered development of electronic commerce, the legal framework must be clear and simple, predictable and consistent with the rules applicable at international level so that it does not adversely affect the competitiveness of European industry or impede innovation in that sector.

(61) If the market is actually to operate by electronic means in the context of globalisation, the European Union and the major non-European areas need to consult each other with a view to making laws and procedures compatible.

(62) Cooperation with third countries should be strengthened in the area of electronic commerce, in particular with applicant countries, the developing countries and the European Union's other trading partners.

(63) The adoption of this Directive will not prevent the Member States from taking into account the various social, societal and cultural implications which are inherent in the advent of the information society; in particular it should not hinder measures which Member States might adopt in conformity with Community law to achieve social, cultural and democratic goals taking into account their linguistic diversity, national and regional specificities as well as their cultural heritage, and to ensure and maintain public access to the widest possible range of information society services; in any case, the development of the information society is to ensure that Community citizens can have access to

the cultural European heritage provided in the digital environment.

(64) Electronic communication offers the Member States an excellent means of providing public services in the cultural, educational and linguistic fields.

(65) The Council, in its resolution of 19 January 1999 on the consumer dimension of the information society[25]), stressed that the protection of consumers deserved special attention in this field; the Commission will examine the degree to which existing consumer protection rules provide insufficient protection in the context of the information society and will identify, where necessary, the deficiencies of this legislation and those issues which could require additional measures; if need be, the Commission should make specific additional proposals to resolve such deficiencies that will thereby have been identified,

HAVE ADOPTED THIS DIRECTIVE:

CHAPTER I
GENERAL PROVISIONS

Article 1
Objective and scope

1. This Directive seeks to contribute to the proper functioning of the internal market by ensuring the free movement of information society services between the Member States.

2. This Directive approximates, to the extent necessary for the achievement of the objective set out in paragraph 1, certain national provisions on information society services relating to the internal market, the establishment of service providers, commercial com-

munications, electronic contracts, the liability of intermediaries, codes of conduct, out-of-court dispute settlements, court actions and cooperation between Member States.

3. This Directive complements Community law applicable to information society services without prejudice to the level of protection for, in particular, public health and consumer interests, as established by Community acts and national legislation implementing them in so far as this does not restrict the freedom to provide information society services.

4. This Directive does not establish additional rules on private international law nor does it deal with the jurisdiction of Courts.

5. This Directive shall not apply to:

(a) the field of taxation;

(b) questions relating to information society services covered by Directives 95/46/EC and 97/66/EC;

(c) questions relating to agreements or practices governed by cartel law;

(d) the following activities of information society services:

– the activities of notaries or equivalent professions to the extent that they involve a direct and specific connection with the exercise of public authority,

– the representation of a client and defence of his interests before the courts,

– gambling activities which involve wagering a stake with monetary value in games of chance, including lotteries and betting transactions.

6. This Directive does not affect measures taken at Community or national level, in the respect of Community law, in order to promote cultural and linguistic diversity and to ensure the defence of pluralism.

---

[25]) OJ C 23, 28. 1. 1999, p. 1.

1

Article 2
Definitions

For the purpose of this Directive, the following terms shall bear the following meanings:

(a) 'information society services': services within the meaning of Article 1(2) of Directive 98/34/EC as amended by Directive 98/48/EC;[26])

---

[26]) *Annotation by the editor:* This provision reads as follows: "2. 'service', any Information Society service, that is to say, any service normally provided for remuneration, at a distance, by electronic means and at the individual request of a recipient of services.

For the purposes of this definition:
– 'at a distance' means that the service is provided without the parties being simultaneously present,
– 'by electronic means' means that the service is sent initially and received at its destination by means of electronic equipment for the processing (including digital compression) and storage of data, and entirely transmitted, conveyed and received by wire, by radio, by optical means or by other electromagnetic means,
– 'at the individual request of a recipient of services' means that the service is provided through the transmission of data on individual request.

An indicative list of services not covered by this definition is set out in Annex V.

This Directive shall not apply to:
– radio broadcasting services,
– television broadcasting services covered by point (a) of Article 1 of Directive 89/552/EEC (*)

(*) OJ L 298, 17. 10. 1989, p. 23. Directive as last amended by Directive 97/36/EC (OJ L 202, 30. 7. 1997, p. 1)."

"ANNEX V

Indicative list of services not covered by the second subparagraph of point 2 of Article 1

1. Services not provided 'at a distance'

Services provided in the physical presence of the provider and the recipient, even if they involve the use of electronic devices

(a) medical examinations or treatment at a doctor's surgery using electronic equipment where the patient is physically present;

(b) 'service provider': any natural or legal person providing an information society service;

(c) 'established service provider': a service provider who effectively pursues an economic activity using a fixed establishment for an indefinite period. The presence and use of the technical

---

(b) consultation of an electronic catalogue in a shop with the customer on site;

(c) plane ticket reservation at a travel agency in the physical presence of the customer by means of a network of computers;

(d) electronic games made available in a video-arcade where the customer is physically present.

2. Services not provided 'by electronic means'

– Services having material content even though provided via electronic devices:

(a) automatic cash or ticket dispensing machines (banknotes, rail tickets);

(b) access to road networks, car parks, etc., charging for use, even if there are electronic devices at the entrance/exit controlling access and/or ensuring correct payment is made,

– Off-line services: distribution of CD roms or software on diskettes,

– Services which are not provided via electronic processing/inventory systems:

(a) voice telephony services;

(b) telefax/telex services;

(c) services provided via voice telephony or fax;

(d) telephone/telefax consultation of a doctor;

(e) telephone/telefax consultation of a lawyer;

(f) telephone/telefax direct marketing.

3. Services not supplied 'at the individual request of a recipient of services'

Services provided by transmitting data without individual demand for simultaneous reception by an unlimited number of individual receivers (point to multipoint transmission):

(a) television broadcasting services (including near-video on-demand services), covered by point (a) of Article 1 of Directive 89/552/EEC;

(b) radio broadcasting services;

(c) (televised) teletext."

1

means and technologies required to provide the service do not, in themselves, constitute an establishment of the provider;

(d) 'recipient of the service': any natural or legal person who, for professional ends or otherwise, uses an information society service, in particular for the purposes of seeking information or making it accessible;

(e) 'consumer': any natural person who is acting for purposes which are outside his or her trade, business or profession;

(f) 'commercial communication': any form of communication designed to promote, directly or indirectly, the goods, services or image of a company, organisation or person pursuing a commercial, industrial or craft activity or exercising a regulated profession. The following do not in themselves constitute commercial communications:

– information allowing direct access to the activity of the company, organisation or person, in particular a domain name or an electronic-mail address,

– communications relating to the goods, services or image of the company, organisation or person compiled in an independent manner, particularly when this is without financial consideration;

(g) 'regulated profession': any profession within the meaning of either Article 1(d) of Council Directive 89/48/ EEC of 21 December 1988 on a general system for the recognition of higher-education diplomas awarded on completion of professional education and training of at least three-years' duration[27]) or of Article 1(f) of Council

Directive 92/51/EEC of 18 June 1992 on a second general system for the recognition of professional education and training to supplement Directive 89/ 48/EEC[28]);

(h) 'coordinated field': requirements laid down in Member States' legal systems applicable to information society service providers or information society services, regardless of whether they are of a general nature or specifically designed for them.

(i) The coordinated field concerns requirements with which the service provider has to comply in respect of:

– the taking up of the activity of an information society service, such as requirements concerning qualifications, authorisation or notification,

– the pursuit of the activity of an information society service, such as requirements concerning the behaviour of the service provider, requirements regarding the quality or content of the service including those applicable to advertising and contracts, or requirements concerning the liability of the service provider;

(ii) The coordinated field does not cover requirements such as:

– requirements applicable to goods as such,

– requirements applicable to the delivery of goods,

– requirements applicable to services not provided by electronic means.

Article 3
Internal market

1. Each Member State shall ensure that the information society services provided by a service provider estab-

---

[27]) OJ L 19, 24. 1. 1989, p. 16.

[28]) OJ L 209, 24. 7. 1992, p. 25. Directive as last amended by Commission Directive 97/38/EC (OJ L 184, 12. 7. 1997, p. 31).

lished on its territory comply with the national provisions applicable in the Member State in question which fall within the coordinated field.

2. Member States may not, for reasons falling within the coordinated field, restrict the freedom to provide information society services from another Member State.

3. Paragraphs 1 and 2 shall not apply to the fields referred to in the Annex.

4. Member States may take measures to derogate from paragraph 2 in respect of a given information society service if the following conditions are fulfilled:

(a) the measures shall be:

(i) necessary for one of the following reasons:

– public policy, in particular the prevention, investigation, detection and prosecution of criminal offences, including the protection of minors and the fight against any incitement to hatred on grounds of race, sex, religion or nationality, and violations of human dignity concerning individual persons,

– the protection of public health,

– public security, including the safeguarding of national security and defence,

– the protection of consumers, including investors;

(ii) taken against a given information society service which prejudices the objectives referred to in point (i) or which presents a serious and grave risk of prejudice to those objectives;

(iii) proportionate to those objectives;

(b) before taking the measures in question and without prejudice to court proceedings, including preliminary proceedings and acts carried out

in the framework of a criminal investigation, the Member State has:

– asked the Member State referred to in paragraph 1 to take measures and the latter did not take such measures, or they were inadequate,

– notified the Commission and the Member State referred to in paragraph 1 of its intention to take such measures.

5. Member States may, in the case of urgency, derogate from the conditions stipulated in paragraph 4(b). Where this is the case, the measures shall be notified in the shortest possible time to the Commission and to the Member State referred to in paragraph 1, indicating the reasons for which the Member State considers that there is urgency.

6. Without prejudice to the Member State's possibility of proceeding with the measures in question, the Commission shall examine the compatibility of the notified measures with Community law in the shortest possible time; where it comes to the conclusion that the measure is incompatible with Community law, the Commission shall ask the Member State in question to refrain from taking any proposed measures or urgently to put an end to the measures in question.

CHAPTER II
PRINCIPLES
Section 1: Establishment and information requirements

Article 4
Principle excluding prior authorisation

1. Member States shall ensure that the taking up and pursuit of the activity of an information society service pro-

vider may not be made subject to prior authorisation or any other requirement having equivalent effect.

2. Paragraph 1 shall be without prejudice to authorisation schemes which are not specifically and exclusively targeted at information society services, or which are covered by Directive 97/13/EC of the European Parliament and of the Council of 10 April 1997 on a common framework for general authorisations and individual licences in the field of telecommunications services[29]).

Article 5
General information to be provided

1. In addition to other information requirements established by Community law, Member States shall ensure that the service provider shall render easily, directly and permanently accessible to the recipients of the service and competent authorities, at least the following information:

(a) the name of the service provider;

(b) the geographic address at which the service provider is established;

(c) the details of the service provider, including his electronic mail address, which allow him to be contacted rapidly and communicated with in a direct and effective manner;

(d) where the service provider is registered in a trade or similar public register, the trade register in which the service provider is entered and his registration number, or equivalent means of identification in that register;

(e) where the activity is subject to an authorisation scheme, the particu-

lars of the relevant supervisory authority;

(f) as concerns the regulated professions:

– any professional body or similar institution with which the service provider is registered,

– the professional title and the Member State where it has been granted,

– a reference to the applicable professional rules in the Member State of establishment and the means to access them;

(g) where the service provider undertakes an activity that is subject to VAT, the identification number referred to in Article 22(1) of the sixth Council Directive 77/388/EEC of 17 May 1977 on the harmonisation of the laws of the Member States relating to turnover taxes – Common system of value added tax: uniform basis of assessment[30]).

2. In addition to other information requirements established by Community law, Member States shall at least ensure that, where information society services refer to prices, these are to be indicated clearly and unambiguously and, in particular, must indicate whether they are inclusive of tax and delivery costs.

Section 2: Commercial communications
Article 6
Information to be provided

In addition to other information requirements established by Community law, Member States shall ensure that

---

[29]) OJ L 117, 7. 5. 1997, p. 15.

[30]) OJ L 145, 13. 6. 1977, p. 1. Directive as last amended by Directive 1999/85/EC (OJ L 277, 28. 10. 1999, p. 34).

commercial communications which are part of, or constitute, an information society service comply at least with the following conditions:

(a) the commercial communication shall be clearly identifiable as such;

(b) the natural or legal person on whose behalf the commercial communication is made shall be clearly identifiable;

(c) promotional offers, such as discounts, premiums and gifts, where permitted in the Member State where the service provider is established, shall be clearly identifiable as such, and the conditions which are to be met to qualify for them shall be easily accessible and be presented clearly and unambiguously;

(d) promotional competitions or games, where permitted in the Member State where the service provider is established, shall be clearly identifiable as such, and the conditions for participation shall be easily accessible and be presented clearly and unambiguously.

Article 7
Unsolicited commercial communication

1. In addition to other requirements established by Community law, Member States which permit unsolicited commercial communication by electronic mail shall ensure that such commercial communication by a service provider established in their territory shall be identifiable clearly and unambiguously as such as soon as it is received by the recipient.

2. Without prejudice to Directive 97/7/EC and Directive 97/66/EC, Member States shall take measures to ensure that service providers undertaking unsolicited commercial communications by electronic mail consult regularly and respect the opt-out registers in which natural persons not wishing to receive such commercial communications can register themselves.

Article 8
Regulated professions

1. Member States shall ensure that the use of commercial communications which are part of, or constitute, an information society service provided by a member of a regulated profession is permitted subject to compliance with the professional rules regarding, in particular, the independence, dignity and honour of the profession, professional secrecy and fairness towards clients and other members of the profession.

2. Without prejudice to the autonomy of professional bodies and associations, Member States and the Commission shall encourage professional associations and bodies to establish codes of conduct at Community level in order to determine the types of information that can be given for the purposes of commercial communication in conformity with the rules referred to in paragraph 1

3. When drawing up proposals for Community initiatives which may become necessary to ensure the proper functioning of the Internal Market with regard to the information referred to in paragraph 2, the Commission shall take due account of codes of conduct applicable at Community level and shall act in close cooperation with the relevant professional associations and bodies.

4. This Directive shall apply in addition to Community Directives concerning access to, and the exercise of, activities of the regulated professions.

Section 3: Contracts concluded by electronic means

Article 9
Treatment of contracts

1. Member States shall ensure that their legal system allows contracts to be concluded by electronic means. Member States shall in particular ensure that the legal requirements applicable to the contractual process neither create obstacles for the use of electronic contracts nor result in such contracts being deprived of legal effectiveness and validity on account of their having been made by electronic means.

2. Member States may lay down that paragraph 1 shall not apply to all or certain contracts falling into one of the following categories:

(a) contracts that create or transfer rights in real estate, except for rental rights;

(b) contracts requiring by law the involvement of courts, public authorities or professions exercising public authority;

(c) contracts of suretyship granted and on collateral securities furnished by persons acting for purposes outside their trade, business or profession;

(d) contracts governed by family law or by the law of succession.

3. Member States shall indicate to the Commission the categories referred to in paragraph 2 to which they do not apply paragraph 1. Member States shall submit to the Commission every five years a report on the application of paragraph 2 explaining the reasons why they consider it necessary to maintain the category referred to in paragraph 2(b) to which they do not apply paragraph 1.

Article 10
Information to be provided

1. In addition to other information requirements established by Community law, Member States shall ensure, except when otherwise agreed by parties who are not consumers, that at least the following information is given by the service provider clearly, comprehensibly and unambiguously and prior to the order being placed by the recipient of the service:

(a) the different technical steps to follow to conclude the contract;

(b) whether or not the concluded contract will be filed by the service provider and whether it will be accessible;

(c) the technical means for identifying and correcting input errors prior to the placing of the order;

(d) the languages offered for the conclusion of the contract.

2. Member States shall ensure that, except when otherwise agreed by parties who are not consumers, the service provider indicates any relevant codes of conduct to which he subscribes and information on how those codes can be consulted electronically.

3. Contract terms and general conditions provided to the recipient must be made available in a way that allows him to store and reproduce them.

4. Paragraphs 1 and 2 shall not apply to contracts concluded exclusively by exchange of electronic mail or by equivalent individual communications.

Article 11
Placing of the order

1. Member States shall ensure, except when otherwise agreed by parties who are not consumers, that in cases where the recipient of the service places

1

his order through technological means, the following principles apply:

– the service provider has to acknowledge the receipt of the recipient's order without undue delay and by electronic means,

– the order and the acknowledgement of receipt are deemed to be received when the parties to whom they are addressed are able to access them.

2. Member States shall ensure that, except when otherwise agreed by parties who are not consumers, the service provider makes available to the recipient of the service appropriate, effective and accessible technical means allowing him to identify and correct input errors, prior to the placing of the order.

3. Paragraph 1, first indent, and paragraph 2 shall not apply to contracts concluded exclusively by exchange of electronic mail or by equivalent individual communications.

Section 4: Liability of intermediary service providers

Article 12
'Mere conduit'

1. Where an information society service is provided that consists of the transmission in a communication network of information provided by a recipient of the service, or the provision of access to a communication network, Member States shall ensure that the service provider is not liable for the information transmitted, on condition that the provider:

(a) does not initiate the transmission;

(b) does not select the receiver of the transmission; and

(c) does not select or modify the information contained in the transmission.

2. The acts of transmission and of provision of access referred to in paragraph 1 include the automatic, intermediate and transient storage of the information transmitted in so far as this takes place for the sole purpose of carrying out the transmission in the communication network, and provided that the information is not stored for any period longer than is reasonably necessary for the transmission.

3. This Article shall not affect the possibility for a court or administrative authority, in accordance with Member States' legal systems, of requiring the service provider to terminate or prevent an infringement.

Article 13
'Caching'

1. Where an information society service is provided that consists of the transmission in a communication network of information provided by a recipient of the service, Member States shall ensure that the service provider is not liable for the automatic, intermediate and temporary storage of that information, performed for the sole purpose of making more efficient the information's onward transmission to other recipients of the service upon their request, on condition that:

(a) the provider does not modify the information;

(b) the provider complies with conditions on access to the information;

(c) the provider complies with rules regarding the updating of the information, specified in a manner widely recognised and used by industry;

(d) the provider does not interfere with the lawful use of technology, widely recognised and used by industry, to obtain data on the use of the information; and

19

1

(e) the provider acts expeditiously to remove or to disable access to the information it has stored upon obtaining actual knowledge of the fact that the information at the initial source of the transmission has been removed from the network, or access to it has been disabled, or that a court or an administrative authority has ordered such removal or disablement.

2. This Article shall not affect the possibility for a court or administrative authority, in accordance with Member States' legal systems, of requiring the service provider to terminate or prevent an infringement.

Article 14
Hosting

1. Where an information society service is provided that consists of the storage of information provided by a recipient of the service, Member States shall ensure that the service provider is not liable for the information stored at the request of a recipient of the service, on condition that:

(a) the provider does not have actual knowledge of illegal activity or information and, as regards claims for damages, is not aware of facts or circumstances from which the illegal activity or information is apparent; or

(b) the provider, upon obtaining such knowledge or awareness, acts expeditiously to remove or to disable access to the information.

2. Paragraph 1 shall not apply when the recipient of the service is acting under the authority or the control of the provider.

3. This Article shall not affect the possibility for a court or administrative authority, in accordance with Member States' legal systems, of requiring the service provider to terminate or pre-

vent an infringement, nor does it affect the possibility for Member States of establishing procedures governing the removal or disabling of access to information.

Article 15
No general obligation to monitor

1. Member States shall not impose a general obligation on providers, when providing the services covered by Articles 12, 13 and 14, to monitor the information which they transmit or store, nor a general obligation actively to seek facts or circumstances indicating illegal activity.

2. Member States may establish obligations for information society service providers promptly to inform the competent public authorities of alleged illegal activities undertaken or information provided by recipients of their service or obligations to communicate to the competent authorities, at their request, information enabling the identification of recipients of their service with whom they have storage agreements.

CHAPTER III
IMPLEMENTATION

Article 16
Codes of conduct

1. Member States and the Commission shall encourage:

(a) the drawing up of codes of conduct at Community level, by trade, professional and consumer associations or organisations, designed to contribute to the proper implementation of Articles 5 to 15;

(b) the voluntary transmission of draft codes of conduct at national or Community level to the Commission;

1

(c) the accessibility of these codes of conduct in the Community languages by electronic means;

(d) the communication to the Member States and the Commission, by trade, professional and consumer associations or organisations, of their assessment of the application of their codes of conduct and their impact upon practices, habits or customs relating to electronic commerce;

(e) the drawing up of codes of conduct regarding the protection of minors and human dignity.

2. Member States and the Commission shall encourage the involvement of associations or organisations representing consumers in the drafting and implementation of codes of conduct affecting their interests and drawn up in accordance with paragraph 1(a). Where appropriate, to take account of their specific needs, associations representing the visually impaired and disabled should be consulted.

Article 17
Out-of-court dispute settlement

1. Member States shall ensure that, in the event of disagreement between an information society service provider and the recipient of the service, their legislation does not hamper the use of out-of-court schemes, available under national law, for dispute settlement, including appropriate electronic means.

2. Member States shall encourage bodies responsible for the out-of-court settlement of, in particular, consumer disputes to operate in a way which provides adequate procedural guarantees for the parties concerned.

3. Member States shall encourage bodies responsible for out-of-court dispute settlement to inform the Commission of the significant decisions they take regarding information society services and to transmit any other information on the practices, usages or customs relating to electronic commerce.

Article 18
Court actions

1. Member States shall ensure that court actions available under national law concerning information society services' activities allow for the rapid adoption of measures, including interim measures, designed to terminate any alleged infringement and to prevent any further impairment of the interests involved.

2. The Annex to Directive 98/27/EC shall be supplemented as follows:

"11. Directive 2000/31/EC of the European Parliament and of the Council of 8 June 2000 on certain legal aspects on information society services, in particular electronic commerce, in the internal market (Directive on electronic commerce) (OJ L 178, 17. 7. 2000, p. 1)."

Article 19
Cooperation

1. Member States shall have adequate means of supervision and investigation necessary to implement this Directive effectively and shall ensure that service providers supply them with the requisite information.

2. Member States shall cooperate with other Member States; they shall, to that end, appoint one or several contact points, whose details they shall communicate to the other Member States and to the Commission.

3. Member States shall, as quickly as possible, and in conformity with national law, provide the assistance and information requested by other Member States or by the Commission,

including by appropriate electronic means.

4. Member States shall establish contact points which shall be accessible at least by electronic means and from which recipients and service providers may:

(a) obtain general information on contractual rights and obligations as well as on the complaint and redress mechanisms available in the event of disputes, including practical aspects involved in the use of such mechanisms;

(b) obtain the details of authorities, associations or organisations from which they may obtain further information or practical assistance.

5. Member States shall encourage the communication to the Commission of any significant administrative or judicial decisions taken in their territory regarding disputes relating to information society services and practices, usages and customs relating to electronic commerce. The Commission shall communicate these decisions to the other Member States.

Article 20
Sanctions

Member States shall determine the sanctions applicable to infringements of national provisions adopted pursuant to this Directive and shall take all measures necessary to ensure that they are enforced. The sanctions they provide for shall be effective, proportionate and dissuasive.

CHAPTER IV
FINAL PROVISIONS

Article 21
Re-examination

1. Before 17 July 2003, and thereafter every two years, the Commission shall submit to the European Parliament, the Council and the Economic and Social Committee a report on the application of this Directive, accompanied, where necessary, by proposals for adapting it to legal, technical and economic developments in the field of information society services, in particular with respect to crime prevention, the protection of minors, consumer protection and to the proper functioning of the internal market.

2. In examining the need for an adaptation of this Directive, the report shall in particular analyse the need for proposals concerning the liability of providers of hyperlinks and location tool services, 'notice and take down' procedures and the attribution of liability following the taking down of content. The report shall also analyse the need for additional conditions for the exemption from liability, provided for in Articles 12 and 13, in the light of technical developments, and the possibility of applying the internal market principles to unsolicited commercial communications by electronic mail.

Article 22
Transposition

1. Member States shall bring into force the laws, regulations and administrative provisions necessary to comply with this Directive before 17 January 2002. They shall forthwith inform the Commission thereof.

2. When Member States adopt the measures referred to in paragraph 1, these shall contain a reference to this Directive or shall be accompanied by such reference at the time of their official publication. The methods of making such reference shall be laid down by Member States.

1

Article 23
Entry into force

This Directive shall enter into force on the day of its publication in the Official Journal of the European Communities.

Article 24
Addressees

This Directive is addressed to the Member States.

ANNEX
DEROGATIONS FROM ARTICLE 3

As provided for in Article 3(3), Article 3(1) and (2) do not apply to:

– copyright, neighbouring rights, rights referred to in Directive 87/54/EEC[31]) and Directive 96/9/EC[32]) as well as industrial property rights,

– the emission of electronic money by institutions in respect of which Member States have applied one of the derogations provided for in Article 8(1) of Directive 2000/46/EC[33]),

---

[31]) OJ L 24, 27. 1. 1987, p. 36.
[32]) OJ L 77, 27. 3. 1996, p. 20.
[33]) Not yet published in the Official Journal.

– Article 44(2) of Directive 85/611/EEC[34]),

– Article 30 and Title IV of Directive 92/49/EEC[35]), Title IV of Directive 92/96/EEC[36]), Articles 7 and 8 of Directive 88/357/EEC[37]) and Article 4 of Directive 90/619/EEC[38]),

– the freedom of the parties to choose the law applicable to their contract,

– contractual obligations concerning consumer contacts,

– formal validity of contracts creating or transferring rights in real estate where such contracts are subject to mandatory formal requirements of the law of the Member State where the real estate is situated,

– the permissibility of unsolicited commercial communications by electronic mail.

---

[34]) OJ L 375, 31. 12. 1985, p. 3. Directive as last amended by Directive 95/26/EC (OJ L 168, 18. 7. 1995, p. 7).
[35]) OJ L 228, 11. 8. 1992, p. 1. Directive as last amended by Directive 95/26/EC.
[36]) OJ L 360, 9. 12. 1992, p. 2. Directive as last amended by Directive 95/26/EC.
[37]) OJ L 172, 4. 7. 1988, p. 1. Directive as last amended by Directive 92/49/EC.
[38]) OJ L 330, 29. 11. 1990, p. 50. Directive as last amended by Directive 92/96/EC.

1

2

Distance Selling Directive
Directive 97/7/EC of the European Parliament and of the Council of 20 May 1997 on the protection of consumers in respect of distance contracts

OJ L 144 , 4. 6. 1997, p. 19, amended by OJ L 271, 9. 10. 2002, p. 16, OJ L 149, 11. 6. 2005, p. 22, OJ L 319, 5. 12. 2007, p. 1

THE EUROPEAN PARLIAMENT AND THE COUNCIL OF THE EUROPEAN UNION,

Having regard to the Treaty establishing the European Community, and in particular Article 100a thereof,

Having regard to the proposal from the Commission[1]),

Having regard to the opinion of the Economic and Social Committee [2]),

Acting in accordance with the procedure laid down in Article 189b of the Treaty [3]), in the light of the joint text approved by the Conciliation Committee on 27 November 1996,

(1) Whereas, in connection with the attainment of the aims of the internal market, measures must be taken for the gradual consolidation of that market;

---

[1]) OJ No C 156, 23. 6. 1992, p. 14 and OJ No C 308, 15. 11. 1993, p. 18.

[2]) OJ No C 19, 25. 1. 1993, p. 111.

[3]) Opinion of the European Parliament of 26 May 1993 (OJ No C 176, 28. 6. 1993, p. 95), Council common position of 29 June 1995 (OJ No C 288, 30. 10. 1995, p. 1) and Decision of the European Parliament of 13 December 1995 (OJ No C 17, 22. 1. 1996, p. 51). Decision of the European Parliament of 16 January 1997 and Council Decision of 20 January 1997.

(2) Whereas the free movement of goods and services affects not only the business sector but also private individuals; whereas it means that consumers should be able to have access to the goods and services of another Member State on the same terms as the population of that State;

(3) Whereas, for consumers, cross–border distance selling could be one of the main tangible results of the completion of the internal market, as noted, *inter alia*, in the communication from the Commission to the Council entitled 'Towards a single market in distribution'; whereas it is essential to the smooth operation of the internal market for consumers to be able to have dealings with a business outside their country, even if it has a subsidiary in the consumer's country of residence;

(4) Whereas the introduction of new technologies is increasing the number of ways for consumers to obtain information about offers anywhere in the Community and to place orders; whereas some Member States have already taken different or diverging measures to protect consumers in respect of distance selling, which has had a detrimental effect on competition between businesses in the internal market; whereas it is therefore necessary to

2

introduce at Community level a minimum set of common rules in this area;

(5) Whereas paragraphs 18 and 19 of the Annex to the Council resolution of 14 April 1975 on a preliminary programme of the European Economic Community for a consumer protection and information policy[4]) point to the need to protect the purchasers of goods or services from demands for payment for unsolicited goods and from high – pressure selling methods;

(6) Whereas paragraph 33 of the communication from the Commission to the Council entitled 'A new impetus for consumer protection policy', which was approved by the Council resolution of 23 June 1986[5]), states that the Commission will submit proposals regarding the use of new information technologies enabling consumers to place orders with suppliers from their homes;

(7) Whereas the Council resolution of 9 November 1989 on future priorities for relaunching consumer protection policy[6]) calls upon the Commission to give priority to the areas referred to in the Annex to that resolution; whereas that Annex refers to new technologies involving teleshopping; whereas the Commission has responded to that resolution by adopting a three – year action plan for consumer protection policy in the European Economic Community (1990–1992); whereas that plan provides for the adoption of a Directive;

(8) Whereas the languages used for distance contracts are a matter for the Member States;

(9) Whereas contracts negotiated at a distance involve the use of one or more means of distance communication; whereas the various means of communication are used as part of an organized distance sales or service-provision scheme not involving the simultaneous presence of the supplier and the consumer; whereas the constant development of those means of communication does not allow an exhaustive list to be compiled but does require principles to be defined which are valid even for those which are not as yet in widespread use;

(10) Whereas the same transaction comprising successive operations or a series of separate operations over a period of time may give rise to different legal descriptions depending on the law of the Member States; whereas the provisions of this Directive cannot be applied differently according to the law of the Member States, subject to their recourse to Article 14; whereas, to that end, there is therefore reason to consider that there must at least be compliance with the provisions of this Directive at the time of the first of a series of successive operations or the first of a series of separate operations over a period of time which may be considered as forming a whole, whether that operation or series of operations are the subject of a single contract or successive, separate contracts;

(11) Whereas the use of means of distance communication must not lead to a reduction in the information provided to the consumer; whereas the information that is required to be sent to the consumer should therefore be determined, whatever the means of communication used; whereas the information supplied must also comply with the other relevant Community rules, in particular those in Council Directive 84/450/EEC of 10 September 1984 relating to the approximation of the laws,

---

[4]) OJ No C 92, 25. 4. 1975, p. 1.
[5]) OJ No C 167, 5. 7. 1986, p. 1.
[6]) OJ No C 294, 22. 11. 1989, p. 1.

2

regulations and administrative provisions of the Member States concerning misleading advertising[7]); whereas, if exceptions are made to the obligation to provide information, it is up to the consumer, on a discretionary basis, to request certain basic information such as the identity of the supplier, the main characteristics of the goods or services and their price;

(12) Whereas in the case of communication by telephone it is appropriate that the consumer receive enough information at the beginning of the conversation to decide whether or not to continue;

(13) Whereas information disseminated by certain electronic technologies is often ephemeral in nature insofar as it is not received on a permanent medium; whereas the consumer must therefore receive written notice in good time of the information necessary for proper performance of the contract;

(14) Whereas the consumer is not able actually to see the product or ascertain the nature of the service provided before concluding the contract; whereas provision should be made, unless otherwise specified in this Directive, for a right of withdrawal from the contract; whereas, if this right is to be more than formal, the costs, if any, borne by the consumer when exercising the right of withdrawal must be limited to the direct costs for returning the goods; whereas this right of withdrawal shall be without prejudice to the consumer's rights under national laws, with particular regard to the receipt of damaged products and services or of products and services not corresponding to the description given in the offer of such products or services; whereas it

is for the Member States to determine the other conditions and arrangements following exercise of the right of withdrawal;

(15) Whereas it is also necessary to prescribe a time limit for performance of the contract if this is not specified at the time of ordering;

(16) Whereas the promotional technique involving the dispatch of a product or the provision of a service to the consumer in return for payment without a prior request from, or the explicit agreement of, the consumer cannot be permitted, unless a substitute product or service is involved;

(17) Whereas the principles set out in Articles 8 and 10 of the European Convention for the Protection of Human Rights and Fundamental Freedoms of 4 November 1950 apply; whereas the consumer's right to privacy, particularly as regards freedom from certain particularly intrusive means of communication, should be recognized; whereas specific limits on the use of such means should therefore be stipulated; whereas Member States should take appropriate measures to protect effectively those consumers, who do not wish to be contacted through certain means of communication, against such contacts, without prejudice to the particular safeguards available to the consumer under Community legislation concerning the protection of personal data and privacy;

(18) Whereas it is important for the minimum binding rules contained in this Directive to be supplemented where appropriate by voluntary arrangements among the traders concerned, in line with Commission recommendation 92/295/EEC of 7 April 1992 on codes of practice for the pro-

---

[7]) OJ No L 250, 19. 9. 1984, p. 17.

tection of consumers in respect of contracts negotiated at a distance[8]);

(19) Whereas in the interest of optimum consumer protection it is important for consumers to be satisfactorily informed of the provisions of this Directive and of codes of practice that may exist in this field;

(20) Whereas non-compliance with this Directive may harm not only consumers but also competitors; whereas provisions may therefore be laid down enabling public bodies or their representatives, or consumer organizations which, under national legislation, have a legitimate interest in consumer protection, or professional organizations which have a legitimate interest in taking action, to monitor the application thereof;

(21) Whereas it is important, with a view to consumer protection, to address the question of cross-border complaints as soon as this is feasible; whereas the Commission published on 14 February 1996 a plan of action on consumer access to justice and the settlement of consumer disputes in the internal market; whereas that plan of action includes specific initiatives to promote out-of-court procedures; whereas objective criteria (Annex II) are suggested to ensure the reliability of those procedures and provision is made for the use of standardized claims forms (Annex III);

(22) Whereas in the use of new technologies the consumer is not in control of the means of communication used; whereas it is therefore necessary to provide that the burden of proof may be on the supplier;

(23) Whereas there is a risk that, in certain cases, the consumer may be deprived of protection under this Directive through the designation of the law of a non-member country as the law applicable to the contract; whereas provisions should therefore be included in this Directive to avert that risk;

(24) Whereas a Member State may ban, in the general interest, the marketing on its territory of certain goods and services through distance contracts; whereas that ban must comply with Community rules; whereas there is already provision for such bans, notably with regard to medicinal products, under Council Directive 89/552/EEC of 3 October 1989 on the coordination of certain provisions laid down by law, regulation or administrative action in Member States concerning the pursuit of television broadcasting activities[9]) and Council Directive 92/28/EEC of 31 March 1992 on the advertising of medicinal products for human use[10]),

HAVE ADOPTED THIS DIRECTIVE:

Article 1
Object

The object of this Directive is to approximate the laws, regulations and administrative provisions of the Member States concerning distance contracts between consumers and suppliers.

Article 2
Definitions

For the purposes of this Directive:

(1) 'distance contract' means any contract concerning goods or services concluded between a supplier and a consumer under an organized distance sales or service-provision scheme run by the supplier, who, for the purpose of

---

[8]) OJ No L 156, 10. 6. 1992, p. 21.

[9]) OJ No L 298, 17. 10. 1989, p. 23.
[10]) OJ No L 113, 30. 4. 1992, p. 13.

2

the contract, makes exclusive use of one or more means of distance communication up to and including the moment at which the contract is concluded;

(2) 'consumer' means any natural person who, in contracts covered by this Directive, is acting for purposes which are outside his trade, business or profession;

(3) 'supplier' means any natural or legal person who, in contracts covered by this Directive, is acting in his commercial or professional capacity;

(4) 'means of distance communication' means any means which, without the simultaneous physical presence of the supplier and the consumer, may be used for the conclusion of a contract between those parties. An indicative list of the means covered by this Directive is contained in Annex I;

(5) 'operator of a means of communication' means any public or private natural or legal person whose trade, business or profession involves making one or more means of distance communication available to suppliers.

Article 3
Exemptions

1. This Directive shall not apply to contracts:

– relating to any financial service to which Directive 2002/65/EC of the European Paliament and of the Council of 23 September 2002 concerning the distance marketing of consumer financial services and amending Council Directive 90/619/EEC and Directives 97/7/EC and 98/27/EC[11]) applies,

– concluded by means of automatic vending machines or automated commercial premises,

---

[11]) OJ L 271, 9. 10. 2002, p. 16.

– concluded with telecommunications operators through the use of public payphones,

– concluded for the construction and sale of immovable property or relating to other immovable property rights, except for rental,

– concluded at an auction.

2. Articles 4, 5, 6 and 7 (1) shall not apply:

– to contracts for the supply of foodstuffs, beverages or other goods intended for everyday consumption supplied to the home of the consumer, to his residence or to his workplace by regular roundsmen,

– to contracts for the provision of accommodation, transport, catering or leisure services, where the supplier undertakes, when the contract is concluded, to provide these services on a specific date or within a specific period; exceptionally, in the case of outdoor leisure events, the supplier can reserve the right not to apply Article 7 (2) in specific circumstances.

Article 4
Prior information

1. In good time prior to the conclusion of any distance contract, the consumer shall be provided with the following information:

(a) the identity of the supplier and, in the case of contracts requiring payment in advance, his address;

(b) the main characteristics of the goods or services;

(c) the price of the goods or services including all taxes;

(d) delivery costs, where appropriate;

(e) the arrangements for payment, delivery or performance;

(f) the existence of a right of withdrawal, except in the cases referred to in Article 6 (3);

(g) the cost of using the means of distance communication, where it is calculated other than at the basic rate;

(h) the period for which the offer or the price remains valid;

(i) where appropriate, the minimum duration of the contract in the case of contracts for the supply of products or services to be performed permanently or recurrently.

2. The information referred to in paragraph 1, the commercial purpose of which must be made clear, shall be provided in a clear and comprehensible manner in any way appropriate to the means of distance communication used, with due regard, in particular, to the principles of good faith in commercial transactions, and the principles governing the protection of those who are unable, pursuant to the legislation of the Member States, to give their consent, such as minors.

3. Moreover, in the case of telephone communications, the identity of the supplier and the commercial purpose of the call shall be made explicitly clear at the beginning of any conversation with the consumer.

Article 5
Written confirmation of information

1. The consumer must receive written confirmation or confirmation in another durable medium available and accessible to him of the information referred to in Article 4 (1) (a) to (f), in good time during the performance of the contract, and at the latest at the time of delivery where goods not for delivery to third parties are concerned, unless the information has already been given to the consumer prior to conclusion of the contract in writing or on another durable medium available and accessible to him.

In any event the following must be provided:

– written information on the conditions and procedures for exercising the right of withdrawal, within the meaning of Article 6, including the cases referred to in the first indent of Article 6 (3),

– the geographical address of the place of business of the supplier to which the consumer may address any complaints,

– information on after-sales services and guarantees which exist,

– the conclusion for cancelling the contract, where it is of unspecified duration or a duration exceeding one year.

2. Paragraph 1 shall not apply to services which are performed through the use of a means of distance communication, where they are supplied on only one occasion and are invoiced by the operator of the means of distance communication. Nevertheless, the consumer must in all cases be able to obtain the geographical address of the place of business of the supplier to which he may address any complaints.

Article 6
Right of withdrawal

1. For any distance contract the consumer shall have a period of at least seven working days in which to withdraw from the contract without penalty and without giving any reason. The only charge that may be made to the consumer because of the exercise of his right of withdrawal is the direct cost of returning the goods.

The period for exercise of this right shall begin:

2

– in the case of goods, from the day of receipt by the consumer where the obligations laid down in Article 5 have been fulfilled,

– in the case of services, from the day of conclusion of the contract or from the day on which the obligations laid down in Article 5 were fulfilled if they are fulfilled after conclusion of the contract, provided that this period does not exceed the three – month period referred to in the following subparagraph.

If the supplier has failed to fulfil the obligations laid down in Article 5, the period shall be three months. The period shall begin:

– in the case of goods, from the day of receipt by the consumer,

– in the case of services, from the day of conclusion of the contract.

If the information referred to in Article 5 is supplied within this three-month period, the seven working day period referred to in the first subparagraph shall begin as from that moment.

2. Where the right of withdrawal has been exercised by the consumer pursuant to this Article, the supplier shall be obliged to reimburse the sums paid by the consumer free of charge. The only charge that may be made to the consumer because of the exercise of his right of withdrawal is the direct cost of returning the goods. Such reimbursement must be carried out as soon as possible and in any case within 30 days.

3. Unless the parties have agreed otherwise, the consumer may not exercise the right of withdrawal provided for in paragraph 1 in respect of contracts:

– for the provision of services if performance has begun, with the consumer's agreement, before the end of the seven working day period referred to in paragraph 1,

– for the supply of goods or services the price of which is dependent on fluctuations in the financial market which cannot be controlled by the supplier,

– for the supply of goods made to the consumer's specifications or clearly personalized or which, by reason of their nature, cannot be returned or are liable to deteriorate or expire rapidly,

– for the supply of audio or video recordings or computer software which were unsealed by the consumer,

– for the supply of newspapers, periodicals and magazines,

– for gaming and lottery services.

4. The Member States shall make provision in their legislation to ensure that:

– if the price of goods or services is fully or partly covered by credit granted by the supplier, or

– if that price is fully or partly covered by credit granted to the consumer by a third party on the basis of an agreement between the third party and the supplier,

the credit agreement shall be cancelled, without any penalty, if the consumer exercises his right to withdraw from the contract in accordance with paragraph 1.

Member States shall determine the detailed rules for cancellation of the credit agreement.

Article 7
Performance

1. Unless the parties have agreed otherwise, the supplier must execute the order within a maximum of 30 days from the day following that on which the consumer forwarded his order to the supplier.

2. Where a supplier fails to perform his side of the contract on the grounds that the goods or services ordered are unavailable, the consumer must be informed of this situation and must be able to obtain a refund of any sums he has paid as soon as possible and in any case within 30 days.

3. Nevertheless, Member States may lay down that the supplier may provide the consumer with goods or services of equivalent quality and price provided that this possibility was provided for prior to the conclusion of the contract or in the contract. The consumer shall be informed of this possibility in a clear and comprehensible manner. The cost of returning the goods following exercise of the right of withdrawal shall, in this case, be borne by the supplier, and the consumer must be informed of this. In such cases the supply of goods or services may not be deemed to constitute inertia selling within the meaning of Article 9.

Article 8
Payment by card

[repealed]*)

Article 9
Inertia selling

Given the prohibition of inertia selling practices laid down in Directive 2005/29/EC of 11 May 2005 of the European Parliament and of the Council concerning unfair business-to-consumer commercial practices in the internal market[12]), Member States shall take the measures necessary to exempt the consumer from the provision of any consideration in cases of unsolicited

---

*) OJ L 319, 5. 12. 2007, p. 1.
12) OJ L 149, 11. 6. 2005, p. 22.

supply, the absence of a response not constituting consent.

Article 10
Restrictions on the use of certain means of distance communication

1. Use by a supplier of the following means requires the prior consent of the consumer:

– automated calling system without human intervention (automatic calling machine),

– facsimile machine (fax).

2. Member States shall ensure that means of distance communication, other than those referred to in paragraph 1, which allow individual communications may be used only where there is no clear objection from the consumer.

Article 11
Judicial or administrative redress

1. Member States shall ensure that adequate and effective means exist to ensure compliance with this Directive in the interests of consumers.

2. The means referred to in paragraph 1 shall include provisions whereby one or more of the following bodies, as determined by national law, may take action under national law before the courts or before the competent administrative bodies to ensure that the national provisions for the implementation of this Directive are applied:

(a) public bodies or their representatives;

(b) consumer organizations having a legitimate interest in protecting consumers;

(c) professional organizations having a legitimate interest in acting.

3. (a) Member States may stipulate that the burden of proof concerning the

existence of prior information, written confirmation, compliance with time-limits or consumer consent can be placed on the supplier.

(b) Member States shall take the measures needed to ensure that suppliers and operators of means of communication, where they are able to do so, cease practices which do not comply with measures adopted pursuant to this Directive.

4. Member States may provide for voluntary supervision by self-regulatory bodies of compliance with the provisions of this Directive and recourse to such bodies for the settlement of disputes to be added to the means which Member States must provided to ensure compliance with the provisions of this Directive.

Article 12
Binding nature

1. The consumer may not waive the rights conferred on him by the transposition of this Directive into national law.

2. Member States shall take the measures needed to ensure that the consumer does not lose the protection granted by this Directive by virtue of the choice of the law of a non-member country as the law applicable to the contract if the latter has close connection with the territory of one or more Member States.

Article 13
Community rules

1. The provisions of this Directive shall apply insofar as there are no particular provisions in rules of Community law governing certain types of distance contracts in their entirety.

2. Where specific Community rules contain provisions governing only certain aspects of the supply of goods or provision of services, those provisions, rather than the provisions of this Directive, shall apply to these specific aspects of the distance contracts.

Article 14
Minimal clause

Member States may introduce or maintain, in the area covered by this Directive, more stringent provisions compatible with the Treaty, to ensure a higher level of consumer protection. Such provisions shall, where appropriate, include a ban, in the general interest, on the marketing of certain goods or services, particularly medicinal products, within their territory by means of distance contracts, with due regard for the Treaty.

Article 15
Implementation

1. Member States shall bring into force the laws, regulations and administrative provisions necessary to comply with this Directive no later than three years after it enters into force. They shall forthwith inform the Commission thereof.

2. When Member States adopt the measures referred to in paragraph 1, these shall contain a reference to this Directive or shall be accompanied by such reference on the occasion of their official publication. The procedure for such reference shall be laid down by Member States.

3. Member States shall communicate to the Commission the text of the provisions of national law which they adopt in the field governed by this Directive.

4. No later than four years after the entry into force of this Directive the Commission shall submit a report to the European Parliament and the Council on the implementation of this Directive, accompanied if appropriate by a proposal for the revision thereof.

Article 16
Consumer information

Member States shall take appropriate measures to inform the consumer of the national law transposing this Directive and shall encourage, where appropriate, professional organizations to inform consumers of their codes of practice.

Article 17
Complaints systems

The Commission shall study the feasibility of establishing effective means to deal with consumers' complaints in respect of distance selling. Within two years after the entry into force of this Directive the Commission shall submit a report to the European Parliament and the Council on the results of the studies, accompanied if appropriate by proposals.

Article 18

This Directive shall enter into force on the day of its publication in the Of-

ficial Journal of the European Communities.

Article 19

This Directive is addressed to the Member States.

ANNEX I

Means of communication covered by Article 2 (4)
 – Unaddressed printed matter
 – Addressed printed matter
 – Standard letter
 – Press advertising with order form
 – Catalogue
 – Telephone with human intervention
 – Telephone without human intervention (automatic calling machine, audiotext)
 – Radio
 – Videophone (telephone with screen)
 – Videotex (microcomputer and television screen) with keyboard or touch screen
 – Electronic mail
 – Facsimile machine (fax)
 – Television (teleshopping).

ANNEX II

*[repealed]**)*

---

*) OJ L 271, 9. 10. 2002, p. 19.

2

3

Distance Selling Directive for Financial Services Directive 2002/65/EC of the European Parliament and of the Council of 23 September 2002 concerning the distance marketing of consumer financial services and amending Council Directive 90/619/EEC and Directives 97/7/EC and 98/27/EC

OJ L 271, 9. 10. 2002, p.16, amended by OJ L 149, 11. 6. 2005, p. 22, OJ L 319, 5. 12. 2007, p. 1

THE EUROPEAN PARLIAMENT AND THE COUNCIL OF THE EUROPEAN UNION,

Having regard to the Treaty establishing the European Community, and in particular Article 47(2), Article 55 and Article 95 thereof,

Having regard to the proposal from the Commission[1]),

Having regard to the opinion of the Economic and Social Committee[2]),

Acting in accordance with the procedure laid down in Article 251 of the Treaty[3]),

Whereas:

(1) It is important, in the context of achieving the aims of the single market,

to adopt measures designed to consolidate progressively this market and those measures must contribute to attaining a high level of consumer protection, in accordance with Articles 95 and 153 of the Treaty.

(2) Both for consumers and suppliers of financial services, the distance marketing of financial services will constitute one of the main tangible results of the completion of the internal market.

(3) Within the framework of the internal market, it is in the interest of consumers to have access without discrimination to the widest possible range of financial services available in the Community so that they can choose those that are best suited to their needs. In order to safeguard freedom of choice, which is an essential consumer right, a high degree of consumer protection is required in order to enhance consumer confidence in distance selling.

(4) It is essential to the smooth operation of the internal market for consumers to be able to negotiate and conclude contracts with a supplier established in other Member States, regardless of whether the supplier is also es-

---

[1]) OJ C 385, 11. 12. 1998, p. 10 and OJ C 177 E, 27. 6. 2000, p. 21.

[2]) OJ C 169, 16. 6. 1999, p. 43.

[3]) Opinion of the European Parliament of 5 May 1999 (OJ C 279, 1. 10. 1999, p. 207), Council Common Position of 19 December 2001 (OJ C 58 E, 5. 3. 2002, p. 32) and Decision of the European Parliament of 14 May 2002 (not yet published in the Official Journal). Council Decision of 26 June 2002 (not yet published in the Official Journal).

tablished in the Member State in which the consumer resides.

(5) Because of their intangible nature, financial services are particularly suited to distance selling and the establishment of a legal framework governing the distance marketing of financial services should increase consumer confidence in the use of new techniques for the distance marketing of financial services, such as electronic commerce.

(6) This Directive should be applied in conformity with the Treaty and with secondary law, including Directive 2000/31/EC[4]) on electronic commerce, the latter being applicable solely to the transactions which it covers.

(7) This Directive aims to achieve the objectives set forth above without prejudice to Community or national law governing freedom to provide services or, where applicable, host Member State control and/or authorisation or supervision systems in the Member States where this is compatible with Community legislation.

(8) Moreover, this Directive, and in particular its provisions relating to information about any contractual clause on law applicable to the contract and/ or on the competent court does not affect the applicability to the distance marketing of consumer financial services of Council Regulation (EC) No 44/2001 of 22 December 2000 on jurisdiction and the recognition and enforcement of judgements in civil and commercial matters[5]) or of the 1980 Rome Convention on the law applicable to contractual obligations.

(9) The achievement of the objectives of the Financial Services Action Plan requires a higher level of con-

sumer protection in certain areas. This implies a greater convergence, in particular, in non harmonised collective investment funds, rules of conduct applicable to investment services and consumer credits. Pending the achievement of the above convergence, a high level of consumer protection should be maintained.

(10) Directive 97/7/EC of the European Parliament and of the Council of 20 May 1997 on the protection of consumers in respect of distance contracts[6]), lays down the main rules applicable to distance contracts for goods or services concluded between a supplier and a consumer. However, that Directive does not cover financial services.

(11) In the context of the analysis conducted by the Commission with a view to ascertaining the need for specific measures in the field of financial services, the Commission invited all the interested parties to transmit their comments, notably in connection with the preparation of its Green Paper entitled 'Financial Services – Meeting Consumers' Expectations'. The consultations in this context showed that there is a need to strengthen consumer protection in this area. The Commission therefore decided to present a specific proposal concerning the distance marketing of financial services.

(12) The adoption by the Member States of conflicting or different consumer protection rules governing the distance marketing of consumer financial services could impede the functioning of the internal market and competition between firms in the market. It is therefore necessary to enact common rules at Community level in this area, consistent with no reduction in overall

---

[4]) OJ L 178, 17. 7. 2000, p. 1.
[5]) OJ L 12, 16. 1. 2001, p. 1.

[6]) OJ L 144, 4. 6. 1997, p. 19.

3

consumer protection in the Member States.

(13) A high level of consumer protection should be guaranteed by this Directive, with a view to ensuring the free movement of financial services. Member States should not be able to adopt provisions other than those laid down in this Directive in the fields it harmonises, unless otherwise specifically indicated in it.

(14) This Directive covers all financial services liable to be provided at a distance. However, certain financial services are governed by specific provisions of Community legislation which continue to apply to those financial services. However, principles governing the distance marketing of such services should be laid down.

(15) Contracts negotiated at a distance involve the use of means of distance communication which are used as part of a distance sales or service-provision scheme not involving the simultaneous presence of the supplier and the consumer. The constant development of those means of communication requires principles to be defined that are valid even for those means which are not yet in widespread use. Therefore, distance contracts are those the offer, negotiation and conclusion of which are carried out at a distance.

(16) A single contract involving successive operations or separate operations of the same nature performed over time may be subject to different legal treatment in the different Member States, but it is important that this Directive be applied in the same way in all the Member States. To that end, it is appropriate that this Directive should be considered to apply to the first of a series of successive operations or separate operations of the same nature performed over time which may be con-

sidered as forming a whole, irrespective of whether that operation or series of operations is the subject of a single contract or several successive contracts.

(17) An 'initial service agreement' may be considered to be for example the opening of a bank account, acquiring a credit card, concluding a portfolio management contract, and 'operations' may be considered to be for example the deposit or withdrawal of funds to or from the bank account, payment by credit card, transactions made within the framework of a portfolio management contract. Adding new elements to an initial service agreement, such as a possibility to use an electronic payment instrument together with one's existing bank account, does not constitute an 'operation' but an additional contract to which this Directive applies. The subscription to new units of the same collective investment fund is considered to be one of 'successive operations of the same nature'.

(18) By covering a service-provision scheme organised by the financial services provider, this Directive aims to exclude from its scope services provided on a strictly occasional basis and outside a commercial structure dedicated to the conclusion of distance contracts.

(19) The supplier is the person providing services at a distance. This Directive should however also apply when one of the marketing stages involves an intermediary. Having regard to the nature and degree of that involvement, the pertinent provisions of this Directive should apply to such an intermediary, irrespective of his or her legal status.

(20) Durable mediums include in particular floppy discs, CD-ROMs, DVDs and the hard drive of the consumer's computer on which the elec-

tronic mail is stored, but they do not include Internet websites unless they fulfil the criteria contained in the definition of a durable medium.

(21) The use of means of distance communications should not lead to an unwarranted restriction on the information provided to the client. In the interests of transparency this Directive lays down the requirements needed to ensure that an appropriate level of information is provided to the consumer both before and after conclusion of the contract. The consumer should receive, before conclusion of the contract, the prior information needed so as to properly appraise the financial service offered to him and hence make a well-informed choice. The supplier should specify how long his offer applies as it stands.

(22) Information items listed in this Directive cover information of a general nature applicable to all kinds of financial services. Other information requirements concerning a given financial service, such as the coverage of an insurance policy, are not solely specified in this Directive. This kind of information should be provided in accordance, where applicable, with relevant Community legislation or national legislation in conformity with Community law.

(23) With a view to optimum protection of the consumer, it is important that the consumer is adequately informed of the provisions of this Directive and of any codes of conduct existing in this area and that he has a right of withdrawal.

(24) When the right of withdrawal does not apply because the consumer has expressly requested the performance of a contract, the supplier should inform the consumer of this fact.

(25) Consumers should be protected against unsolicited services. Consumers should be exempt from any obligation in the case of unsolicited services, the absence of a reply not being construed as signifying consent on their part. However, this rule should be without prejudice to the tacit renewal of contracts validly concluded between the parties whenever the law of the Member States permits such tacit renewal.

(26) Member States should take appropriate measures to protect effectively consumers who do not wish to be contacted through certain means of communication or at certain times. This Directive should be without prejudice to the particular safeguards available to consumers under Community legislation concerning the protection of personal data and privacy.

(27) With a view to protecting consumers, there is a need for suitable and effective complaint and redress procedures in the Member States with a view to settling potential disputes between suppliers and consumers, by using, where appropriate, existing procedures.

(28) Member States should encourage public or private bodies established with a view to settling disputes out of court to cooperate in resolving cross-border disputes. Such cooperation could in particular entail allowing consumers to submit to extra-judicial bodies in the Member State of their residence complaints concerning suppliers established in other Member States. The establishment of FIN-NET offers increased assistance to consumers when using cross-border services.

(29) This Directive is without prejudice to extension by Member States, in accordance with Community law, of

3

the protection provided by this Directive to non-profit organisations and persons making use of financial services in order to become entrepreneurs.

(30) This Directive should also cover cases where the national legislation includes the concept of a consumer making a binding contractual statement.

(31) The provisions in this Directive on the supplier's choice of language should be without prejudice to provisions of national legislation, adopted in conformity with Community law governing the choice of language.

(32) The Community and the Member States have entered into commitments in the context of the General Agreement on Trade in Services (GATS) concerning the possibility for consumers to purchase banking and investment services abroad. The GATS entitles Member States to adopt measures for prudential reasons, including measures to protect investors, depositors, policy-holders and persons to whom a financial service is owed by the supplier of the financial service. Such measures should not impose restrictions going beyond what is required to ensure the protection of consumers.

(33) In view of the adoption of this Directive, the scope of Directive 97/7/EC and Directive 98/27/EC of the European Parliament and of the Council of 19 May 1998 on injunctions for the protection of consumers' interests[7]) and the scope of the cancellation period in Council Directive 90/619/EEC of 8 November 1990 on the coordination of laws, regulations and administrative provisions relating to direct life assurance, laying down provisions to facili-

tate the effective exercise of freedom to provide services[8]) should be adapted.

(34) Since the objectives of this Directive, namely the establishment of common rules on the distance marketing of consumer financial services cannot be sufficiently achieved by the Member States and can therefore be better achieved at Community level, the Community may adopt measures, in accordance with the principles of subsidiarity as set out in Article 5 of the Treaty. In accordance with the principle of proportionality, as set out in that Article, this Directive does not go beyond what is necessary to achieve that objective,

HAVE ADOPTED THIS DIRECTIVE:

Article 1
Object and scope

1. The object of this Directive is to approximate the laws, regulations and administrative provisions of the Member States concerning the distance marketing of consumer financial services.

2. In the case of contracts for financial services comprising an initial service agreement followed by successive operations or a series of separate operations of the same nature performed over time, the provisions of this Directive shall apply only to the initial agreement.

In case there is no initial service agreement but the successive operations or the separate operations of the same nature performed over time are performed between the same contractual parties, Articles 3 and 4 apply only when the first operation is performed. Where, however, no operation

---

[7]) OJ L 166, 11. 6. 1998, p. 51. Directive as last amended by Directive 2000/31/EC (OJ L 178, 17. 7. 2001, p. 1).

[8]) OJ L 330, 29. 11. 1990, p. 50. Directive as last amended by Directive 92/96/EEC (OJ L 360, 9. 12. 1992, p. 1).

of the same nature is performed for more than one year, the next operation will be deemed to be the first in a new series of operations and, accordingly, Articles 3 and 4 shall apply.

Article 2
Definitions

For the purposes of this Directive:

(a) 'distance contract' means any contract concerning financial services concluded between a supplier and a consumer under an organised distance sales or service-provision scheme run by the supplier, who, for the purpose of that contract, makes exclusive use of one or more means of distance communication up to and including the time at which the contract is concluded;

(b) 'financial service' means any service of a banking, credit, insurance, personal pension, investment or payment nature;

(c) 'supplier' means any natural or legal person, public or private, who, acting in his commercial or professional capacity, is the contractual provider of services subject to distance contracts;

(d) 'consumer' means any natural person who, in distance contracts covered by this Directive, is acting for purposes which are outside his trade, business or profession;

(e) 'means of distance communication' refers to any means which, without the simultaneous physical presence of the supplier and the consumer, may be used for the distance marketing of a service between those parties;

(f) 'durable medium' means any instrument which enables the consumer to store information addressed personally to him in a way accessible for future reference for a period of time adequate for the purposes of the information and which allows the unchanged reproduction of the information stored;

(g) 'operator or supplier of a means of distance communication' means any public or private, natural or legal person whose trade, business or profession involves making one or more means of distance communication available to suppliers.

Article 3
Information to the consumer prior to the conclusion of the distance contract

1. In good time before the consumer is bound by any distance contract or offer, he shall be provided with the following information concerning:

(1) the supplier

(a) the identity and the main business of the supplier, the geographical address at which the supplier is established and any other geographical address relevant for the customer's relations with the supplier;

(b) the identity of the representative of the supplier established in the consumer's Member State of residence and the geographical address relevant for the customer's relations with the representative, if such a representative exists;

(c) when the consumer's dealings are with any professional other than the supplier, the identity of this professional, the capacity in which he is acting vis-à-vis the consumer, and the geographical address relevant for the customer's relations with this professional;

(d) where the supplier is registered in a trade or similar public register, the trade register in which the supplier is entered and his registration number or an equivalent means of identification in that register;

3

(e) where the supplier's activity is subject to an authorisation scheme, the particulars of the relevant supervisory authority;

(2) the financial service

(a) a description of the main characteristics of the financial service;

(b) the total price to be paid by the consumer to the supplier for the financial service, including all related fees, charges and expenses, and all taxes paid via the supplier or, when an exact price cannot be indicated, the basis for the calculation of the price enabling the consumer to verify it;

(c) where relevant notice indicating that the financial service is related to instruments involving special risks related to their specific features or the operations to be executed or whose price depends on fluctuations in the financial markets outside the supplier's control and that historical performances are no indicators for future performances;

(d) notice of the possibility that other taxes and/or costs may exist that are not paid via the supplier or imposed by him;

(e) any limitations of the period for which the information provided is valid;

(f) the arrangements for payment and for performance;

(g) any specific additional cost for the consumer of using the means of distance communication, if such additional cost is charged;

(3) the distance contract

(a) the existence or absence of a right of withdrawal in accordance with Article 6 and, where the right of withdrawal exists, its duration and the conditions for exercising it, including information on the amount which the consumer may be required to pay on the basis of Article 7(1), as well as the consequences of non-exercise of that right;

(b) the minimum duration of the distance contract in the case of financial services to be performed permanently or recurrently;

(c) information on any rights the parties may have to terminate the contract early or unilaterally by virtue of the terms of the distance contract, including any penalties imposed by the contract in such cases;

(d) practical instructions for exercising the right of withdrawal indicating, *inter alia*, the address to which the notification of a withdrawal should be sent;

(e) the Member State or States whose laws are taken by the supplier as a basis for the establishment of relations with the consumer prior to the conclusion of the distance contract;

(f) any contractual clause on law applicable to the distance contract and/or on competent court;

(g) in which language, or languages, the contractual terms and conditions, and the prior information referred to in this Article are supplied, and furthermore in which language, or languages, the supplier, with the agreement of the consumer, undertakes to communicate during the duration of this distance contract;

(4) redress

(a) whether or not there is an out-of-court complaint and redress mechanism for the consumer that is party to the distance contract and, if so, the methods for having access to it;

(b) the existence of guarantee funds or other compensation arrangements, not covered by Directive 94/19/EC of the European Parliament and of the Council of 30 May 1994 on deposit guarantee schemes[9]) and Directive

___
[9]) OJ L 135, 31. 5. 1994, p. 5.

3

97/9/EC of the European Parliament and of the Council of 3 March 1997 on investor compensation schemes[10]).

2. The information referred to in paragraph 1, the commercial purpose of which must be made clear, shall be provided in a clear and comprehensible manner in any way appropriate to the means of distance communication used, with due regard, in particular, to the principles of good faith in commercial transactions, and the principles governing the protection of those who are unable, pursuant to the legislation of the Member States, to give their consent, such as minors.

3. In the case of voice telephony communications

(a) the identity of the supplier and the commercial purpose of the call initiated by the supplier shall be made explicitly clear at the beginning of any conversation with the consumer;

(b) subject to the explicit consent of the consumer only the following information needs to be given:

– the identity of the person in contact with the consumer and his link with the supplier,

– a description of the main characteristics of the financial service,

– the total price to be paid by the consumer to the supplier for the financial service including all taxes paid via the supplier or, when an exact price cannot be indicated, the basis for the calculation of the price enabling the consumer to verify it,

– notice of the possibility that other taxes and/or costs may exist that are not paid via the supplier or imposed by him,

– the existence or absence of a right of withdrawal in accordance with Article 6 and, where the right of withdrawal exists, its duration and the conditions for exercising it, including information on the amount which the consumer may be required to pay on the basis of Article 7(1).

The supplier shall inform the consumer that other information is available on request and of what nature this information is. In any case the supplier shall provide the full information when he fulfils his obligations under Article 5.

4. Information on contractual obligations, to be communicated to the consumer during the pre-contractual phase, shall be in conformity with the contractual obligations which would result from the law presumed to be applicable to the distance contract if the latter were concluded.

Article 4
Additional information requirements

1. Where there are provisions in the Community legislation governing financial services which contain prior information requirements additional to those listed in Article 3(1), these requirements shall continue to apply.

2. Pending further harmonisation, Member States may maintain or introduce more stringent provisions on prior information requirements when the provisions are in conformity with Community law.

3. Member States shall communicate to the Commission national provisions on prior information requirements under paragraphs 1 and 2 of this Article when these requirements are additional to those listed in Article 3(1). The Commission shall take account of the communicated national provisions when drawing up the report referred to in Article 20(2).

---

[10]) OJ L 84, 26. 3. 1997, p. 22.

3

4. The Commission shall, with a view to creating a high level of transparency by all appropriate means, ensure that information, on the national provisions communicated to it, is made available to consumers and suppliers.

5. Where Directive 2007/64/EC of the European Parliament and of the Council of 13 November 2007 on payment services in the internal market[11]) is also applicable, the information provisions under Article 3(1) of this Directive, with the exception of paragraphs (2)(c) to (g), (3)(a), (d) and (e), and (4)(b), shall be replaced with Articles 36, 37, 41 and 42 of that Directive.

Article 5
Communication of the contractual terms and conditions and of the prior information

1. The supplier shall communicate to the consumer all the contractual terms and conditions and the information referred to in Article 3(1) and Article 4 on paper or on another durable medium available and accessible to the consumer in good time before the consumer is bound by any distance contract or offer.

2. The supplier shall fulfil his obligation under paragraph 1 immediately after the conclusion of the contract, if the contract has been concluded at the consumer's request using a means of distance communication which does not enable providing the contractual terms and conditions and the information in conformity with paragraph 1.

3. At any time during the contractual relationship the consumer is entitled, at his request, to receive the contractual terms and conditions on paper. In addition, the consumer is en-

titled to change the means of distance communication used, unless this is incompatible with the contract concluded or the nature of the financial service provided.

Article 6
Right of withdrawal

1. The Member States shall ensure that the consumer shall have a period of 14 calendar days to withdraw from the contract without penalty and without giving any reason. However, this period shall be extended to 30 calendar days in distance contracts relating to life insurance covered by Directive 90/619/EEC and personal pension operations.

The period for withdrawal shall begin:

– either from the day of the conclusion of the distance contract, except in respect of the said life assurance, where the time limit will begin from the time when the consumer is informed that the distance contract has been concluded, or

– from the day on which the consumer receives the contractual terms and conditions and the information in accordance with Article 5(1) or (2), if that is later than the date referred to in the first indent.

Member States, in addition to the right of withdrawal, may provide that the enforceability of contracts relating to investment services is suspended for the same period provided for in this paragraph.

2. The right of withdrawal shall not apply to:

(a) financial services whose price depends on fluctuations in the financial market outside the suppliers control, which may occur during the withdrawal period, such as services related to:

– foreign exchange,

---

11) OJ L 319, 5. 12. 2007, p. 1.

3

– money market instruments,

– transferable securities,

– units in collective investment undertakings,

– financial-futures contracts, including equivalent cash-settled instruments,

– forward interest-rate agreements (FRAs),

– interest-rate, currency and equity swaps,

– options to acquire or dispose of any instruments referred to in this point including equivalent cash-settled instruments. This category includes in particular options on currency and on interest rates;

(b) travel and baggage insurance policies or similar short-term insurance policies of less than one month's duration;

(c) contracts whose performance has been fully completed by both parties at the consumer's express request before the consumer exercises his right of withdrawal.

3. Member States may provide that the right of withdrawal shall not apply to:

(a) any credit intended primarily for the purpose of acquiring or retaining property rights in land or in an existing or projected building, or for the purpose of renovating or improving a building, or

(b) any credit secured either by mortgage on immovable property or by a right related to immovable property, or

(c) declarations by consumers using the services of an official, provided that the official confirms that the consumer is guaranteed the rights under Article 5(1).

This paragraph shall be without prejudice to the right to a reflection time to the benefit of the consumers that are resident in those Member States where it exists, at the time of the adoption of this Directive.

4. Member States making use of the possibility set out in paragraph 3 shall communicate it to the Commission.

5. The Commission shall make available the information communicated by Member States to the European Parliament and the Council and shall ensure that it is also available to consumers and suppliers who request it.

6. If the consumer exercises his right of withdrawal he shall, before the expiry of the relevant deadline, notify this following the practical instructions given to him in accordance with Article 3(1)(3)(d) by means which can be proved in accordance with national law. The deadline shall be deemed to have been observed if the notification, if it is on paper or on another durable medium available and accessible to the recipient, is dispatched before the deadline expires.

7. This Article does not apply to credit agreements cancelled under the conditions of Article 6(4) of Directive 97/7/EC or Article 7 of Directive 94/47/EC of the European Parliament and of the Council of 26 October 1994 on the protection of purchasers in respect of certain aspects of contracts relating to the purchase of the right to use immovable properties on a timeshare basis[12]).

If to a distance contract of a given financial service another distance contract has been attached concerning services provided by the supplier or by a third party on the basis of an agreement between the third party and the supplier, this additional distance contract

---

[12]) OJ L 280, 29. 10. 1994, p. 83.

3

shall be cancelled, without any penalty, if the consumer exercises his right of withdrawal as provided for in Article 6(1).

8. The provisions of this Article are without prejudice to the Member States' laws and regulations governing the cancellation or termination or non-enforceability of a distance contract or the right of a consumer to fulfil his contractual obligations before the time fixed in the distance contract. This applies irrespective of the conditions for and the legal effects of the winding-up of the contract.

Article 7

Payment of the service provided before withdrawal

1. When the consumer exercises his right of withdrawal under Article 6(1) he may only be required to pay, without any undue delay, for the service actually provided by the supplier in accordance with the contract. The performance of the contract may only begin after the consumer has given his approval. The amount payable shall not:

– exceed an amount which is in proportion to the extent of the service already provided in comparison with the full coverage of the contract,

– in any case be such that it could be construed as a penalty.

2. Member States may provide that the consumer cannot be required to pay any amount when withdrawing from an insurance contract.

3. The supplier may not require the consumer to pay any amount on the basis of paragraph 1 unless he can prove that the consumer was duly informed about the amount payable, in conformity with Article 3(1)(3)(a). However, in no case may he require such payment if he has commenced the performance of the contract before the expiry of the withdrawal period provided for in Article 6(1) without the consumer's prior request.

4. The supplier shall, without any undue delay and no later than within 30 calendar days, return to the consumer any sums he has received from him in accordance with the distance contract, except for the amount referred to in paragraph 1. This period shall begin from the day on which the supplier receives the notification of withdrawal.

5. The consumer shall return to the supplier any sums and/or property he has received from the supplier without any undue delay and no later than within 30 calendar days. This period shall begin from the day on which the consumer dispatches the notification of withdrawal.

Article 8

Payment by card

[repealed]*)

Article 9

Given the prohibition of inertia selling practices laid down in Directive 2005/29/EC of 11 May 2005 of the European Parliament and of the Council concerning unfair business-to-consumer commercial practices in the internal market[13]) and without prejudice to Member States' legislation on the tacit renewal of distance contracts, when such rules permit tacit renewal, Member States shall take measures to exempt the consumer from any obligation in the event of unsolicited supplies, the absence of a reply not constituting consent.

---

*) OJ L 319, 5. 12. 2007, p. 1.
[13]) OJ L 149, 11. 6. 2005, p. 22.

Article 10
Unsolicited communications

1. The use by a supplier of the following distance communication techniques shall require the consumer's prior consent:

(a) automated calling systems without human intervention (automatic calling machines);

(b) fax machines.

2. Member States shall ensure that means of distance communication other than those referred to in paragraph 1, when they allow individual communications:

(a) shall not be authorised unless the consent of the consumers concerned has been obtained, or

(b) may only be used if the consumer has not expressed his manifest objection.

3. The measures referred to in paragraphs 1 and 2 shall not entail costs for consumers.

Article 11
Sanctions

Member States shall provide for appropriate sanctions in the event of the supplier's failure to comply with national provisions adopted pursuant to this Directive.

They may provide for this purpose in particular that the consumer may cancel the contract at any time, free of charge and without penalty.

These sanctions must be effective, proportional and dissuasive.

Article 12
Imperative nature of this Directive's provisions

1. Consumers may not waive the rights conferred on them by this Directive.

2. Member States shall take the measures needed to ensure that the consumer does not lose the protection granted by this Directive by virtue of the choice of the law of a non-member country as the law applicable to the contract, if this contract has a close link with the territory of one or more Member States.

Article 13
Judicial and administrative redress

1. Member States shall ensure that adequate and effective means exist to ensure compliance with this Directive in the interests of consumers.

2. The means referred to in paragraph 1 shall include provisions whereby one or more of the following bodies, as determined by national law, may take action in accordance with national law before the courts or competent administrative bodies to ensure that the national provisions for the implementation of this Directive are applied:

(a) public bodies or their representatives;

(b) consumer organisations having a legitimate interest in protecting consumers;

(c) professional organisations having a legitimate interest in acting.

3. Member States shall take the measures necessary to ensure that operators and suppliers of means of distance communication put an end to practices that have been declared to be contrary to this Directive, on the basis of a judicial decision, an administrative decision or a decision issued by a supervisory authority notified to them, where those operators or suppliers are in a position to do so.

Article 14
Out-of-court redress

1. Member States shall promote the setting up or development of

3

adequate and effective out-of-court complaints and redress procedures for the settlement of consumer disputes concerning financial services provided at distance.

2. Member States shall, in particular, encourage the bodies responsible for out-of-court settlement of disputes to cooperate in the resolution of cross-border disputes concerning financial services provided at distance.

Article 15
Burden of proof

Without prejudice to Article 7(3), Member States may stipulate that the burden of proof in respect of the supplier's obligations to inform the consumer and the consumer's consent to conclusion of the contract and, where appropriate, its performance, can be placed on the supplier.

Any contractual term or condition providing that the burden of proof of the respect by the supplier of all or part of the obligations incumbent on him pursuant to this Directive should lie with the consumer shall be an unfair term within the meaning of Council Directive 93/13/EEC of 5 April 1993 on unfair terms in consumer contracts[14]).

Article 16
Transitional measures

Member States may impose national rules which are in conformity with this Directive on suppliers established in a Member State which has not yet transposed this Directive and whose law has no obligations corresponding to those provided for in this Directive.

---

[14]) OJ L 95, 21. 4. 1993, p. 29.

Article 17
Directive 90/619/EC

In Article 15(1) of Directive 90/619/EEC the first subparagraph shall be replaced by the following:

"1. Each Member State shall prescribe that a policyholder who concludes an individual life-assurance contract shall have a period of 30 calendar days, from the time when he was informed that the contract had been concluded, within which to cancel the contract."

Article 18
Directive 97/7/EC

Directive 97/7/EC is hereby amended as follows:

1. the first indent of Article 3(1) shall be replaced by the following:
"– relating to any financial service to which Directive 2002/65/EC of the European Parliament and of the Council of 23 September 2002 concerning the distance marketing of consumer financial services and amending Council Directive 90/619/EEC and Directives 97/7/EC and 98/27/EC[15]) applies,";

2. Annex II shall be deleted.

Article 19
Directive 98/27/EC

The following point shall be added to the Annex of Directive 98/27/EC:
"11. Directive 2002/65/EC of the European Parliament and of the Council of 23 September 2002 concerning the distance marketing of consumer financial services and amending Council Directive 90/619/EEC and Directives 97/7/EC and 98/27/EC[16])."

---

[15]) OJ L 271, 9. 10. 2002, p. 16.
[16]) OJ L 271, 9. 10. 2002, p. 16.

3

Article 20
Review

1. Following the implementation of this Directive, the Commission shall examine the functioning of the internal market in financial services in respect of the marketing of those services. It should seek to analyse and detail the difficulties that are, or might be faced by both consumers and suppliers, in particular arising from differences between national provisions regarding information and right of withdrawal.

2. Not later than 9 April 2006 the Commission shall report to the European Parliament and the Council on the problems facing both consumers and suppliers seeking to buy and sell financial services, and shall submit, where appropriate, proposals to amend and/or further harmonise the information and right of withdrawal provisions in Community legislation concerning financial services and/or those covered in Article 3.

Article 21
Transposition

1. Member States shall bring into force the laws, regulations and administrative provisions necessary to comply with this Directive not later than 9 October 2004. They shall forthwith inform the Commission thereof.

When Member States adopt these measures, they shall contain a reference to this Directive or shall be accompanied by such a reference on the occasion of their official publication. The methods of making such reference shall be laid down by Member States.

2. Member States shall communicate to the Commission the text of the main provisions of national law which they adopt in the field governed by this Directive together with a table showing how the provisions of this Directive correspond to the national provisions adopted.

Article 22
Entry into force

This Directive shall enter into force on the day of its publication in the Official Journal of the European Communities.

Article 23
Addressees

This Directive is addressed to the Member States.

4

E-Signature Directive
Directive 1999/93/EC of the European Parliament and of the Council of 13 December 1999 on a Community framework for electronic signatures

OJ L 13, 19. 1. 2000, p. 12

THE EUROPEAN PARLIAMENT AND THE COUNCIL OF THE EUROPEAN UNION,

Having regard to the Treaty establishing the European Community, and in particular Articles 47(2), 55 and 95 thereof,

Having regard to the proposal from the Commission [1]),

Having regard to the opinion of the Economic and Social Committee[2]),

Having regard to the opinion of the Committee of the Regions[3]),

Acting in accordance with the procedure laid down in Article 251 of the Treaty[4]),

Whereas:

(1) On 16 April 1997 the Commission presented to the European Parliament, the Council, the Economic and Social Committee and the Committee of the Regions a Communication on a European Initiative in Electronic Commerce;

(2) On 8 October 1997 the Commission presented to the European Parliament, the Council, the Economic and Social Committee and the Committee of the Regions a Communication on ensuring security and trust in electronic communication – towards a European framework for digital signatures and encryption;

(3) On 1 December 1997 the Council invited the Commission to submit as soon as possible a proposal for a Directive of the European Parliament and of the Council on digital signatures;

(4) Electronic communication and commerce necessitate 'electronic signatures' and related services allowing data authentication; divergent rules with respect to legal recognition of electronic signatures and the accreditation of certification-service providers in the Member States may create a significant barrier to the use of electronic communications and electronic commerce; on the other hand, a clear Community framework regarding the conditions applying to electronic signatures will strengthen confidence in, and general acceptance of, the new technologies; legislation in the Member States should

---

[1]) OJ C 325, 23. 10. 1998, p. 5.
[2]) OJ C 40, 15. 2. 1999, p. 29.
[3]) OJ C 93, 6. 4. 1999, p. 33.
[4]) Opinion of the European Parliament of 13 January 1999 (OJ C 104, 14. 4. 1999, p. 49), Council Common Position of 28 June 1999 (OJ C 243, 27. 8. 1999, p. 33) and Decision of the European Parliament of 27 October 1999 (not yet published in the Official Journal). Council Decision of 30 November 1999.

4

not hinder the free movement of goods and services in the internal market;

(5) The interoperability of electronic-signature products should be promoted; in accordance with Article 14 of the Treaty, the internal market comprises an area without internal frontiers in which the free movement of goods is ensured; essential requirements specific to electronic-signature products must be met in order to ensure free movement within the internal market and to build trust in electronic signatures, without prejudice to Council Regulation (EC) No 3381/94 of 19 December 1994 setting up a Community regime for the control of exports of dual-use goods[5]) and Council Decision 94/942/CFSP of 19 December 1994 on the joint action adopted by the Council concerning the control of exports of dual-use goods[6]);

(6) This Directive does not harmonise the provision of services with respect to the confidentiality of information where they are covered by national provisions concerned with public policy or public security;

(7) The internal market ensures the free movement of persons, as a result of which citizens and residents of the European Union increasingly need to deal with authorities in Member States other than the one in which they reside; the availability of electronic communication could be of great service in this respect;

(8) Rapid technological development and the global character of the Internet necessitate an approach which is open to various technologies and services capable of authenticating data electronically;

(9) Electronic signatures will be used in a large variety of circumstances and applications, resulting in a wide range of new services and products related to or using electronic signatures; the definition of such products and services should not be limited to the issuance and management of certificates, but should also encompass any other service and product using, or ancillary to, electronic signatures, such as registration services, time-stamping services, directory services, computing services or consultancy services related to electronic signatures;

(10) The internal market enables certification-service-providers to develop their cross-border activities with a view to increasing their competitiveness, and thus to offer consumers and businesses new opportunities to exchange information and trade electronically in a secure way, regardless of frontiers; in order to stimulate the Community-wide provision of certification services over open networks, certification-service-providers should be free to provide their services without prior authorisation; prior authorisation means not only any permission whereby the certification-service-provider concerned has to obtain a decision by national authorities before being allowed to provide its certification services, but also any other measures having the same effect;

(11) Voluntary accreditation schemes aiming at an enhanced level of service-provision may offer certification-service-providers the appropriate framework for developing further their services towards the levels of trust, security and quality demanded by the evolving market; such schemes should

[5]) OJ L 367, 31. 12. 1994, p. 1. Regulation as amended by Regulation (EC) No 837/95 (OJ L 90, 21. 4. 1995, p. 1).
[6]) OJ L 367, 31. 12. 1994, p. 8. Decision as last amended by Decision 99/193/CFSP (OJ L 73, 19. 3. 1999, p. 1).

4

encourage the development of best practice among certification-service-providers; certification-service-providers should be left free to adhere to and benefit from such accreditation schemes;

(12) Certification services can be offered either by a public entity or a legal or natural person, when it is established in accordance with the national law; whereas Member States should not prohibit certification-service-providers from operating outside voluntary accreditation schemes; it should be ensured that such accreditation schemes do not reduce competition for certification services;

(13) Member States may decide how they ensure the supervision of compliance with the provisions laid down in this Directive; this Directive does not preclude the establishment of private-sector-based supervision systems; this Directive does not oblige certification-service-providers to apply to be supervised under any applicable accreditation scheme;

(14) It is important to strike a balance between consumer and business needs;

(15) Annex III covers requirements for secure signature-creation devices to ensure the functionality of advanced electronic signatures; it does not cover the entire system environment in which such devices operate; the functioning of the internal market requires the Commission and the Member States to act swiftly to enable the bodies charged with the conformity assessment of secure signature devices with Annex III to be designated; in order to meet market needs conformity assessment must be timely and efficient;

(16) This Directive contributes to the use and legal recognition of electronic signatures within the Community; a regulatory framework is not needed for electronic signatures exclusively used within systems, which are based on voluntary agreements under private law between a specified number of participants; the freedom of parties to agree among themselves the terms and conditions under which they accept electronically signed data should be respected to the extent allowed by national law; the legal effectiveness of electronic signatures used in such systems and their admissibility as evidence in legal proceedings should be recognised;

(17) This Directive does not seek to harmonise national rules concerning contract law, particularly the formation and performance of contracts, or other formalities of a non-contractual nature concerning signatures; for this reason the provisions concerning the legal effect of electronic signatures should be without prejudice to requirements regarding form laid down in national law with regard to the conclusion of contracts or the rules determining where a contract is concluded;

(18) The storage and copying of signature-creation data could cause a threat to the legal validity of electronic signatures;

(19) Electronic signatures will be used in the public sector within national and Community administrations and in communications between such administrations and with citizens and economic operators, for example in the public procurement, taxation, social security, health and justice systems;

(20) Harmonised criteria relating to the legal effects of electronic signatures will preserve a coherent legal framework across the Community; national law lays down different requirements for the legal validity of handwritten signatures; whereas certificates

4

can be used to confirm the identity of a person signing electronically; advanced electronic signatures based on qualified certificates aim at a higher level of security; advanced electronic signatures which are based on a qualified certificate and which are created by a secure-signature-creation device can be regarded as legally equivalent to hand-written signatures only if the requirements for hand-written signatures are fulfilled;

(21) In order to contribute to the general acceptance of electronic authentication methods it has to be ensured that electronic signatures can be used as evidence in legal proceedings in all Member States; the legal recognition of electronic signatures should be based upon objective criteria and not be linked to authorisation of the certification-service-provider involved; national law governs the legal spheres in which electronic documents and electronic signatures may be used; this Directive is without prejudice to the power of a national court to make a ruling regarding conformity with the requirements of this Directive and does not affect national rules regarding the unfettered judicial consideration of evidence;

(22) Certification-service-providers providing certification-services to the public are subject to national rules regarding liability;

(23) The development of international electronic commerce requires cross-border arrangements involving third countries; in order to ensure interoperability at a global level, agreements on multilateral rules with third countries on mutual recognition of certification services could be beneficial;

(24) In order to increase user confidence in electronic communication and electronic commerce, certifica-tion-service-providers must observe data protection legislation and individual privacy;

(25) provisions on the use of pseudonyms in certificates should not prevent Member States from requiring identification of persons pursuant to Community or national law;

(26) The measures necessary for the implementation of this Directive are to be adopted in accordance with Council Decision 1999/468/EC of 28 June 1999 laying down the procedures for the exercise of implementing powers conferred on the Commission[7]);

(27) Two years after its implementation the Commission will carry out a review of this Directive so as, inter alia, to ensure that the advance of technology or changes in the legal environment have not created barriers to achieving the aims stated in this Directive; it should examine the implications of associated technical areas and submit a report to the European Parliament and the Council on this subject;

(28) In accordance with the principles of subsidiarity and proportionality as set out in Article 5 of the Treaty, the objective of creating a harmonised legal framework for the provision of electronic signatures and related services cannot be sufficiently achieved by the Member States and can therefore be better achieved by the Community; this Directive does not go beyond what is necessary to achieve that objective,

HAVE ADOPTED THIS DIRECTIVE:

Article 1
Scope

The purpose of this Directive is to facilitate the use of electronic signa-

---

[7]) OJ L 184, 17. 7. 1999, p. 23.

4

tures and to contribute to their legal recognition. It establishes a legal framework for electronic signatures and certain certification-services in order to ensure the proper functioning of the internal market.

It does not cover aspects related to the conclusion and validity of contracts or other legal obligations where there are requirements as regards form prescribed by national or Community law nor does it affect rules and limits, contained in national or Community law, governing the use of documents.

Article 2
Definitions

For the purpose of this Directive:

1. 'electronic signature' means data in electronic form which are attached to or logically associated with other electronic data and which serve as a method of authentication;

2. 'advanced electronic signature' means an electronic signature which meets the following requirements:

(a) it is uniquely linked to the signatory;

(b) it is capable of identifying the signatory;

(c) it is created using means that the signatory can maintain under his sole control; and

(d) it is linked to the data to which it relates in such a manner that any subsequent change of the data is detectable;

3. 'signatory' means a person who holds a signature-creation device and acts either on his own behalf or on behalf of the natural or legal person or entity he represents;

4. 'signature-creation data' means unique data, such as codes or private cryptographic keys, which are used by the signatory to create an electronic signature;

5. 'signature-creation device' means configured software or hardware used to implement the signature-creation data;

6. 'secure-signature-creation device' means a signature-creation device which meets the requirements laid down in Annex III;

7. 'signature-verification-data' means data, such as codes or public cryptographic keys, which are used for the purpose of verifying an electronic signature;

8. 'signature-verification device' means configured software or hardware used to implement the signature-verification-data;

9. 'certificate' means an electronic attestation which links signature-verification data to a person and confirms the identity of that person;

10. 'qualified certificate' means a certificate which meets the requirements laid down in Annex I and is provided by a certification-service-provider who fulfils the requirements laid down in Annex II;

11. 'certification-service-provider' means an entity or a legal or natural person who issues certificates or provides other services related to electronic signatures;

12. 'electronic-signature product' means hardware or software, or relevant components thereof, which are intended to be used by a certification-service-provider for the provision of electronic-signature services or are intended to be used for the creation or verification of electronic signatures;

13. 'voluntary accreditation' means any permission, setting out rights and obligations specific to the provision of certification services, to be granted upon request by the certification-service-provider concerned, by the public or private body charged with the elab-

4

oration of, and supervision of compliance with, such rights and obligations, where the certification-service-provider is not entitled to exercise the rights stemming from the permission until it has received the decision by the body.

Article 3
Market access

1. Member States shall not make the provision of certification services subject to prior authorisation.

2. Without prejudice to the provisions of paragraph 1, Member States may introduce or maintain voluntary accreditation schemes aiming at enhanced levels of certification-service provision. All conditions related to such schemes must be objective, transparent, proportionate and non-discriminatory. Member States may not limit the number of accredited certification-service-providers for reasons which fall within the scope of this Directive.

3. Each Member State shall ensure the establishment of an appropriate system that allows for supervision of certification-service-providers which are established on its territory and issue qualified certificates to the public.

4. The conformity of secure signature-creation-devices with the requirements laid down in Annex III shall be determined by appropriate public or private bodies designated by Member States. The Commission shall, pursuant to the procedure laid down in Article 9, establish criteria for Member States to determine whether a body should be designated.

A determination of conformity with the requirements laid down in Annex III made by the bodies referred to in the first subparagraph shall be recognised by all Member States.

5. The Commission may, in accordance with the procedure laid down in Article 9, establish and publish reference numbers of generally recognised standards for electronic-signature products in the Official Journal of the European Communities. Member States shall presume that there is compliance with the requirements laid down in Annex II, point (f), and Annex III when an electronic signature product meets those standards.

6. Member States and the Commission shall work together to promote the development and use of signature-verification devices in the light of the recommendations for secure signature-verification laid down in Annex IV and in the interests of the consumer.

7. Member States may make the use of electronic signatures in the public sector subject to possible additional requirements. Such requirements shall be objective, transparent, proportionate and non-discriminatory and shall relate only to the specific characteristics of the application concerned. Such requirements may not constitute an obstacle to cross-border services for citizens.

Article 4
Internal market principles

1. Each Member State shall apply the national provisions which it adopts pursuant to this Directive to certification-service-providers established on its territory and to the services which they provide. Member States may not restrict the provision of certification-services originating in another Member State in the fields covered by this Directive.

4

2. Member States shall ensure that electronic-signature products which comply with this Directive are permitted to circulate freely in the internal market.

Article 5
Legal effects of electronic signatures

1. Member States shall ensure that advanced electronic signatures which are based on a qualified certificate and which are created by a secure-signature-creation device:

(a) satisfy the legal requirements of a signature in relation to data in electronic form in the same manner as a handwritten signature satisfies those requirements in relation to paper-based data; and

(b) are admissible as evidence in legal proceedings.

2. Member States shall ensure that an electronic signature is not denied legal effectiveness and admissibility as evidence in legal proceedings solely on the grounds that it is:

– in electronic form, or

– not based upon a qualified certificate, or

– not based upon a qualified certificate issued by an accredited certification-service-provider, or

– not created by a secure signature-creation device.

Article 6
Liability

1. As a minimum, Member States shall ensure that by issuing a certificate as a qualified certificate to the public or by guaranteeing such a certificate to the public a certification-service-provider is liable for damage caused to any entity or legal or natural person who reasonably relies on that certificate:

(a) as regards the accuracy at the time of issuance of all information contained in the qualified certificate and as regards the fact that the certificate contains all the details prescribed for a qualified certificate;

(b) for assurance that at the time of the issuance of the certificate, the signatory identified in the qualified certificate held the signature-creation data corresponding to the signature-verification data given or identified in the certificate;

(c) for assurance that the signature-creation data and the signature-verification data can be used in a complementary manner in cases where the certification-service-provider generates them both;

unless the certification-service-provider proves that he has not acted negligently.

2. As a minimum Member States shall ensure that a certification-service-provider who has issued a certificate as a qualified certificate to the public is liable for damage caused to any entity or legal or natural person who reasonably relies on the certificate for failure to register revocation of the certificate unless the certification-service-provider proves that he has not acted negligently.

3. Member States shall ensure that a certification-service-provider may indicate in a qualified certificate limitations on the use of that certificate. provided that the limitations are recognisable to third parties. The certification-service-provider shall not be liable for damage arising from use of a qualified certificate which exceeds the limitations placed on it.

4

4. Member States shall ensure that a certification-service-provider may indicate in the qualified certificate a limit on the value of transactions for which the certificate can be used, provided that the limit is recognisable to third parties.

The certification-service-provider shall not be liable for damage resulting from this maximum limit being exceeded.

5. The provisions of paragraphs 1 to 4 shall be without prejudice to Council Directive 93/13/EEC of 5 April 1993 on unfair terms in consumer contracts[8]).

Article 7
International aspects

1. Member States shall ensure that certificates which are issued as qualified certificates to the public by a certification-service-provider established in a third country are recognised as legally equivalent to certificates issued by a certification-service-provider established within the Community if:

(a) the certification-service-provider fulfils the requirements laid down in this Directive and has been accredited under a voluntary accreditation scheme established in a Member State; or

(b) a certification-service-provider established within the Community which fulfils the requirements laid down in this Directive guarantees the certificate; or

(c) the certificate or the certification-service-provider is recognised under a bilateral or multilateral agreement between the Community and third countries or international organisations.

---

[8]) OJ L 95, 21. 4. 1993, p. 29.

2. In order to facilitate cross-border certification services with third countries and legal recognition of advanced electronic signatures originating in third countries, the Commission shall make proposals, where appropriate, to achieve the effective implementation of standards and international agreements applicable to certification services. In particular, and where necessary, it shall submit proposals to the Council for appropriate mandates for the negotiation of bilateral and multilateral agreements with third countries and international organisations. The Council shall decide by qualified majority.

3. Whenever the Commission is informed of any difficulties encountered by Community undertakings with respect to market access in third countries, it may, if necessary, submit proposals to the Council for an appropriate mandate for the negotiation of comparable rights for Community undertakings in these third countries. The Council shall decide by qualified majority.

Measures taken pursuant to this paragraph shall be without prejudice to the obligations of the Community and of the Member States under relevant international agreements.

Article 8
Data protection

1. Member States shall ensure that certification-service-providers and national bodies responsible for accreditation or supervision comply with the requirements laid down in Directive 95/46/EC of the European Parliament and of the Council of 24 October 1995 on tile protection of individuals with regard to the processing of personal

4

data and on the free movement of such data[9]).

2. Member States shall ensure that a certification-service-provider which issues certificates to the public may collect personal data only directly from the data subject, or after the explicit consent of the data subject, and only insofar as it is necessary for the purposes of issuing and maintaining the certificate. The data may not be collected or processed for any other purposes without the explicit consent of the data subject.

3. Without prejudice to the legal effect given to pseudonyms under national law, Member States shall not prevent certification service providers from indicating in the certificate a pseudonym instead of the signatory's name.

Article 9
Committee

1. The Commission shall be assisted by an 'Electronic-Signature Committee', hereinafter referred to as 'the committee'.

2. Where reference is made to this paragraph, Articles 4 and 7 of Decision 1999/468/EC shall apply, having regard to the provisions of Article 8 thereof.

The period laid down in Article 4(3) of Decision 1999/468/EC shall be set at three months.

3. The Committee shall adopt its own rules of procedure.

Article 10
Tasks of the committee

The committee shall clarify the requirements laid down in the Annexes of this Directive, the criteria referred to in Article 3(4) and the generally recog-

---

[9]) OJ L 281, 23. 11. 1995, p. 31.

nised standards for electronic signature products established and published pursuant to Article 3(5), in accordance with the procedure laid down in Article 9(2).

Article 11
Notification

1. Member States shall notify to the Commission and the other Member States the following:

(a) information on national voluntary accreditation schemes, including any additional requirements pursuant to Article 3(7);

(b) the names and addresses of the national bodies responsible for accreditation and supervision as well as of the bodies referred to in Article 3(4);

(c) the names and addresses of all accredited national certification service providers.

2. Any information supplied under paragraph 1 and changes in respect of that information shall be notified by the Member States as soon as possible.

Article 12
Review

1. The Commission shall review the operation of this Directive and report thereon to the European Parliament and to the Council by 19 July 2003 at the latest.

2. The review shall *inter alia* assess whether the scope of this Directive should be modified, taking account of technological, market and legal developments. The report shall in particular include an assessment, on the basis of experience gained, of aspects of harmonisation. The report shall be accompanied, where appropriate, by legislative proposals.

Article 13
Implementation

1. Member States shall bring into force the laws, regulations and administrative provisions necessary to comply with this Directive before 19 July 2001. They shall forthwith inform the Commission thereof.

When Member States adopt these measures, they shall contain a reference to this Directive or shall be accompanied by such a reference on the occasion of their official publication. The methods of making such reference shall be laid down by the Member States.

2. Member States shall communicate to the Commission the text of the main provisions of domestic law which they adopt in the field governed by this Directive.

Article 14
Entry into force

This Directive shall enter into force on the day of its publication in the Official Journal of the European Communities.

Article 15
Addressees

This Directive is addressed to the Member States.

ANNEX I
Requirements for qualified certificates

Qualified certificates must contain:

(a) an indication that the certificate is issued as a qualified certificate;

(b) the identification of the certification-service-provider and the State in which it is established;

(c) the name of the signatory or a pseudonym, which shall be identified as such;

(d) provision for a specific attribute of the signatory to be included if relevant, depending on the purpose for which the certificate is intended;

(e) signature-verification data which correspond to signature-creation data under the control of the signatory;

(f) an indication of the beginning and end of the period of validity of the certificate;

(g) the identity code of the certificate;

(h) the advanced electronic signature of the certification-service-provider issuing it;

(i) limitations on the scope of use of the certificate, if applicable; and

(j) limits on the value of transactions for which the certificate can be used, if applicable.

ANNEX II
Requirements for certification-service-providers issuing qualified certificates

Certification-service-providers must:

(a) demonstrate the reliability necessary for providing certification services;

(b) ensure the operation of a prompt and secure directory and a secure and immediate revocation service;

(c) ensure that the date and time when a certificate is issued or revoked can be determined precisely;

(d) verify, by appropriate means in accordance with national law, the identity and, if applicable, any specific attributes of the person to which a qualified certificate is issued;

(e) employ personnel who possess the expert knowledge, experience, and qualifications necessary for the services provided, in particular competence at

4

managerial level, expertise in electronic signature technology and familiarity with proper security procedures; they must also apply administrative and management procedures which are adequate and correspond to recognised standards;

(f) use trustworthy systems and products which are protected against modification and ensure the technical and cryptographic security of the process supported by them;

(g) take measures against forgery of certificates, and, in cases where the certification-service-provider generates signature-creation data, guarantee confidentiality during the process of generating such data;

(h) maintain sufficient financial resources to operate in conformity with the requirements laid down in the Directive, in particular to bear the risk of liability for damages, for example, by obtaining appropriate insurance;

(i) record all relevant information concerning a qualified certificate for an appropriate period of time, in particular for the purpose of providing evidence of certification for the purposes of legal proceedings. Such recording may be done electronically;

(j) not store or copy signature-creation data of the person to whom the certification-service-provider provided key management services;

(k) before entering into a contractual relationship with a person seeking a certificate to support his electronic signature inform that person by a durable means of communication of the precise terms and conditions regarding the use of the certificate, including any limitations on its use, the existence of a voluntary accreditation scheme and procedures for complaints and dispute settlement. Such information, which may be transmitted elec-

tronically, must be in writing and in redily understandable language. Relevant parts of this information must also be made available on request to third-parties relying on the certificate;

(l) use trustworthy systems to store certificates in a verifiable form so that:

– only authorised persons can make entries and changes,

– information can be checked for authenticity,

– certificates are publicly available for retrieval in only those cases for which the certificate-holder's consent has been obtained, and

– any technical changes compromising these security requirements are apparent to the operator.

ANNEX III
Requirements for secure signature-creation devices

1. Secure signature-creation devices must, by appropriate technical and procedural means, ensure at the least that:

(a) the signature-creation-data used for signature generation can practically occur only once, and that their secrecy is reasonably assured;

(b) the signature-creation-data used for signature generation cannot, with reasonable assurance, be derived and the signature is protected against forgery using currently available technology;

(c) the signature-creation-data used for signature generation can be reliably protected by the legitimate signatory against the use of others.

2. Secure signature-creation devices must not alter the data to be signed or prevent such data from being presented to the signatory prior to the signature process.

4

ANNEX IV
Recommendations for secure signature verification

During the signature-verification process it should be ensured with reasonable certainty that:

(a) the data used for verifying the signature correspond to the data displayed to the verifier;

(b) the signature is reliably verified and the result of that verification is correctly displayed;

(c) the verifier can, as necessary, reliably establish the contents of the signed data;

(d) the authenticity and validity of the certificate required at the time of signature verification are reliably verified;

(e) the result of verification and the signatory's identity are correctly displayed;

(f) the use of a pseudonym is clearly indicated; and

(g) any security-relevant changes can be detected.

5

Information Society Copyright Directive
Directive 2001/29/EC of the European Parliament and of the Council of 22 May 2001 on the harmonisation of certain aspects of copyright and related rights in the information society

OJ L 167, 22. 6. 2001, p. 10, corrected by OJ L 6, 10. 1. 2002, p. 70

THE EUROPEAN PARLIAMENT AND THE COUNCIL OF THE EUROPEAN UNION,

Having regard to the Treaty establishing the European Community, and in particular Articles 47(2), 55 and 95 thereof,

Having regard to the proposal from the Commission[1]),

Having regard to the opinion of the Economic and Social Committee[2]),

Acting in accordance with the procedure laid down in Article 251 of the Treaty[3]),

Whereas:

(1) The Treaty provides for the establishment of an internal market and the institution of a system ensuring that competition in the internal market is not distorted. Harmonisation of the

---

[1]) OJ C 108, 7. 4. 1998, p. 6 and OJ C 180, 25. 6. 1999, p. 6.

[2]) OJ C 407, 28. 12. 1998, p. 30.

[3]) Opinion of the European Parliament of 10 February 1999 (OJ C 150, 28. 5. 1999, p. 171), Council Common Position of 28 September 2000 (OJ C 344, 1. 12. 2000, p. 1) and Decision of the European Parliament of 14 February 2001 (not yet published in the Official Journal). Council Decision of 9 April 2001.

laws of the Member States on copyright and related rights contributes to the achievement of these objectives.

(2) The European Council, meeting at Corfu on 24 and 25 June 1994, stressed the need to create a general and flexible legal framework at Community level in order to foster the development of the information society in Europe. This requires, *inter alia*, the existence of an internal market for new products and services. Important Community legislation to ensure such a regulatory framework is already in place or its adoption is well under way. Copyright and related rights play an important role in this context as they protect and stimulate the development and marketing of new products and services and the creation and exploitation of their creative content.

(3) The proposed harmonisation will help to implement the four freedoms of the internal market and relates to compliance with the fundamental principles of law and especially of property, including intellectual property, and freedom of expression and the public interest.

(4) A harmonised legal framework on copyright and related rights, through increased legal certainty and

while providing for a high level of protection of intellectual property, will foster substantial investment in creativity and innovation, including network infrastructure, and lead in turn to growth and increased competitiveness of European industry, both in the area of content provision and information technology and more generally across a wide range of industrial and cultural sectors. This will safeguard employment and encourage new job creation.

(5) Technological development has multiplied and diversified the vectors for creation, production and exploitation. While no new concepts for the protection of intellectual property are needed, the current law on copyright and related rights should be adapted and supplemented to respond adequately to economic realities such as new forms of exploitation.

(6) Without harmonisation at Community level, legislative activities at national level which have already been initiated in a number of Member States in order to respond to the technological challenges might result in significant differences in protection and thereby in restrictions on the free movement of services and products incorporating, or based on, intellectual property, leading to a refragmentation of the internal market and legislative inconsistency. The impact of such legislative differences and uncertainties will become more significant with the further development of the information society, which has already greatly increased transborder exploitation of intellectual property. This development will and should further increase. Significant legal differences and uncertainties in protection may hinder economies of scale for new products and services containing copyright and related rights.

(7) The Community legal framework for the protection of copyright and related rights must, therefore, also be adapted and supplemented as far as is necessary for the smooth functioning of the internal market. To that end, those national provisions on copyright and related rights which vary considerably from one Member State to another or which cause legal uncertainties hindering the smooth functioning of the internal market and the proper development of the information society in Europe should be adjusted, and inconsistent national responses to the technological developments should be avoided, whilst differences not adversely affecting the functioning of the internal market need not be removed or prevented.

(8) The various social, societal and cultural implications of the information society require that account be taken of the specific features of the content of products and services.

(9) Any harmonisation of copyright and related rights must take as a basis a high level of protection, since such rights are crucial to intellectual creation. Their protection helps to ensure the maintenance and development of creativity in the interests of authors, performers, producers, consumers, culture, industry and the public at large. Intellectual property has therefore been recognised as an integral part of property.

(10) If authors or performers are to continue their creative and artistic work, they have to receive an appropriate reward for the use of their work, as must producers in order to be able to finance this work. The investment required to produce products such as phonograms, films or multimedia products, and services such as "on-demand" services, is considerable. Ad-

equate legal protection of intellectual property rights is necessary in order to guarantee the availability of such a reward and provide the opportunity for satisfactory returns on this investment.

(11) A rigorous, effective system for the protection of copyright and related rights is one of the main ways of ensuring that European cultural creativity and production receive the necessary resources and of safeguarding the independence and dignity of artistic creators and performers.

(12) Adequate protection of copyright works and subject-matter of related rights is also of great importance from a cultural standpoint. Article 151 of the Treaty requires the Community to take cultural aspects into account in its action.

(13) A common search for, and consistent application at European level of, technical measures to protect works and other subject-matter and to provide the necessary information on rights are essential insofar as the ultimate aim of these measures is to give effect to the principles and guarantees laid down in law.

(14) This Directive should seek to promote learning and culture by protecting works and other subject-matter while permitting exceptions or limitations in the public interest for the purpose of education and teaching.

(15) The Diplomatic Conference held under the auspices of the World Intellectual Property Organisation (WIPO) in December 1996 led to the adoption of two new Treaties, the "WIPO Copyright Treaty" and the "WIPO Performances and Phonograms Treaty", dealing respectively with the protection of authors and the protection of performers and phonogram producers. Those Treaties update

the international protection for copyright and related rights significantly, not least with regard to the so-called "digital agenda", and improve the means to fight piracy world-wide. The Community and a majority of Member States have already signed the Treaties and the process of making arrangements for the ratification of the Treaties by the Community and the Member States is under way. This Directive also serves to implement a number of the new international obligations.

(16) Liability for activities in the network environment concerns not only copyright and related rights but also other areas, such as defamation, misleading advertising, or infringement of trademarks, and is addressed horizontally in Directive 2000/31/EC of the European Parliament and of the Council of 8 June 2000 on certain legal aspects of information society services, in particular electronic commerce, in the internal market ("Directive on electronic commerce")[4], which clarifies and harmonises various legal issues relating to information society services including electronic commerce. This Directive should be implemented within a timescale similar to that for the implementation of the Directive on electronic commerce, since that Directive provides a harmonised framework of principles and provisions relevant inter alia to important parts of this Directive. This Directive is without prejudice to provisions relating to liability in that Directive.

(17) It is necessary, especially in the light of the requirements arising out of the digital environment, to ensure that collecting societies achieve a higher level of rationalisation and transparen-

---

[4) OJ L 178, 17. 7. 2000, p. 1.

5

cy with regard to compliance with competition rules.

(18) This Directive is without prejudice to the arrangements in the Member States concerning the management of rights such as extended collective licences.

(19) The moral rights of rightholders should be exercised according to the legislation of the Member States and the provisions of the Berne Convention for the Protection of Literary and Artistic Works, of the WIPO Copyright Treaty and of the WIPO Performances and Phonograms Treaty. Such moral rights remain outside the scope of this Directive.

(20) This Directive is based on principles and rules already laid down in the Directives currently in force in this area, in particular Directives 91/250/EEC[5]), 92/100/EEC[6]), 93/83/EEC[7]), 93/98/EEC[8]) and 96/9/EC[9]), and it develops those principles and rules

[5]) Council Directive 91/250/EEC of 14 May 1991 on the legal protection of computer programs (OJ L 122, 17. 5. 1991, p. 42). Directive as amended by Directive 93/98/EEC.
[6]) Council Directive 92/100/EEC of 19 November 1992 on rental right and lending right and on certain rights related to copyright in the field of intellectual property (OJ L 346, 27. 11. 1992, p. 61). Directive as amended by Directive 93/98/EEC.
[7]) Council Directive 93/83/EEC of 27 September 1993 on the coordination of certain rules concerning copyright and rights related to copyright applicable to satellite broadcasting and cable retransmission (OJ L 248, 6. 10. 1993, p. 15).
[8]) Council Directive 93/98/EEC of 29 October 1993 harmonising the term of protection of copyright and certain related rights (OJ L 290, 24. 11. 1993, p. 9).
[9]) Directive 96/9/EC of the European Parliament and of the Council of 11 March 1996 on the legal protection of databases (OJ L 77, 27. 3. 1996, p. 20).

and places them in the context of the information society. The provisions of this Directive should be without prejudice to the provisions of those Directives, unless otherwise provided in this Directive.

(21) This Directive should define the scope of the acts covered by the reproduction right with regard to the different beneficiaries. This should be done in conformity with the acquis communautaire. A broad definition of these acts is needed to ensure legal certainty within the internal market.

(22) The objective of proper support for the dissemination of culture must not be achieved by sacrificing strict protection of rights or by tolerating illegal forms of distribution of counterfeited or pirated works.

(23) This Directive should harmonise further the author's right of communication to the public. This right should be understood in a broad sense covering all communication to the public not present at the place where the communication originates. This right should cover any such transmission or retransmission of a work to the public by wire or wireless means, including broadcasting. This right should not cover any other acts.

(24) The right to make available to the public subject-matter referred to in Article 3(2) should be understood as covering all acts of making available such subject-matter to members of the public not present at the place where the act of making available originates, and as not covering any other acts.

(25) The legal uncertainty regarding the nature and the level of protection of acts of on-demand transmission of copyright works and subject-matter protected by related rights over networks should be overcome by providing for harmonised protection at Com-

5

munity level. It should be made clear that all rightholders recognised by this Directive should have an exclusive right to make available to the public copyright works or any other subject-matter by way of interactive on-demand transmissions. Such interactive on-demand transmissions are characterised by the fact that members of the public may access them from a place and at a time individually chosen by them.

(26) With regard to the making available in on-demand services by broadcasters of their radio or television productions incorporating music from commercial phonograms as an integral part thereof, collective licensing arrangements are to be encouraged in order to facilitate the clearance of the rights concerned.

(27) The mere provision of physical facilities for enabling or making a communication does not in itself amount to communication within the meaning of this Directive.

(28) Copyright protection under this Directive includes the exclusive right to control distribution of the work incorporated in a tangible article. The first sale in the Community of the original of a work or copies thereof by the rightholder or with his consent exhausts the right to control resale of that object in the Community. This right should not be exhausted in respect of the original or of copies thereof sold by the rightholder or with his consent outside the Community. Rental and lending rights for authors have been established in Directive 92/100/EEC. The distribution right provided for in this Directive is without prejudice to the provisions relating to the rental and lending rights contained in Chapter I of that Directive.

(29) The question of exhaustion does not arise in the case of services and on-line services in particular. This also applies with regard to a material copy of a work or other subject-matter made by a user of such a service with the consent of the rightholder. Therefore, the same applies to rental and lending of the original and copies of works or other subject-matter which are services by nature. Unlike CD-ROM or CD-I, where the intellectual property is incorporated in a material medium, namely an item of goods, every on-line service is in fact an act which should be subject to authorisation where the copyright or related right so provides.

(30) The rights referred to in this Directive may be transferred, assigned or subject to the granting of contractual licences, without prejudice to the relevant national legislation on copyright and related rights.

(31) A fair balance of rights and interests between the different categories of rightholders, as well as between the different categories of rightholders and users of protected subject-matter must be safeguarded. The existing exceptions and limitations to the rights as set out by the Member States have to be reassessed in the light of the new electronic environment. Existing differences in the exceptions and limitations to certain restricted acts have direct negative effects on the functioning of the internal market of copyright and related rights. Such differences could well become more pronounced in view of the further development of transborder exploitation of works and cross-border activities. In order to ensure the proper functioning of the internal market, such exceptions and limitations should be defined more harmoniously. The degree of their harmonisation should be based on their impact on the smooth functioning of the internal market.

5

(32) This Directive provides for an exhaustive enumeration of exceptions and limitations to the reproduction right and the right of communication to the public. Some exceptions or limitations only apply to the reproduction right, where appropriate. This list takes due account of the different legal traditions in Member States, while, at the same time, aiming to ensure a functioning internal market. Member States should arrive at a coherent application of these exceptions and limitations, which will be assessed when reviewing implementing legislation in the future.

(33) The exclusive right of reproduction should be subject to an exception to allow certain acts of temporary reproduction, which are transient or incidental reproductions, forming an integral and essential part of a technological process and carried out for the sole purpose of enabling either efficient transmission in a network between third parties by an intermediary, or a lawful use of a work or other subject-matter to be made. The acts of reproduction concerned should have no separate economic value on their own. To the extent that they meet these conditions, this exception should include acts which enable browsing as well as acts of caching to take place, including those which enable transmission systems to function efficiently, provided that the intermediary does not modify the information and does not interfere with the lawful use of technology, widely recognised and used by industry, to obtain data on the use of the information. A use should be considered lawful where it is authorised by the rightholder or not restricted by law.

(34) Member States should be given the option of providing for certain exceptions or limitations for cases such as educational and scientific pur-

poses, for the benefit of public institutions such as libraries and archives, for purposes of news reporting, for quotations, for use by people with disabilities, for public security uses and for uses in administrative and judicial proceedings.

(35) In certain cases of exceptions or limitations, rightholders should receive fair compensation to compensate them adequately for the use made of their protected works or other subject-matter. When determining the form, detailed arrangements and possible level of such fair compensation, account should be taken of the particular circumstances of each case. When evaluating these circumstances, a valuable criterion would be the possible harm to the rightholders resulting from the act in question. In cases where rightholders have already received payment in some other form, for instance as part of a licence fee, no specific or separate payment may be due. The level of fair compensation should take full account of the degree of use of technological protection measures referred to in this Directive. In certain situations where the prejudice to the rightholder would be minimal, no obligation for payment may arise.

(36) The Member States may provide for fair compensation for rightholders also when applying the optional provisions on exceptions or limitations which do not require such compensation.

(37) Existing national schemes on reprography, where they exist, do not create major barriers to the internal market. Member States should be allowed to provide for an exception or limitation in respect of reprography.

(38) Member States should be allowed to provide for an exception or limitation to the reproduction right for

certain types of reproduction of audio, visual and audio-visual material for private use, accompanied by fair compensation. This may include the introduction or continuation of remuneration schemes to compensate for the prejudice to rightholders. Although differences between those remuneration schemes affect the functioning of the internal market, those differences, with respect to analogue private reproduction, should not have a significant impact on the development of the information society. Digital private copying is likely to be more widespread and have a greater economic impact. Due account should therefore be taken of the differences between digital and analogue private copying and a distinction should be made in certain respects between them.

(39) When applying the exception or limitation on private copying, Member States should take due account of technological and economic developments, in particular with respect to digital private copying and remuneration schemes, when effective technological protection measures are available. Such exceptions or limitations should not inhibit the use of technological measures or their enforcement against circumvention.

(40) Member States may provide for an exception or limitation for the benefit of certain non-profit making establishments, such as publicly accessible libraries and equivalent institutions, as well as archives. However, this should be limited to certain special cases covered by the reproduction right. Such an exception or limitation should not cover uses made in the context of on-line delivery of protected works or other subject-matter. This Directive should be without prejudice to the Member States' option to derogate from the exclusive public lending right in accordance with Article 5 of Directive 92/100/EEC. Therefore, specific contracts or licences should be promoted which, without creating imbalances, favour such establishments and the disseminative purposes they serve.

(41) When applying the exception or limitation in respect of ephemeral recordings made by broadcasting organisations it is understood that a broadcaster's own facilities include those of a person acting on behalf of and under the responsibility of the broadcasting organisation.

(42) When applying the exception or limitation for non-commercial educational and scientific research purposes, including distance learning, the non-commercial nature of the activity in question should be determined by that activity as such. The organisational structure and the means of funding of the establishment concerned are not the decisive factors in this respect.

(43) It is in any case important for the Member States to adopt all necessary measures to facilitate access to works by persons suffering from a disability which constitutes an obstacle to the use of the works themselves, and to pay particular attention to accessible formats.

(44) When applying the exceptions and limitations provided for in this Directive, they should be exercised in accordance with international obligations. Such exceptions and limitations may not be applied in a way which prejudices the legitimate interests of the rightholder or which conflicts with the normal exploitation of his work or other subject-matter. The provision of such exceptions or limitations by Member States should, in particular, duly reflect the increased economic im-

pact that such exceptions or limitations may have in the context of the new electronic environment. Therefore, the scope of certain exceptions or limitations may have to be even more limited when it comes to certain new uses of copyright works and other subject-matter.

(45) The exceptions and limitations referred to in Article 5(2), (3) and (4) should not, however, prevent the definition of contractual relations designed to ensure fair compensation for the rightholders insofar as permitted by national law.

(46) Recourse to mediation could help users and rightholders to settle disputes. The Commission, in cooperation with the Member States within the Contact Committee, should undertake a study to consider new legal ways of settling disputes concerning copyright and related rights.

(47) Technological development will allow rightholders to make use of technological measures designed to prevent or restrict acts not authorised by the rightholders of any copyright, rights related to copyright or the *sui generis* right in databases. The danger, however, exists that illegal activities might be carried out in order to enable or facilitate the circumvention of the technical protection provided by these measures. In order to avoid fragmented legal approaches that could potentially hinder the functioning of the internal market, there is a need to provide for harmonised legal protection against circumvention of effective technological measures and against provision of devices and products or services to this effect.

(48) Such legal protection should be provided in respect of technological measures that effectively restrict acts not authorised by the rightholders of any copyright, rights related to copyright or the *sui generis* right in databases without, however, preventing the normal operation of electronic equipment and its technological development. Such legal protection implies no obligation to design devices, products, components or services to correspond to technological measures, so long as such device, product, component or service does not otherwise fall under the prohibition of Article 6. Such legal protection should respect proportionality and should not prohibit those devices or activities which have a commercially significant purpose or use other than to circumvent the technical protection. In particular, this protection should not hinder research into cryptography.

(49) The legal protection of technological measures is without prejudice to the application of any national provisions which may prohibit the private possession of devices, products or components for the circumvention of technological measures.

(50) Such a harmonised legal protection does not affect the specific provisions on protection provided for by Directive 91/250/EEC. In particular, it should not apply to the protection of technological measures used in connection with computer programs, which is exclusively addressed in that Directive. It should neither inhibit nor prevent the development or use of any means of circumventing a technological measure that is necessary to enable acts to be undertaken in accordance with the terms of Article 5(3) or Article 6 of Directive 91/250/EEC. Articles 5 and 6 of that Directive exclusively determine exceptions to the exclusive rights applicable to computer programs.

5

(51) The legal protection of technological measures applies without prejudice to public policy, as reflected in Article 5, or public security. Member States should promote voluntary measures taken by rightholders, including the conclusion and implementation of agreements between rightholders and other parties concerned, to accommodate achieving the objectives of certain exceptions or limitations provided for in national law in accordance with this Directive. In the absence of such voluntary measures or agreements within a reasonable period of time, Member States should take appropriate measures to ensure that rightholders provide beneficiaries of such exceptions or limitations with appropriate means of benefiting from them, by modifying an implemented technological measure or by other means. However, in order to prevent abuse of such measures taken by rightholders, including within the framework of agreements, or taken by a Member State, any technological measures applied in implementation of such measures should enjoy legal protection.

(52) When implementing an exception or limitation for private copying in accordance with Article 5(2)(b), Member States should likewise promote the use of voluntary measures to accommodate achieving the objectives of such exception or limitation. If, within a reasonable period of time, no such voluntary measures to make reproduction for private use possible have been taken, Member States may take measures to enable beneficiaries of the exception or limitation concerned to benefit from it. Voluntary measures taken by rightholders, including agreements between rightholders and other parties concerned, as well as measures taken by Member States, do not prevent rightholders from using technological measures which are consistent with the exceptions or limitations on private copying in national law in accordance with Article 5(2)(b), taking account of the condition of fair compensation under that provision and the possible differentiation between various conditions of use in accordance with Article 5(5), such as controlling the number of reproductions. In order to prevent abuse of such measures, any technological measures applied in their implementation should enjoy legal protection.

(53) The protection of technological measures should ensure a secure environment for the provision of interactive on-demand services, in such a way that members of the public may access works or other subject-matter from a place and at a time individually chosen by them. Where such services are governed by contractual arrangements, the first and second subparagraphs of Article 6(4) should not apply. Non-interactive forms of online use should remain subject to those provisions.

(54) Important progress has been made in the international standardisation of technical systems of identification of works and protected subject-matter in digital format. In an increasingly networked environment, differences between technological measures could lead to an incompatibility of systems within the Community. Compatibility and interoperability of the different systems should be encouraged. It would be highly desirable to encourage the development of global systems.

(55) Technological development will facilitate the distribution of works, notably on networks, and this will entail the need for rightholders to identify better the work or other subject-matter, the author or any other rightholder, and to provide information about the

terms and conditions of use of the work or other subject-matter in order to render easier the management of rights attached to them. Rightholders should be encouraged to use markings indicating, in addition to the information referred to above, inter alia their authorisation when putting works or other subject-matter on networks.

(56) There is, however, the danger that illegal activities might be carried out in order to remove or alter the electronic copyright-management information attached to it, or otherwise to distribute, import for distribution, broadcast, communicate to the public or make available to the public works or other protected subject-matter from which such information has been removed without authority. In order to avoid fragmented legal approaches that could potentially hinder the functioning of the internal market, there is a need to provide for harmonised legal protection against any of these activities.

(57) Any such rights-management information systems referred to above may, depending on their design, at the same time process personal data about the consumption patterns of protected subject-matter by individuals and allow for tracing of on-line behaviour. These technical means, in their technical functions, should incorporate privacy safeguards in accordance with Directive 95/46/EC of the European Parliament and of the Council of 24 October 1995 on the protection of individuals with regard to the processing of personal data and the free movement of such data[10]).

(58) Member States should provide for effective sanctions and remedies for infringements of rights and obligations as set out in this Directive. They should take all the measures necessary to ensure that those sanctions and remedies are applied. The sanctions thus provided for should be effective, proportionate and dissuasive and should include the possibility of seeking damages and/or injunctive relief and, where appropriate, of applying for seizure of infringing material.

(59) In the digital environment, in particular, the services of intermediaries may increasingly be used by third parties for infringing activities. In many cases such intermediaries are best placed to bring such infringing activities to an end. Therefore, without prejudice to any other sanctions and remedies available, rightholders should have the possibility of applying for an injunction against an intermediary who carries a third party's infringement of a protected work or other subject-matter in a network. This possibility should be available even where the acts carried out by the intermediary are exempted under Article 5. The conditions and modalities relating to such injunctions should be left to the national law of the Member States.

(60) The protection provided under this Directive should be without prejudice to national or Community legal provisions in other areas, such as industrial property, data protection, conditional access, access to public documents, and the rule of media exploitation chronology, which may affect the protection of copyright or related rights.

(61) In order to comply with the WIPO Performances and Phonograms Treaty, Directives 92/100/EEC and 93/98/EEC should be amended,

HAVE ADOPTED THIS DIRECTIVE:

---

[10]) OJ L 281, 23. 11. 1995, p. 31.

5

CHAPTER I
OBJECTIVE AND SCOPE

Article 1
Scope

1. This Directive concerns the legal protection of copyright and related rights in the framework of the internal market, with particular emphasis on the information society.

2. Except in the cases referred to in Article 11, this Directive shall leave intact and shall in no way affect existing Community provisions relating to:

(a) the legal protection of computer programs;

(b) rental right, lending right and certain rights related to copyright in the field of intellectual property;

(c) copyright and related rights applicable to broadcasting of programmes by satellite and cable retransmission;

(d) the term of protection of copyright and certain related rights;

(e) the legal protection of databases.

CHAPTER II
RIGHTS AND EXCEPTIONS

Article 2
Reproduction right

Member States shall provide for the exclusive right to authorise or prohibit direct or indirect, temporary or permanent reproduction by any means and in any form, in whole or in part:

(a) for authors, of their works;

(b) for performers, of fixations of their performances;

(c) for phonogram producers, of their phonograms;

(d) for the producers of the first fixations of films, in respect of the original and copies of their films;

(e) for broadcasting organisations, of fixations of their broadcasts, whether those broadcasts are transmitted by wire or over the air, including by cable or satellite.

Article 3
Right of communication to the public of works and right of making available to the public other subject-matter

1. Member States shall provide authors with the exclusive right to authorise or prohibit any communication to the public of their works, by wire or wireless means, including the making available to the public of their works in such a way that members of the public may access them from a place and at a time individually chosen by them.

2. Member States shall provide for the exclusive right to authorise or prohibit the making available to the public, by wire or wireless means, in such a way that members of the public may access them from a place and at a time individually chosen by them:

(a) for performers, of fixations of their performances;

(b) for phonogram producers, of their phonograms;

(c) for the producers of the first fixations of films, of the original and copies of their films;

(d) for broadcasting organisations, of fixations of their broadcasts, whether these broadcasts are transmitted by wire or over the air, including by cable or satellite.

3. The rights referred to in paragraphs 1 and 2 shall not be exhausted by any act of communication to the public or making available to the public as set out in this Article.

5

Article 4
Distribution right

1. Member States shall provide for authors, in respect of the original of their works or of copies thereof, the exclusive right to authorise or prohibit any form of distribution to the public by sale or otherwise.

2. The distribution right shall not be exhausted within the Community in respect of the original or copies of the work, except where the first sale or other transfer of ownership in the Community of that object is made by the rightholder or with his consent.

Article 5
Exceptions and limitations

1. Temporary acts of reproduction referred to in Article 2, which are transient or incidental which are an integral and essential part of a technological process and the sole purpose of which is to enable:

(a) a transmission in a network between third parties by an intermediary, or

(b) a lawful use

of a work or other subject-matter to be made, and which have no independent economic significance, shall be exempted from the reproduction right provided for in Article 2.

2. Member States may provide for exceptions or limitations to the reproduction right provided for in Article 2 in the following cases:

(a) in respect of reproductions on paper or any similar medium, effected by the use of any kind of photographic technique or by some other process having similar effects, with the exception of sheet music, provided that the rightholders receive fair compensation;

(b) in respect of reproductions on any medium made by a natural person for private use and for ends that are neither directly nor indirectly commercial, on condition that the rightholders receive fair compensation which takes account of the application or non-application of technological measures referred to in Article 6 to the work or subject-matter concerned;

(c) in respect of specific acts of reproduction made by publicly accessible libraries, educational establishments or museums, or by archives, which are not for direct or indirect economic or commercial advantage;

(d) in respect of ephemeral recordings of works made by broadcasting organisations by means of their own facilities and for their own broadcasts; the preservation of these recordings in official archives may, on the grounds of their exceptional documentary character, be permitted;

(e) in respect of reproductions of broadcasts made by social institutions pursuing non-commercial purposes, such as hospitals or prisons, on condition that the rightholders receive fair compensation.

3. Member States may provide for exceptions or limitations to the rights provided for in Articles 2 and 3 in the following cases:

(a) use for the sole purpose of illustration for teaching or scientific research, as long as the source, including the author's name, is indicated, unless this turns out to be impossible and to the extent justified by the non-commercial purpose to be achieved;

(b) uses, for the benefit of people with a disability, which are directly related to the disability and of a non-commercial nature, to the extent required by the specific disability;

5

(c) reproduction by the press, communication to the public or making available of published articles on current economic, political or religious topics or of broadcast works or other subject-matter of the same character, in cases where such use is not expressly reserved, and as long as the source, including the author's name, is indicated, or use of works or other subject-matter in connection with the reporting of current events, to the extent justified by the informatory purpose and as long as the source, including the author's name, is indicated, unless this turns out to be impossible;

(d) quotations for purposes such as criticism or review, provided that they relate to a work or other subject-matter which has already been lawfully made available to the public, that, unless this turns out to be impossible, the source, including the author's name, is indicated, and that their use is in accordance with fair practice, and to the extent required by the specific purpose;

(e) use for the purposes of public security or to ensure the proper performance or reporting of administrative, parliamentary or judicial proceedings;

(f) use of political speeches as well as extracts of public lectures or similar works or subject-matter to the extent justified by the informatory purpose and provided that the source, including the author's name, is indicated, except where this turns out to be impossible;

(g) use during religious celebrations or official celebrations organised by a public authority;

(h) use of works, such as works of architecture or sculpture, made to be located permanently in public places;

(i) incidental inclusion of a work or other subject-matter in other material;

(j) use for the purpose of advertising the public exhibition or sale of artistic works, to the extent necessary to promote the event, excluding any other commercial use;

(k) use for the purpose of caricature, parody or pastiche;

(l) use in connection with the demonstration or repair of equipment;

(m) use of an artistic work in the form of a building or a drawing or plan of a building for the purposes of reconstructing the building;

(n) use by communication or making available, for the purpose of research or private study, to individual members of the public by dedicated terminals on the premises of establishments referred to in paragraph 2(c) of works and other subject-matter not subject to purchase or licensing terms which are contained in their collections;

(o) use in certain other cases of minor importance where exceptions or limitations already exist under national law, provided that they only concern analogue uses and do not affect the free circulation of goods and services within the Community, without prejudice to the other exceptions and limitations contained in this Article.

4. Where the Member States may provide for an exception or limitation to the right of reproduction pursuant to paragraphs 2 and 3, they may provide similarly for an exception or limitation to the right of distribution as referred to in Article 4 to the extent justified by the purpose of the authorised act of reproduction.

5. The exceptions and limitations provided for in paragraphs 1, 2, 3 and 4 shall only be applied in certain special cases which do not conflict with a normal exploitation of the work or other

5

subject-matter and do not unreasonably prejudice the legitimate interests of the rightholder.

CHAPTER III
PROTECTION OF TECHNOLOGICAL MEASURES AND RIGHTS-MANAGEMENT INFORMATION
Article 6
Obligations as to technological measures

1. Member States shall provide adequate legal protection against the circumvention of any effective technological measures, which the person concerned carries out in the knowledge, or with reasonable grounds to know, that he or she is pursuing that objective.

2. Member States shall provide adequate legal protection against the manufacture, import, distribution, sale, rental, advertisement for sale or rental, or possession for commercial purposes of devices, products or components or the provision of services which:

(a) are promoted, advertised or marketed for the purpose of circumvention of, or

(b) have only a limited commercially significant purpose or use other than to circumvent, or

(c) are primarily designed, produced, adapted or performed for the purpose of enabling or facilitating the circumvention of,

any effective technological measures.

3. For the purposes of this Directive, the expression "technological measures" means any technology, device or component that, in the normal course of its operation, is designed to prevent or restrict acts, in respect of works or other subject-matter, which are not authorised by the rightholder of any copyright or any right related to copyright as provided for by law or the *sui generis* right provided for in Chapter III of Directive 96/9/EC. Technological measures shall be deemed "effective" where the use of a protected work or other subject-matter is controlled by the rightholders through application of an access control or protection process, such as encryption, scrambling or other transformation of the work or other subject-matter or a copy control mechanism, which achieves the protection objective.

4. Notwithstanding the legal protection provided for in paragraph 1, in the absence of voluntary measures taken by rightholders, including agreements between rightholders and other parties concerned, Member States shall take appropriate measures to ensure that rightholders make available to the beneficiary of an exception or limitation provided for in national law in accordance with Article 5(2)(a), (2)(c), (2)(d), (2)(e), (3)(a), (3)(b) or (3)(e) the means of benefiting from that exception or limitation, to the extent necessary to benefit from that exception or limitation and where that beneficiary has legal access to the protected work or subject-matter concerned.

A Member State may also take such measures in respect of a beneficiary of an exception or limitation provided for in accordance with Article 5(2)(b), unless reproduction for private use has already been made possible by rightholders to the extent necessary to benefit from the exception or limitation concerned and in accordance with the provisions of Article 5(2)(b) and (5), without preventing rightholders from adopting adequate measures regarding

5

the number of reproductions in accordance with these provisions.

The technological measures applied voluntarily by rightholders, including those applied in implementation of voluntary agreements, and technological measures applied in implementation of the measures taken by Member States, shall enjoy the legal protection provided for in paragraph 1.

The provisions of the first and second subparagraphs shall not apply to works or other subject-matter made available to the public on agreed contractual terms in such a way that members of the public may access them from a place and at a time individually chosen by them.

When this Article is applied in the context of Directives 92/100/EEC and 96/9/EC, this paragraph shall apply *mutatis mutandis.*

Article 7
Obligations concerning rights-management information

1. Member States shall provide for adequate legal protection against any person knowingly performing without authority any of the following acts:

(a) the removal or alteration of any electronic rights-management information;

(b) the distribution, importation for distribution, broadcasting, communication or making available to the public of works or other subject-matter protected under this Directive or under Chapter III of Directive 96/9/EC from which electronic rights-management information has been removed or altered without authority,

if such person knows, or has reasonable grounds to know, that by so doing he is inducing, enabling, facilitating or concealing an infringement of any copyright or any rights related to copyright as provided by law, or of the *sui generis* right provided for in Chapter III of Directive 96/9/EC.

2. For the purposes of this Directive, the expression "rights-management information" means any information provided by rightholders which identifies the work or other subject-matter referred to in this Directive or covered by the *sui generis* right provided for in Chapter III of Directive 96/9/EC, the author or any other rightholder, or information about the terms and conditions of use of the work or other subject-matter, and any numbers or codes that represent such information.

The first subparagraph shall apply when any of these items of information is associated with a copy of, or appears in connection with the communication to the public of, a work or other subjectmatter referred to in this Directive or covered by the *sui generis* right provided for in Chapter III of Directive 96/9/EC.

CHAPTER IV
COMMON PROVISIONS
Article 8
Sanctions and remedies

1. Member States shall provide appropriate sanctions and remedies in respect of infringements of the rights and obligations set out in this Directive and shall take all the measures necessary to ensure that those sanctions and remedies are applied. The sanctions thus provided for shall be effective, proportionate and dissuasive.

2. Each Member State shall take the measures necessary to ensure that

rightholders whose interests are affected by an infringing activity carried out on its territory can bring an action for damages and/or apply for an injunction and, where appropriate, for the seizure of infringing material as well as of devices, products or components referred to in Article 6(2).

3. Member States shall ensure that rightholders are in a position to apply for an injunction against intermediaries whose services are used by a third party to infringe a copyright or related right.

Article 9
Continued application of other legal provisions

This Directive shall be without prejudice to provisions concerning in particular patent rights, trade marks, design rights, utility models, topographies of semi-conductor products, type faces, conditional access, access to cable of broadcasting services, protection of national treasures, legal deposit requirements, laws on restrictive practices and unfair competition, trade secrets, security, confidentiality, data protection and privacy, access to public documents, the law of contract.

Article 10
Application over time

1. The provisions of this Directive shall apply in respect of all works and other subject-matter referred to in this Directive which are, on 22 December 2002, protected by the Member States' legislation in the field of copyright and related rights, or which meet the criteria for protection under the provisions of this Directive or the provisions referred to in Article 1(2).

2. This Directive shall apply without prejudice to any acts concluded and rights acquired before 22 December 2002.

Article 11
Technical adaptations

1. Directive 92/100/EEC is hereby amended as follows:
   (a) Article 7 shall be deleted;
   (b) Article 10(3) shall be replaced by the following:
   "3. The limitations shall only be applied in certain special cases which do not conflict with a normal exploitation of the subject-matter and do not unreasonably prejudice the legitimate interests of the rightholder."

2. Article 3(2) of Directive 93/98/EEC shall be replaced by the following:
   "2. The rights of producers of phonograms shall expire 50 years after the fixation is made. However, if the phonogram has been lawfully published within this period, the said rights shall expire 50 years from the date of the first lawful publication. If no lawful publication has taken place within the period mentioned in the first sentence, and if the phonogram has been lawfully communicated to the public within this period, the said rights shall expire 50 years from the date of the first lawful communication to the public.

   However, where through the expiry of the term of protection granted pursuant to this paragraph in its version before amendment by Directive 2001/29/EC of the European Parliament and of the Council of 22 May 2001 on the harmonisation of certain aspects of copyright and related rights in the information society[11]) the rights of producers of phonograms are no longer

---

[11]) OJ L 167, 22. 6. 2001, p. 10.

protected on 22 December 2002, this paragraph shall not have the effect of protecting those rights anew."

Article 12
Final provisions

1. Not later than 22 December 2004 and every three years thereafter, the Commission shall submit to the European Parliament, the Council and the Economic and Social Committee a report on the application of this Directive, in which, *inter alia,* on the basis of specific information supplied by the Member States, it shall examine in particular the application of Articles 5, 6 and 8 in the light of the development of the digital market. In the case of Article 6, it shall examine in particular whether that Article confers a sufficient level of protection and whether acts which are permitted by law are being adversely affected by the use of effective technological measures. Where necessary, in particular to ensure the functioning of the internal market pursuant to Article 14 of the Treaty, it shall submit proposals for amendments to this Directive.

2. Protection of rights related to copyright under this Directive shall leave intact and shall in no way affect the protection of copyright.

3. A contact committee is hereby established. It shall be composed of representatives of the competent authorities of the Member States. It shall be chaired by a representative of the Commission and shall meet either on the initiative of the chairman or at the request of the delegation of a Member State.

4. The tasks of the committee shall be as follows:

(a) to examine the impact of this Directive on the functioning of the internal market, and to highlight any difficulties;

(b) to organise consultations on all questions deriving from the application of this Directive;

(c) to facilitate the exchange of information on relevant developments in legislation and case-law, as well as relevant economic, social, cultural and technological developments;

(d) to act as a forum for the assessment of the digital market in works and other items, including private copying and the use of technological measures.

Article 13
Implementation

1. Member States shall bring into force the laws, regulations and administrative provisions necessary to comply with this Directive before 22 December 2002. They shall forthwith inform the Commission thereof.

When Member States adopt these measures, they shall contain a reference to this Directive or shall be accompanied by such reference on the occasion of their official publication. The methods of making such reference shall be laid down by Member States.

2. Member States shall communicate to the Commission the text of the provisions of domestic law which they adopt in the field governed by this Directive.

Article 14
Entry into force

This Directive shall enter into force on the day of its publication in the Official Journal of the European Communities.

Article 15
Addressees

This Directive is addressed to the Member States.

6

Database Directive
Directive 96/9/EC of the European Parliament and of the Council of 11 March 1996 on the legal protection of databases

OJ L 77, 27. 3. 1996, p. 20

THE EUROPEAN PARLIAMENT AND THE COUNCIL OF THE EUROPEAN UNION,

Having regard to the Treaty establishing the European Community, and in particular Article 57 (2), 66 and 100a thereof,

Having regard to the proposal from the Commission [1]),

Having regard to the opinion of the Economic and Social Committee [2]),

Acting in accordance with the procedure laid down in Article 189b of the Treaty[3]),

(1) Whereas databases are at present not sufficiently protected in all Member States by existing legislation; whereas such protection, where it exists, has different attributes;

(2) Whereas such differences in the legal protection of databases offered by the legislation of the Member States

have direct negative effects on the functioning of the internal market as regards databases and in particular on the freedom of natural and legal persons to provide on-line database goods and services on the basis of harmonized legal arrangements throughout the Community; whereas such differences could well become more pronounced as Member States introduce new legislation in this field, which is now taking on an increasingly international dimension;

(3) Whereas existing differences distorting the functioning of the internal market need to be removed and new ones prevented from arising, while differences not adversely affecting the functioning of the internal market or the development of an information market within the Community need not be removed or prevented from arising;

(4) Whereas copyright protection for databases exists in varying forms in the Member States according to legislation or case-law, and whereas, if differences in legislation in the scope and conditions of protection remain between the Member States, such unharmonized intellectual property rights can have the effect of preventing the free movement of goods or services within the Community;

---

[1]) OJ No C 156, 23. 6. 1992, p. 4 and OJ No C 308, 15. 11. 1993, p. 1.

[2]) OJ No C 19, 25. 1. 1993, p. 3.

[3]) Opinion of the European Parliament of 23 June 1993 (OJ No C 194, 19. 7. 1993, p. 144), Common Position of the Council of 10 July 1995 (OJ No C 288, 30. 10. 1995, p. 14), Decision of the European Parliament of 14 December 1995 (OJ No C 17, 22. 1. 1996) and Council Decision of 26 February 1996.

6

(5) Whereas copyright remains an appropriate form of exclusive right for authors who have created databases;

(6) Whereas, nevertheless, in the absence of a harmonized system of unfair-competition legislation or of case-law, other measures are required in addition to prevent the unauthorized extraction and/or re-utilization of the contents of a database;

(7) Whereas the making of databases requires the investment of considerable human, technical and financial resources while such databases can be copied or accessed at a fraction of the cost needed to design them independently;

(8) Whereas the unauthorized extraction and/or re-utilization of the contents of a database constitute acts which can have serious economic and technical consequences;

(9) Whereas databases are a vital tool in the development of an information market within the Community; whereas this tool will also be of use in many other fields;

(10) Whereas the exponential growth, in the Community and world-wide, in the amount of information generated and processed annually in all sectors of commerce and industry calls for investment in all the Member States in advanced information processing systems;

(11) Whereas there is at present a very great imbalance in the level of investment in the database sector both as between the Member States and between the Community and the world's largest database-producing third countries;

(12) Whereas such an investment in modern information storage and processing systems will not take place within the Community unless a stable

and uniform legal protection regime is introduced for the protection of the rights of makers of databases;

(13) Whereas this Directive protects collections, sometimes called 'compilations', of works, data or other materials which are arranged, stored and accessed by means which include electronic, electromagnetic or electro-optical processes or analogous processes;

(14) Whereas protection under this Directive should be extended to cover non-electronic databases;

(15) Whereas the criteria used to determine whether a database should be protected by copyright should be defined to the fact that the selection or the arrangement of the contents of the database is the author's own intellectual creation; whereas such protection should cover the structure of the database;

(16) Whereas no criterion other than originality in the sense of the author's intellectual creation should be applied to determine the eligibility of the database for copyright protection, and in particular no aesthetic or qualitative criteria should be applied;

(17) Whereas the term 'database' should be understood to include literary, artistic, musical or other collections of works or collections of other material such as texts, sound, images, numbers, facts, and data; whereas it should cover collections of independent works, data or other materials which are systematically or methodically arranged and can be individually accessed; whereas this means that a recording or an audiovisual, cinematographic, literary or musical work as such does not fall within the scope of this Directive;

(18) Whereas this Directive is without prejudice to the freedom of authors

to decide whether, or in what manner, they will allow their works to be included in a database, in particular whether or not the authorization given is exclusive; whereas the protection of databases by the *sui generis* right is without prejudice to existing rights over their contents, and whereas in particular where an author or the holder of a related right permits some of his works or subject matter to be included in a database pursuant to a non-exclusive agreement, a third party may make use of those works or subject matter subject to the required consent of the author or of the holder of the related right without the sui generis right of the maker of the database being invoked to prevent him doing so, on condition that those works or subject matter are neither extracted from the database nor re-utilized on the basis thereof;

(19) Whereas, as a rule, the compilation of several recordings of musical performances on a CD does not come within the scope of this Directive, both because, as a compilation, it does not meet the conditions for copyright protection and because it does not represent a substantial enough investment to be eligible under the *sui generis* right;

(20) Whereas protection under this Directive may also apply to the materials necessary for the operation or consultation of certain databases such as thesaurus and indexation systems;

(21) Whereas the protection provided for in this Directive relates to databases in which works, data or other materials have been arranged systematically or methodically; whereas it is not necessary for those materials to have been physically stored in an organized manner;

(22) Whereas electronic databases within the meaning of this Directive may also include devices such as CD-ROM and CD-i;

(23) Whereas the term 'database' should not be taken to extend to computer programs used in the making or operation of a database, which are protected by Council Directive 91/250/EEC of 14 May 1991 on the legal protection of computer programs[4]);

(24) Whereas the rental and lending of databases in the field of copyright and related rights are governed exclusively by Council Directive 92/100/EEC of 19 November 1992 on rental right and lending right and on certain rights related to copyright in the field of intellectual property[5]);

(25) Whereas the term of copyright is already governed by Council Directive 93/98/EEC of 29 October 1993 harmonizing the term of protection of copyright and certain related rights[6]);

(26) Whereas works protected by copyright and subject matter protected by related rights, which are incorporated into a database, remain nevertheless protected by the respective exclusive rights and may not be incorporated into, or extracted from, the database without the permission of the rightholder or his successors in title;

(27) Whereas copyright in such works and related rights in subject matter thus incorporated into a database are in no way affected by the existence of a separate right in the selection or arrangement of these works and subject matter in a database;

(28) Whereas the moral rights of the natural person who created the database belong to the author and should

---

[4]) OJ No L 122, 17. 5. 1991, p. 42. Directive as last amended by Directive 93/98/EEC (OJ No L 290, 24. 11. 1993, p. 9.)
[5]) OJ No L 346, 27. 11. 1992, p. 61.
[6]) OJ No L 290, 24. 11. 1993, p. 9.

6

be exercised according to the legislation of the Member States and the provisions of the Berne Convention for the Protection of Literary and Artistic Works; whereas such moral rights remain outside the scope of this Directive;

(29) Whereas the arrangements applicable to databases created by employees are left to the discretion of the Member States; whereas, therefore nothing in this Directive prevents Member States from stipulating in their legislation that where a database is created by an employee in the execution of his duties or following the instructions given by his employer, the employer exclusively shall be entitled to exercise all economic rights in the database so created, unless otherwise provided by contract;

(30) Whereas the author's exclusive rights should include the right to determine the way in which his work is exploited and by whom, and in particular to control the distribution of his work to unauthorized persons;

(31) Whereas the copyright protection of databases includes making databases available by means other than the distribution of copies;

(32) Whereas Member States are required to ensure that their national provisions are at least materially equivalent in the case of such acts subject to restrictions as are provided for by this Directive;

(33) Whereas the question of exhaustion of the right of distribution does not arise in the case of on-line databases, which come within the field of provision of services; whereas this also applies with regard to a material copy of such a database made by the user of such a service with the consent of the rightholder; whereas, unlike CD-ROM

or CD-i, where the intellectual property is incorporated in a material medium, namely an item of goods, every on-line service is in fact an act which will have to be subject to authorization where the copyright so provides;

(34) Whereas, nevertheless, once the rightholder has chosen to make available a copy of the database to a user, whether by an on-line service or by other means of distribution, that lawful user must be able to access and use the database for the purposes and in the way set out in the agreement with the rightholder, even if such access and use necessitate performance of otherwise restricted acts;

(35) Whereas a list should be drawn up of exceptions to restricted acts, taking into account the fact that copyright as covered by this Directive applies only to the selection or arrangements of the contents of a database; whereas Member States should be given the option of providing for such exceptions in certain cases; whereas, however, this option should be exercised in accordance with the Berne Convention and to the extent that the exceptions relate to the structure of the database; whereas a distinction should be drawn between exceptions for private use and exceptions for reproduction for private purposes, which concerns provisions under national legislation of some Member States on levies on blank media or recording equipment;

(36) Whereas the term 'scientific research' within the meaning of this Directive covers both the natural sciences and the human sciences;

(37) Whereas Article 10 (1) of the Berne Convention is not affected by this Directive;

(38) Whereas the increasing use of digital recording technology exposes

the database maker to the risk that the contents of his database may be copied and rearranged electronically, without his authorization, to produce a database of identical content which, however, does not infringe any copyright in the arrangement of his database;

(39) Whereas, in addition to aiming to protect the copyright in the original selection or arrangement of the contents of a database, this Directive seeks to safeguard the position of makers of databases against misappropriation of the results of the financial and professional investment made in obtaining and collection the contents by protecting the whole or substantial parts of a database against certain acts by a user or competitor;

(40) Whereas the object of this *sui generis* right is to ensure protection of any investment in obtaining, verifying or presenting the contents of a database for the limited duration of the right; whereas such investment may consist in the deployment of financial resources and/or the expending of time, effort and energy;

(41) Whereas the objective of the *sui generis* right is to give the maker of a database the option of preventing the unauthorized extraction and/or re-utilization of all or a substantial part of the contents of that database; whereas the maker of a database is the person who takes the initiative and the risk of investing; whereas this excludes subcontractors in particular from the definition of maker;

(42) Whereas the special right to prevent unauthorized extraction and/or re-utilization relates to acts by the user which go beyond his legitimate rights and thereby harm the investment; whereas the right to prohibit extraction and/or re-utilization of all or a substantial part of the contents relates

not only to the manufacture of a parasitical competing product but also to any user who, through his acts, causes significant detriment, evaluated qualitatively or quantitatively, to the investment;

(43) Whereas, in the case of on-line transmission, the right to prohibit re-utilization is not exhausted either as regards the database or as regards a material copy of the database or of part thereof made by the addressee of the transmission with the consent of the rightholder;

(44) Whereas, when on-screen display of the contents of a database necessitates the permanent or temporary transfer of all or a substantial part of such contents to another medium, that act should be subject to authorization by the rightholder;

(45) Whereas the right to prevent unauthorized extraction and/or re-utilization does not in any way constitute an extension of copyright protection to mere facts or data;

(46) Whereas the existence of a right to prevent the unauthorized extraction and/or re-utilization of the whole or a substantial part of works, data or materials from a database should not give rise to the creation of a new right in the works, data or materials themselves;

(47) Whereas, in the interests of competition between suppliers of information products and services, protection by the *sui generis* right must not be afforded in such a way as to facilitate abuses of a dominant position, in particular as regards the creation and distribution of new products and services which have an intellectual, documentary, technical, economic or commercial added value; whereas, therefore, the provisions of this Directive are without prejudice to the application of

6

Community or national competition rules;

(48) Whereas the objective of this Directive, which is to afford an appropriate and uniform level of protection of databases as a means to secure the remuneration of the maker of the database, is different from the aim of Directive 95/46/EC of the European Parliament and of the Council of 24 October 1995 on the protection of individuals with regard to the processing of personal data and on the free movement of such data[7]), which is to guarantee free circulation of personal data on the basis of harmonized rules designed to protect fundamental rights, notably the right to privacy which is recognized in Article 8 of the European Convention for the Protection of Human Rights and Fundamental Freedoms; whereas the provisions of this Directive are without prejudice to data protection legislation;

(49) Whereas, notwithstanding the right to prevent extraction and/or re-utilization of all or a substantial part of a database, it should be laid down that the maker of a database or rightholder may not prevent a lawful user of the database from extracting and re-utilizing insubstantial parts; whereas, however, that user may not unreasonably prejudice either the legitimate interests of the holder of the *sui generis* right or the holder of copyright or a related right in respect of the works or subject matter contained in the database;

(50) Whereas the Member States should be given the option of providing for exceptions to the right to prevent the unauthorized extraction and/or re-utilization of a substantial part of the contents of a database in the case of ex-

traction for private purposes, for the purposes of illustration for teaching or scientific research, or where extraction and/or re-utilization are/is carried out in the interests of public security or for the purposes of an administrative or judicial procedure; whereas such operations must not prejudice the exclusive rights of the maker to exploit the database and their purpose must not be commercial;

(51) Whereas the Member States, where they avail themselves of the option to permit a lawful user of a database to extract a substantial part of the contents for the purposes of illustration for teaching or scientific research, may limit that permission to certain categories of teaching or scientific research institution;

(52) Whereas those Member States which have specific rules providing for a right comparable to the *sui generis* right provided for in this Directive should be permitted to retain, as far as the new right is concerned, the exceptions traditionally specified by such rules;

(53) Whereas the burden of proof regarding the date of completion of the making of a database lies with the maker of the database;

(54) Whereas the burden of proof that the criteria exist for concluding that a substantial modification of the contents of a database is to be regarded as a substantial new investment lies with the maker of the database resulting from such investment;

(55) Whereas a substantial new investment involving a new term of protection may include a substantial verification of the contents of the database;

(56) Whereas the right to prevent unauthorized extraction and/or re-utilization in respect of a database should

---

[7]) OJ No L 281, 23. 11. 1995, p. 31.

6

apply to databases whose makers are nationals or habitual residents of third countries or to those produced by legal persons not established in a Member State, within the meaning of the Treaty, only if such third countries offer comparable protection to databases produced by nationals of a Member State or persons who have their habitual residence in the territory of the Community;

(57) Whereas, in addition to remedies provided under the legislation of the Member States for infringements of copyright or other rights, Member States should provide for appropriate remedies against unauthorized extraction and/or re-utilization of the contents of a database;

(58) Whereas, in addition to the protection given under this Directive to the structure of the database by copyright, and to its contents against unauthorized extraction and/or re-utilization under the *sui generis* right, other legal provisions in the Member States relevant to the supply of database goods and services continue to apply;

(59) Whereas this Directive is without prejudice to the application to databases composed of audiovisual works of any rules recognized by a Member State's legislation concerning the broadcasting of audiovisual programmes;

(60) Whereas some Member States currently protect under copyright arrangements databases which do not meet the criteria for eligibility for copyright protection laid down in this Directive; whereas, even if the databases concerned are eligible for protection under the right laid down in this Directive to prevent unauthorized extraction and/or re-utilization of their contents, the term of protection under that right is considerably shorter than that which

they enjoy under the national arrangements currently in force; whereas harmonization of the criteria for determining whether a database is to be protected by copyright may not have the effect of reducing the term of protection currently enjoyed by the rightholders concerned; whereas a derogation should be laid down to that effect; whereas the effects of such derogation must be confined to the territories of the Member States concerned,

HAVE ADOPTED THIS DIRECTIVE:

CHAPTER I
SCOPE
Article 1
Scope

1. This Directive concerns the legal protection of databases in any form.

2. For the purposes of this Directive, 'database' shall mean a collection of independent works, data or other materials arranged in a systematic or methodical way and individually accessible by electronic or other means.

3. Protection under this Directive shall not apply to computer programs used in the making or operation of databases accessible by electronic means.

Article 2
Limitations on the scope

This Directive shall apply without prejudice to Community provisions relating to:

(a) the legal protection of computer programs;

(b) rental right, lending right and certain rights related to copyright in the field of intellectual property;

(c) the term of protection of copyright and certain related rights.

6

CHAPTER II
COPYRIGHT

Article 3
Object of protection

1. In accordance with this Directive, databases which, by reason of the selection or arrangement of their contents, constitute the author's own intellectual creation shall be protected as such by copyright. No other criteria shall be applied to determine their eligibility for that protection.

2. The copyright protection of databases provided for by this Directive shall not extend to their contents and shall be without prejudice to any rights subsisting in those contents themselves.

Article 4
Database authorship

1. The author of a database shall be the natural person or group of natural persons who created the base or, where the legislation of the Member States so permits, the legal person designated as the rightholder by that legislation.

2. Where collective works are recognized by the legislation of a Member State, the economic rights shall be owned by the person holding the copyright.

3. In respect of a database created by a group of natural persons jointly, the exclusive rights shall be owned jointly.

Article 5
Restricted acts

In respect of the expression of the database which is protectable by copyright, the author of a database shall have the exclusive right to carry out or to authorize:

(a) temporary or permanent reproduction by any means and in any form, in whole or in part;

(b) translation, adaptation, arrangement and any other alteration;

(c) any form of distribution to the public of the database or of copies thereof. The first sale in the Community of a copy of the database by the rightholder or with his consent shall exhaust the right to control resale of that copy within the Community;

(d) any communication, display or performance to the public;

(e) any reproduction, distribution, communication, display or performance to the public of the results of the acts referred to in (b).

Article 6
Exceptions to restricted acts

1. The performance by the lawful user of a database or of a copy thereof of any of the acts listed in Article 5 which is necessary for the purposes of access to the contents of the databases and normal use of the contents by the lawful user shall not require the authorization of the author of the database. Where the lawful user is authorized to use only part of the database, this provision shall apply only to that part.

2. Member States shall have the option of providing for limitations on the rights set out in Article 5 in the following cases:

(a) in the case of reproduction for private purposes of a non-electronic database;

(b) where there is use for the sole purpose of illustration for teaching or scientific research, as long as the source is indicated and to the extent justified by the non-commercial purpose to be achieved;

6

(c) where there is use for the purposes of public security of for the purposes of an administrative or judicial procedure;

(d) where other exceptions to copyright which are traditionally authorized under national law are involved, without prejudice to points (a), (b) and (c).

3. In accordance with the Berne Convention for the protection of Literary and Artistic Works, this Article may not be interpreted in such a way as to allow its application to be used in a manner which unreasonably prejudices the rightholder's legitimate interests or conflicts with normal exploitation of the database.

CHAPTER III
SUI GENERIS RIGHT
Article 7
Object of protection

1. Member States shall provide for a right for the maker of a database which shows that there has been qualitatively and/or quantitatively a substantial investment in either the obtaining, verification or presentation of the contents to prevent extraction and/or re-utilization of the whole or of a substantial part, evaluated qualitatively and/or quantitatively, of the contents of that database.

2. For the purposes of this Chapter:

(a) 'extraction' shall mean the permanent or temporary transfer of all or a substantial part of the contents of a database to another medium by any means or in any form;

(b) 're-utilization' shall mean any form of making available to the public all or a substantial part of the contents of a database by the distribution of copies, by renting, by on-line or other forms of transmission. The first sale of a copy of a database within the Community by the rightholder or with his consent shall exhaust the right to control resale of that copy within the Community;

Public lending is not an act of extraction or re-utilization.

3. The right referred to in paragraph 1 may be transferred, assigned or granted under contractual licence.

4. The right provided for in paragraph 1 shall apply irrespective of the eligibility of that database for protection by copyright or by other rights. Moreover, it shall apply irrespective of eligibility of the contents of that database for protection by copyright or by other rights. Protection of databases under the right provided for in paragraph 1 shall be without prejudice to rights existing in respect of their contents.

5. The repeated and systematic extraction and/or re-utilization of insubstantial parts of the contents of the database implying acts which conflict with a normal exploitation of that database or which unreasonably prejudice the legitimate interests of the maker of the database shall not be permitted.

Article 8
Rights and obligations
of lawful users

1. The maker of a database which is made available to the public in whatever manner may not prevent a lawful user of the database from extracting and/or re-utilizing insubstantial parts of its contents, evaluated qualitatively and/or quantitatively, for any purposes whatsoever. Where the lawful user is authorized to extract and/or re-utilize only part of the database, this paragraph shall apply only to that part.

2. A lawful user of a database which is made available to the public in whatever manner may not perform acts which conflict with normal exploitation of the database or unreasonably prejudice the legitimate interests of the maker of the database.

3. A lawful user of a database which is made available to the public in any manner may not cause prejudice to the holder of a copyright or related right in respect of the works or subject matter contained in the database.

Article 9
Exceptions to the *sui generis* right

Member States may stipulate that lawful users of a database which is made available to the public in whatever manner may, without the authorization of its maker, extract or re-utilize a substantial part of its contents:

(a) in the case of extraction for private purposes of the contents of a non-electronic database;

(b) in the case of extraction for the purposes of illustration for teaching or scientific research, as long as the source is indicated and to the extent justified by the non-commercial purpose to be achieved;

(c) in the case of extraction and/or re-utilization for the purposes of public security or an administrative or judicial procedure.

Article 10
Term of protection

1. The right provided for in Article 7 shall run from the date of completion of the making of the database. It shall expire fifteen years from the first of January of the year following the date of completion.

2. In the case of a database which is made available to the public in whatever manner before expiry of the period provided for in paragraph 1, the term of protection by that right shall expire fifteen years from the first of January of the year following the date when the database was first made available to the public.

3. Any substantial change, evaluated qualitatively or quantitatively, to the contents of a database, including any substantial change resulting from the accumulation of successive additions, deletions or alterations, which would result in the database being considered to be a substantial new investment, evaluated qualitatively or quantitatively, shall qualify the database resulting from that investment for its own term of protection.

Article 11
Beneficiaries of protection under the *sui generis* right

1. The right provided for in Article 7 shall apply to database whose makers or rightholders are nationals of a Member State or who have their habitual residence in the territory of the Community.

2. Paragraph 1 shall also apply to companies and firms formed in accordance with the law of a Member State and having their registered office, central administration or principal place of business within the Community; however, where such a company or firm has only its registered office in the territory of the Community, its operations must be genuinely linked on an ongoing basis with the economy of a Member State.

3. Agreements extending the right provided for in Article 7 to databases made in third countries and falling out-

side the provisions of paragraphs 1 and 2 shall be concluded by the Council acting on a proposal from the Commission. The term of any protection extended to databases by virtue of that procedure shall not exceed that available pursuant to Article 10.

CHAPTER IV
COMMON PROVISIONS

Article 12
Remedies

Member States shall provide appropriate remedies in respect of infringements of the rights provided for in this Directive.

Article 13
Continued application of other legal provisions

This Directive shall be without prejudice to provisions concerning in particular copyright, rights related to copyright or any other rights or obligations subsisting in the data, works or other materials incorporated into a database, patent rights, trade marks, design rights, the protection of national treasures, laws on restrictive practices and unfair competition, trade secrets, security, confidentiality, data protection and privacy, access to public documents, and the law of contract.

Article 14
Application over time

1. Protection pursuant to this Directive as regards copyright shall also be available in respect of databases created prior to the date referred to Article 16 (1) which on that date fulfil the requirements laid down in this Directive as regards copyright protection of databases.

2. Notwithstanding paragraph 1, where a database protected under copyright arrangements in a Member State on the date of publication of this Directive does not fulfil the eligibility criteria for copyright protection laid down in Article 3 (1), this Directive shall not result in any curtailing in that Member State of the remaining term of protection afforded under those arrangements.

3. Protection pursuant to the provisions of this Directive as regards the right provided for in Article 7 shall also be available in respect of databases the making of which was completed not more than fifteen years prior to the date referred to in Article 16 (1) and which on that date fulfil the requirements laid down in Article 7.

4. The protection provided for in paragraphs 1 and 3 shall be without prejudice to any acts concluded and rights acquired before the date referred to in those paragraphs.

5. In the case of a database the making of which was completed not more than fifteen years prior to the date referred to in Article 16 (1), the term of protection by the right provided for in Article 7 shall expire fifteen years from the first of January following that date.

Article 15
Binding nature of certain provisions

Any contractual provision contrary to Articles 6 (1) and 8 shall be null and void.

Article 16
Final provisions

1. Member States shall bring into force the laws, regulations and administrative provisions necessary to

comply with this Directive before 1 January 1998.

When Member States adopt these provisions, they shall contain a reference to this Directive or shall be accompanied by such reference on the occasion of their official publication. The methods of making such reference shall be laid down by Member States.

2. Member States shall communicate to the Commission the text of the provisions of domestic law which they adopt in the field governed by this Directive.

3. Not later than at the end of the third year after the date referred to in paragraph 1, and every three years thereafter, the Commission shall submit to the European Parliament, the Council and the Economic and Social Committee a report on the application of this Directive, in which, inter alia, on the basis of specific information supplied by the Member States, it shall examine in particular the application of the *sui generis* right, including Articles 8 and 9, and shall verify especially whether the application of this right has led to abuse of a dominant position or other interference with free competition which would justify appropriate measures being taken, including the establishment of non-voluntary licensing arrangements. Where necessary, it shall submit proposals for adjustment of this Directive in line with developments in the area of databases.

Article 17

This Directive is addressed to the Member States.

6

7

Software Copyright Directive
Council Directive 91/250/EEC of 14 May 1991
on the legal protection of computer programs

OJ L 122, 17. 5. 1991, p. 42, amended by OJ L 290, 24. 11. 1993, p.9

THE COUNCIL OF THE EUROPEAN COMMUNITIES,

Having regard to the Treaty establishing the European Economic Community and in particular Article 100a thereof,

Having regard to the proposal from the Commission [1]),

In cooperation with the European Parliament [2]),

Having regard to the opinion of the Economic and Social Committee [3]),

Whereas computer programs are at present not clearly protected in all Member States by existing legislation and such protection, where it exists, has different attributes;

Whereas the development of computer programs requires the investment of considerable human, technical and financial resources while computer programs can be copied at a fraction of the cost needed to develop them independently;

Whereas computer programs are playing an increasingly important role in a broad range of industries and computer program technology can accordingly be considered as being of fundamental importance for the Community's industrial development;

Whereas certain differences in the legal protection of computer programs offered by the laws of the Member States have direct and negative effects on the functioning of the common market as regards computer programs and such differences could well become greater as Member States introduce new legislation on this subject;

Whereas existing differences having such effects need to be removed and new ones prevented from arising, while differences not adversely affecting the functioning of the common market to a substantial degree need not be removed or prevented from arising;

Whereas the Community's legal framework on the protection of computer programs can accordingly in the first instance be limited to establishing that Member States should accord protection to computer programs under copyright law as literary works and, further, to establishing who and what should be protected, the exclusive rights on which protected persons should be able to rely in order to authorize or prohibit certain acts and for how long the protection should apply;

---

[1]) OJ No C 91, 12. 4. 1989, p. 4; and OJ No C 320, 20. 12. 1990, p. 22.

[2]) OJ No C 231, 17. 9. 1990, p. 78; and Decision of 17 April 1991. (Not yet published in the Official Journal).

[3]) OJ No C 329, 30. 12. 1989, p. 4.

7

Whereas, for the purpose of this Directive, the term 'computer program' shall include programs in any form, including those which are incorporated into hardware; whereas this term also includes preparatory design work leading to the development of a computer program provided that the nature of the preparatory work is such that a computer program can result from it at a later stage;

Whereas, in respect of the criteria to be applied in determining whether or not a computer program is an original work, no tests as to the qualitative or aesthetic merits of the program should be applied;

Whereas the Community is fully committed to the promotion of international standardization;

Whereas the function of a computer program is to communicate and work together with other components of a computer system and with users and, for this purpose, a logical and, where appropriate, physical interconnection and interaction is required to permit all elements of software and hardware to work with other software and hardware and with users in all the ways in which they are intended to function;

Whereas the parts of the program which provide for such interconnection and interaction between elements of software and hardware are generally known as 'interfaces';

Whereas this functional interconnection and interaction is generally known as 'interoperability'; whereas such interoperability can be defined as the ability to exchange information and mutually to use the information which has been exchanged;

Whereas, for the avoidance of doubt, it has to be made clear that only the expression of a computer program is protected and that ideas and principles which underlie any element of a program, including those which underlie its interfaces, are not protected by copyright under this Directive;

Whereas, in accordance with this principle of copyright, to the extent that logic, algorithms and programming languages comprise ideas and principles, those ideas and principles are not protected under this Directive;

Whereas, in accordance with the legislation and jurisprudence of the Member States and the international copyright conventions, the expression of those ideas and principles is to be protected by copyright;

Whereas, for the purposes of this Directive, the term 'rental' means the making available for use, for a limited period of time and for profit-making purposes, of a computer program or a copy thereof; whereas this term does not include public lending, which, accordingly, remains outside the scope of this Directive;

Whereas the exclusive rights of the author to prevent the unauthorized reproduction of his work have to be subject to a limited exception in the case of a computer program to allow the reproduction technically necessary for the use of that program by the lawful acquirer;

Whereas this means that the acts of loading and running necessary for the use of a copy of a program which has been lawfully acquired, and the act of correction of its errors, may not be prohibited by contract; whereas, in the absence of specific contractual provisions, including when a copy of the program has been sold, any other act necessary for the use of the copy of a program

7

may be performed in accordance with its intended purpose by a lawful acquirer of that copy;

Whereas a person having a right to use a computer program should not be prevented from performing acts necessary to observe, study or test the functioning of the program, provided that these acts do not infringe the copyright in the program;

Whereas the unauthorized reproduction, translation, adaptation or transformation of the form of the code in which a copy of a computer program has been made available constitutes an infringement of the exclusive rights of the author;

Whereas, nevertheless, circumstances may exist when such a reproduction of the code and translation of its form within the meaning of Article 4 (a) and (b) are indispensable to obtain the necessary information to achieve the interoperability of an independently created program with other programs;

Whereas it has therefore to be considered that in these limited circumstances only, performance of the acts of reproduction and translation by or on behalf of a person having a right to use a copy of the program is legitimate and compatible with fair practice and must therefore be deemed not to require the authorization of the rightholder;

Whereas an objective of this exception is to make it possible to connect all components of a computer system, including those of different manufacturers, so that they can work together;

Whereas such an exception to the author's exclusive rights may not be used in a way which prejudices the legitimate interests of the rightholder or which conflicts with a normal exploitation of the program;

Whereas, in order to remain in accordance with the provisions of the Berne Convention for the Protection of Literary and Artistic Works, the term of protection should be the life of the author and fifty years from the first of January of the year following the year of his death or, in the case of an anonymous or pseudonymous work, 50 years from the first of January of the year following the year in which the work is first published;

Whereas protection of computer programs under copyright laws should be without prejudice to the application, in appropriate cases, of other forms of protection; whereas, however, any contractual provisions contrary to Article 6 or to the exceptions provided for in Article 5 (2) and (3) should be null and void;

Whereas the provisions of this Directive are without prejudice to the application of the competition rules under Articles 85 and 86 of the Treaty if a dominant supplier refuses to make information available which is necessary for interoperability as defined in this Directive;

Whereas the provisions of this Directive should be without prejudice to specific requirements of Community law already enacted in respect of the publication of interfaces in the telecommunications sector or Council Decisions relating to standardization in the field of information technology and telecommunication;

Whereas this Directive does not affect derogations provided for under national legislation in accordance with the Berne Convention on points not covered by this Directive,

HAS ADOPTED THIS DIRECTIVE:

Article 1
Object of protection

1. In accordance with the provisions of this Directive, Member States shall protect computer programs, by copyright, as literary works within the meaning of the Berne Convention for the Protection of Literary and Artistic Works. For the purposes of this Directive, the term 'computer programs' shall include their preparatory design material.

2. Protection in accordance with this Directive shall apply to the expression in any form of a computer program. Ideas and principles which underlie any element of a computer program, including those which underlie its interfaces, are not protected by copyright under this Directive.

3. A computer program shall be protected if it is original in the sense that it is the author's own intellectual creation. No other criteria shall be applied to determine its eligibility for protection.

Article 2
Authorship of computer programs

1. The author of a computer program shall be the natural person or group of natural persons who has created the program or, where the legislation of the Member State permits, the legal person designated as the rightholder by that legislation. Where collective works are recognized by the legislation of a Member State, the person considered by the legislation of the Member State to have created the work shall be deemed to be its author.

2. In respect of a computer program created by a group of natural persons jointly, the exclusive rights shall be owned jointly.

3. Where a computer program is created by an employee in the execution of his duties or following the instructions given by his employer, the employer exclusively shall be entitled to exercise all economic rights in the program so created, unless otherwise provided by contract.

Article 3
Beneficiaries of protection

Protection shall be granted to all natural or legal persons eligible under national copyright legislation as applied to literary works.

Article 4
Restricted Acts

Subject to the provisions of Articles 5 and 6, the exclusive rights of the rightholder within the meaning of Article 2, shall include the right to do or to authorize:

(a) the permanent or temporary reproduction of a computer program by any means and in any form, in part or in whole. Insofar as loading, displaying, running, transmission or storage of the computer program necessitate such reproduction, such acts shall be subject to authorization by the rightholder;

(b) the translation, adaptation, arrangement and any other alteration of a computer program and the reproduction of the results thereof, without prejudice to the rights of the person who alters the program;

(c) any form of distribution to the public, including the rental, of the original computer program or of copies thereof. The first sale in the Community of a copy of a program by the rightholder or with his consent shall exhaust the distribution right within the Community of that copy, with the exception

7

of the right to control further rental of the program or a copy thereof.

Article 5
Exceptions to the restricted acts

1. In the absence of specific contractual provisions, the acts referred to in Article 4 (a) and (b) shall not require authorization by the rightholder where they are necessary for the use of the computer program by the lawful acquirer in accordance with its intended purpose, including for error correction.

2. The making of a back-up copy by a person having a right to use the computer program may not be prevented by contract insofar as it is necessary for that use.

3. The person having a right to use a copy of a computer program shall be entitled, without the authorization of the rightholder, to observe, study or test the functioning of the program in order to determine the ideas and principles which underlie any element of the program if he does so while performing any of the acts of loading, displaying, running, transmitting or storing the program which he is entitled to do.

Article 6
Decompilation

1. The authorization of the rightholder shall not be required where reproduction of the code and translation of its form within the meaning of Article 4 (a) and (b) are indispensable to obtain the information necessary to achieve the interoperability of an independently created computer program with other programs, provided that the following conditions are met:

(a) these acts are performed by the licensee or by another person having a right to use a copy of a program, or on their behalf by a person authorized to do so;

(b) the information necessary to achieve interoperability has not previously been readily available to the persons referred to in subparagraph (a); and

(c) these acts are confined to the parts of the original program which are necessary to achieve interoperability.

2. The provisions of paragraph 1 shall not permit the information obtained through its application:

(a) to be used for goals other than to achieve the interoperability of the independently created computer program;

(b) to be given to others, except when necessary for the interoperability of the independently created computer program; or

(c) to be used for the development, production or marketing of a computer program substantially similar in its expression, or for any other act which infringes copyright.

3. In accordance with the provisions of the Berne Convention for the protection of Literary and Artistic Works, the provisions of this Article may not be interpreted in such a way as to allow its application to be used in a manner which unreasonably prejudices the right holder's legitimate interests or conflicts with a normal exploitation of the computer program.

Article 7
Special measures of protection

1. Without prejudice to the provisions of Articles 4, 5 and 6, Member States shall provide, in accordance with their national legislation, appropriate remedies against a person committing

any of the acts listed in subparagraphs (a), (b) and (c) below:

(a) any act of putting into circulation a copy of a computer program knowing, or having reason to believe, that it is an infringing copy;

(b) the possession, for commercial purposes, of a copy of a computer program knowing, or having reason to believe, that it is an infringing copy;

(c) any act of putting into circulation, or the possession for commercial purposes of, any means the sole intended purpose of which is to facilitate the unauthorized removal or circumvention of any technical device which may have been applied to protect a computer program.

2. Any infringing copy of a computer program shall be liable to seizure in accordance with the legislation of the Member State concerned.

3. Member States may provide for the seizure of any means referred to in paragraph 1 (c).

Article 8
Term of protection

[repealed]*)

Article 9
Continued application of other legal provisions

1. The provisions of this Directive shall be without prejudice to any other

---

*) *Annotation by the editor:* Repealed by OJ L 290, 24. 11. 1993, p. 9.

legal provisions such as those concerning patent rights, trade-marks, unfair competition, trade secrets, protection of semi-conductor products or the law of contract. Any contractual provisions contrary to Article 6 or to the exceptions provided for in Article 5 (2) and (3) shall be null and void.

2. The provisions of this Directive shall apply also to programs created before 1 January 1993 without prejudice to any acts concluded and rights acquired before that date.

Article 10
Final provisions

1. Member States shall bring into force the laws, regulations and administrative provisions necessary to comply with this Directive before 1 January 1993.

When Member States adopt these measures, the latter shall contain a reference to this Directive or shall be accompanied by such reference on the occasion of their official publication. The methods of making such a reference shall be laid down by the Member States.

2. Member States shall communicate to the Commission the provisions of national law which they adopt in the field governed by this Directive.

Article 11

This Directive is addressed to the Member States.

8

Conditional Access Directive
Directive 98/84/EC of the European Parliament and of the Council of 20 November 1998 on the legal protection of services based on, or consisting of, conditional access

OJ L 320, 28. 11. 1998, p. 54

THE EUROPEAN PARLIAMENT AND THE COUNCIL OF THE EUROPEAN UNION,

Having regard to the Treaty establishing the European Community, and in particular Articles 57(2), 66 and 100a thereof,

Having regard to the proposal from the Commission [1]),

Having regard to the opinion of the Economic and Social Committee [2]),

Acting in accordance with the procedure laid down in Article 189b of the Treaty [3]),

(1) Whereas the objectives of the Community as laid down in the Treaty include creating an ever closer union among the peoples of Europe and ensuring economic and social progress, by eliminating the barriers which divide them;

(2) Whereas the cross-border provision of broadcasting and information

society services may contribute, from the individual point of view, to the full effectiveness of freedom of expression as a fundamental right and, from the collective point of view, to the achievement of the objectives laid down in the Treaty;

(3) Whereas the Treaty provides for the free movement of all services which are normally provided for remuneration; whereas this right, as applied to broadcasting and information society services, is also a specific manifestation in Community law of a more general principle, namely freedom of expression as enshrined in Article 10 of the European Convention for the Protection of Human Rights and Fundamental Freedoms; whereas that Article explicitly recognizes the right of citizens to receive and impart information regardless of frontiers and whereas any restriction of that right must be based on due consideration of other legitimate interests deserving of legal protection;

(4) Whereas the Commission undertook a wide-ranging consultation based on the Green Paper 'Legal Protection of Encrypted Services in the Internal Market'; whereas the results of that consultation confirmed the need for a Community legal instrument ensuring the legal protection of all those

[1]) OJ C 314, 16. 10. 1997, p. 7 and OJ C 203, 30. 6. 1998, p. 12.
[2]) OJ C 129, 27. 4. 1998, p. 16.
[3]) Opinion of the European Parliament of 30 April 1998 (OJ C 152, 18. 5. 1998, p. 59), Council Common Position of 29 June 1998 (OJ C 262, 19. 8. 1998, p. 34) and Decision of the European Parliament of 8 October 1998 (OJ C 328, 26. 10. 1998). Council Decision of 9 November 1998.

8

services whose remuneration relies on conditional access;

(5) Whereas the European Parliament, in its Resolution of 13 May 1997 on the Green Paper [4]), called on the Commission to present a proposal for a Directive covering all encoded services in respect of which encoding is used to ensure payment of a fee, and agreed that this should include information society services provided at a distance by electronic means and at the individual request of a service receiver, as well as broadcasting services;

(6) Whereas the opportunities offered by digital technologies provide the potential for increasing consumer choice and contributing to cultural pluralism, by developing an even wider range of services within the meaning of Articles 59 and 60 of the Treaty; whereas the viability of those services will often depend on the use of conditional access in order to obtain the remuneration of the service provider; whereas, accordingly, the legal protection of service providers against illicit devices which allow access to these services free of charge seems necessary in order to ensure the economic viability of the services;

(7) Whereas the importance of this issue was recognized by the Commission Communication on 'A European Initiative in Electronic Commerce';

(8) Whereas, in accordance with Article 7a of the Treaty, the internal market is to comprise an area without internal frontiers in which the free movement of services and goods is ensured; whereas Article 128(4) of the Treaty requires the Community to take cultural aspects into account in its action under other provisions of the

---

[4]) OJ C 167, 2. 6. 1997, p. 31.

Treaty; whereas by virtue of Article 130(3) of the Treaty, the Community must, through the policies and activities it pursues, contribute to creating the conditions necessary for the competitiveness of its industry;

(9) Whereas this Directive is without prejudice to possible future Community or national provisions meant to ensure that a number of broadcasting services, recognized as being of public interest, are not based on conditional access;

(10) Whereas this Directive is without prejudice to the cultural aspects of any further Community action concerning new services;

(11) Whereas the disparity between national rules concerning the legal protection of services based on, or consisting of, conditional access is liable to create obstacles to the free movement of services and goods;

(12) Whereas the application of the Treaty is not sufficient to remove these internal market obstacles; whereas those obstacles should therefore be removed by providing for an equivalent level of protection between Member States; whereas this implies an approximation of the national rules relating to the commercial activities which concern illicit devices;

(13) Whereas it seems necessary to ensure that Member States provide appropriate legal protection against the placing on the market, for direct or indirect financial gain, of an illicit device which enables or facilitates without authority the circumvention of any technological measures designed to protect the remuneration of a legally provided service;

(14) Whereas those commercial activities which concern illicit devices include commercial communications covering all forms of advertising, direct marketing, sponsorship, sales promo-

tion and public relations promoting such products and services;

(15) Whereas those commercial activities are detrimental to consumers who are misled about the origin of illicit devices; whereas a high level of consumer protection is needed in order to fight against this kind of consumer fraud; whereas Article 129a(1) of the Treaty provides that the Community should contribute to the achievement of a high level of consumer protection by the measures it adopts pursuant to Article 100 a thereof;

(16) Whereas, therefore, the legal framework for the creation of a single audiovisual area laid down in Council Directive 89/552/EEC of 3 October 1989 on the coordination of certain provisions laid down by law, regulation or administrative action in Member States concerning the pursuit of television broadcasting activities⁵) should be supplemented with reference to conditional access techniques as laid down in this Directive, in order, not least, to ensure equal treatment of the suppliers of cross-border broadcasts, regardless of their place of establishment;

(17) Whereas, in accordance with the Council Resolution of 29 June 1995 on the effective uniform application of Community law and on the penalties applicable for breaches of Community law in the internal market⁶), Member States are required to take action to ensure that Community law is duly applied with the same effectiveness and thoroughness as national law;

(18) Whereas, in accordance with Article 5 of the Treaty, Member States

⁵) OJ L 298, 17. 10. 1989, p. 23. Directive as amended by Directive 97/36/EC of the European Parliament and of the Council (OJ L 202, 30. 7. 1997, p. 60).
⁶) OJ C 188, 22. 7. 1995, p. 1.

are required to take all appropriate measures to guarantee the application and effectiveness of Community law, in particular by ensuring that the sanctions chosen are effective, dissuasive and proportionate and the remedies appropriate;

(19) Whereas the approximation of the laws, regulations and administrative provisions of the Member States should be limited to what is needed in order to achieve the objectives of the internal market, in accordance with the principle of proportionality as set out in the third paragraph of Article 3 b of the Treaty;

(20) Whereas the distribution of illicit devices includes transfer by any means and putting such devices on the market for circulation inside or outside the Community;

(21) Whereas this Directive is without prejudice to the application of any national provisions which may prohibit the private possession of illicit devices, to the application of Community competition rules and to the application of Community rules concerning intellectual property rights;

(22) Whereas national law concerning sanctions and remedies for infringing commercial activities may provide that the activities have to be carried out in the knowledge or with reasonable grounds for knowing that the devices in question were illicit;

(23) Whereas the sanctions and remedies provided for under this Directive are without prejudice to any other sanction or remedy for which provision may be made under national law, such as preventive measures in general or seizure of illicit devices; whereas Member States are not obliged to provide criminal sanctions for infringing activities covered by this Directive; whereas Member States' provisions for actions

8

for damages are to be be in conformity with their national legislative and judicial systems;

(24) Whereas this Directive is without prejudice to the application of national rules which do not fall within the field herein coordinated, such as those adopted for the protection of minors, including those in compliance with Directive 89/552/EEC, or national provisions concerned with public policy or public security,

HAVE ADOPTED THIS DIRECTIVE:

Article 1
Scope

The objective of this Directive is to approximate provisions in the Member States concerning measures against illicit devices which give unauthorised access to protected services.

Article 2
Definitions

For the purposes of this Directive:

(a) *protected service* shall mean any of the following services, where provided against remuneration and on the basis of conditional access:

– television broadcasting, as defined in Article 1(a) of Directive 89/552/EEC,

– radio broadcasting, meaning any transmission by wire or over the air, including by satellite, of radio programmes intended for reception by the public,

– information society services within the meaning of Article 1(2) of Directive 98/34/EC of the European Parliament and of the Council of 22 June 1998 laying down a procedure for the provision of information in the field of technical standards and regulations

and of rules on information society services[7]),

or the provision of conditional access to the above services considered as a service in its own right;

(b) *conditional access* shall mean any technical measure and/or arrangement whereby access to the protected service in an intelligible form is made conditional upon prior individual authorisation;

(c) *conditional access device* shall mean any equipment or software designed or adapted to give access to a protected service in an intelligible form;

(d) *associated service* shall mean the installation, maintenance or replacement of conditional access devices, as well as the provision of commercial communication services in relation to them or to protected services;

(e) *illicit device* shall mean any equipment or software designed or adapted to give access to a protected service in an intelligible form without the authorisation of the service provider;

(f) *field coordinated by this Directive* shall mean any provision relating to the infringing activities specified in Article 4.

Article 3
Internal market principles

1. Each Member State shall take the measures necessary to prohibit on its territory the activities listed in Article 4, and to provide for the sanctions and remedies laid down in Article 5.

2. Without prejudice to paragraph 1, Member States may not:

---

[7]) OJ L 204, 21. 7. 1998, p. 37. Directive as amended by Directive 98/48/EC (OJ L 217, 5. 8. 1998, p. 18).

(a) restrict the provision of protected services, or associated services, which originate in another Member State; or

(b) restrict the free movement of conditional access devices;

for reasons falling within the field coordinated by this Directive.

Article 4
Infringing activities

Member States shall prohibit on their territory all of the following activities:

(a) the manufacture, import, distribution, sale, rental or possession for commercial purposes of illicit devices;

(b) the installation, maintenance or replacement for commercial purposes of an illicit device;

(c) the use of commercial communications to promote illicit devices.

Article 5
Sanctions and remedies

1. The sanctions shall be effective, dissuasive and proportionate to the potential impact of the infringing activity.

2. Member States shall take the necessary measures to ensure that providers of protected services whose interests are affected by an infringing activity as specified in Article 4, carried out on their territory, have access to appropriate remedies, including bringing an action for damages and obtaining an injunction or other preventive measure, and where appropriate, applying for disposal outside commercial channels of illicit devices.

Article 6
Implementation

1. Member States shall bring into force the laws, regulations and administrative provisions necessary to comply with this Directive by 28 May 2000. They shall notify them to the Commission forthwith.

When Member States adopt such measures, they shall contain a reference to this Directive or shall be accompanied by such reference at the time of their official publication. The methods of making such reference shall be laid down by Member States.

2. Member States shall communicate to the Commission the text of the provisions of national law which they adopt in the field coordinated by this Directive.

Article 7
Reports

Not later than three years after the entry into force of this Directive, and every two years thereafter, the Commission shall present a report to the European Parliament, the Council and the Economic and Social Committee concerning the implementation of this Directive accompanied, where appropriate, by proposals, in particular as regards the definitions under Article 2, for adapting it in light of technical and economic developments and of the consultations carried out by the Commission.

Article 8
Entry into force

This Directive shall enter into force on the day of its publication in the Official Journal of the European Communities.

Article 9
Addressees

This Directive is addressed to the Member States.

9

E-Money Directive
Directive 2000/46/EC of the European Parliament and of the Council of 18 September 2000 on the taking up, pursuit of and prudential supervision of the business of electronic money institutions

OJ L 275, 27. 10. 2000, p. 39

THE EUROPEAN PARLIAMENT AND THE COUNCIL OF THE EUROPEAN UNION,

Having regard to the Treaty establishing the European Community, and in particular the first and third sentences of Article 47(2) thereof,

Having regard to the proposal from the Commission[1],

Having regard to the opinion of the Economic and Social Committee[2],

Having regard to the opinion of the European Central Bank[3],

Acting in accordance with the procedure laid down in Article 251 of the Treaty[4],

Whereas:

(1) Credit institutions within the meaning of Article 1, point 1, first subparagraph (b) of Directive 2000/12/EC[5]) are limited in the scope of their activities.

(2) It is necessary to take account of the specific characteristics of these institutions and to provide the appropriate measures necessary to coordinate and harmonise Member States' laws, regulations and administrative provisions relating to the taking up, pursuit and prudential supervision of the business of electronic money institutions.

(3) For the purposes of this Directive, electronic money can be considered an electronic surrogate for coins and banknotes, which is stored on an electronic device such as a chip card or computer memory and which is generally intended for the purpose of effecting electronic payments of limited amounts.

(4) The approach adopted is appropriate to achieve only the essential harmonisation necessary and sufficient to secure the mutual recognition of auth-

---

[1] OJ C 317, 15. 10. 1998, p. 7.
[2] OJ C 101, 12. 4. 1999, p. 64.
[3] OJ C 189, 6. 7. 1999, p. 7.
[4] Opinion of the European Parliament of 15 April 1999 (OJ C 219, 30. 7. 1999, p. 415), confirmed on 27 October 1999, Council Common Position of 29 November 1999 (OJ C 26, 28. 1. 2000, p. 1) and Decision of the European Parliament of 11 April 2000 (not yet published in the Official Journal). Decision of the Council of 16 June 2000.

[5] Directive 2000/12/EC of the European Parliament and of the Council of 20 March 2000 relating to the taking up and pursuit of the business of credit institutions (OJ L 126, 26. 5. 2000, p. 1). Directive as last amended by Directive 2000/28/EC (see page 37 of this Official Journal).

orisation and prudential supervision of electronic money institutions, making possible the granting of a single licence recognised throughout the Community and designed to ensure bearer confidence and the application of the principle of home Member State prudential supervision.

(5) Within the wider context of the rapidly evolving electronic commerce it is desirable to provide a regulatory framework that assists electronic money in delivering its full potential benefits and that avoids hampering technological innovation in particular. Therefore, this Directive introduces a technology-neutral legal framework that harmonises the prudential supervision of electronic money institutions to the extent necessary for ensuring their sound and prudent operation and their financial integrity in particular.

(6) Credit institutions, by virtue of point 5 of Annex I to Directive 2000/12/EC, are already allowed to issue and administer means of payment including electronic money and to carry on such activities Community-wide subject to mutual recognition and to the comprehensive prudential supervisory system applying to them in accordance with the European banking Directives.

(7) The introduction of a separate prudential supervisory regime for electronic money institutions, which, although calibrated on the prudential supervisory regime applying to other credit institutions and Directive 2000/12/EC except Title V, Chapters 2 and 3 thereof in particular, differs from that regime, is justified and desirable because the issuance of electronic money does not constitute in itself, in view of its specific character as an electronic surrogate for coins and banknotes, a deposit-taking activity pursuant to Article 3 of Directive 2000/12/

EC, if the received funds are immediately exchanged for electronic money.

(8) The receipt of funds from the public in exchange for electronic money, which results in a credit balance left on account with the issuing institution, constitutes the receipt of deposits or other repayable funds for the purpose of Directive 2000/12/EC.

(9) It is necessary for electronic money to be redeemable to ensure bearer confidence. Redeemability does not imply, in itself, that the funds received in exchange for electronic money shall be regarded as deposits or other repayable funds for the purpose of Directive 2000/12/EC.

(10) Redeemability should always be understood to be at par value.

(11) In order to respond to the specific risks associated with the issuance of electronic money this prudential supervisory regime must be more targeted and, accordingly, less cumbersome than the prudential supervisory regime applying to credit institutions, notably as regards reduced initial capital requirements and the non-application of Directive 93/6/EEC[6]) and Title V, Chapter 2, Sections II and III of Directive 2000/12/EC.

(12) However, it is necessary to preserve a level playing field between electronic money institutions and other credit institutions issuing electronic money and, thus, to ensure fair competition among a wider range of institutions to the benefit of bearers. This is achieved since the abovementioned less cumbersome features of the prudential

---

[6]) Council Directive 93/6/EEC of 15 March 1993 on the capital adequacy of investment firms and credit institutions (OJ L 141, 11. 6. 1993, p. 1). Directive as last amended by Directive 98/33/EC (OJ L 204, 21. 7. 1998, p. 29).

supervisory regime applying to electronic money institutions are balanced by provisions that are more stringent than those applying to other credit institutions, notably as regards restrictions on the business activities which electronic money institutions may carry on and, particularly, prudent limitations of their investments aimed at ensuring that their financial liabilities related to outstanding electronic money are backed at all times by sufficiently liquid low risk assets.

(13) Pending the harmonisation of prudential supervision of outsourced activities for credit institutions it is appropriate that electronic money institutions have sound and prudent management and control procedures. With a view to the possibility of operational and other ancilliary functions related to the issuance of electronic money being performed by undertakings which are not subject to prudential supervision it is essential that electronic money institutions have in place internal structures which should respond to the financial and non-financial risks to which they are exposed.

(14) The issuance of electronic money may affect the stability of the financial system and the smooth operation of payments systems. Close cooperation in assessing the integrity of electronic money schemes is called for.

(15) It is appropriate to afford competent authorities the possibility of waiving some or all of the requirements imposed by this Directive for electronic money institutions which operate only within the territories of the respective Member States.

(16) Adoption of this Directive constitutes the most appropriate means of achieving the desired objectives. This Directive is limited to the minimum necessary to achieve these objectives and does not go beyond what is necessary for this purpose.

(17) provision should be made for the review of this Directive in the light of experience of developments in the market and the protection of bearers of electronic money.

(18) The Banking Advisory Committee has been consulted on the adoption of this Directive,

HAVE ADOPTED THIS DIRECTIVE:

Article 1
Scope, definitions and restriction of activities

1. This Directive shall apply to electronic money institutions.

2. It shall not apply to the institutions referred to in Article 2(3) of Directive 2000/12/EC.

3. For the purposes of this Directive:

(a) 'electronic money institution' shall mean an undertaking or any other legal person, other than a credit institution as defined in Article 1, point 1, first subparagraph (a) of Directive 2000/12/EC which issues means of payment in the form of electronic money;

(b) 'electronic money' shall mean monetary value as represented by a claim on the issuer which is:

(i) stored on an electronic device;

(ii) issued on receipt of funds of an amount not less in value than the monetary value issued;

(iii) accepted as means of payment by undertakings other than the issuer.

4. Member States shall prohibit persons or undertakings that are not credit institutions, as defined in Article 1, point 1, first subparagraph of Directive 2000/12/EC, from carrying on the business of issuing electronic money.

5. The business activities of electronic money institutions other than the issuing of electronic money shall be restricted to:

(a) the provision of closely related financial and non-financial services such as the administering of electronic money by the performance of operational and other ancillary functions related to its issuance, and the issuing and administering of other means of payment but excluding the granting of any form of credit; and

(b) the storing of data on the electronic device on behalf of other undertakings or public institutions.

Electronic money institutions shall not have any holdings in other undertakings except where these undertakings perform operational or other ancillary functions related to electronic money issued or distributed by the institution concerned.

Article 2
Application of Banking Directives

1. Save where otherwise expressly provided for, only references to credit institutions in Directive 91/308/EEC[7]) and Directive 2000/12/EC except Title V, Chapter 2 thereof shall apply to electronic money institutions.

2. Articles 5, 11, 13, 19, 20(7), 51 and 59 of Directive 2000/12/EC shall not apply. The mutual recognition arrangements provided for in Directive 2000/12/EC shall not apply to electronic money institutions' business activities other than the issuance of electronic money.

---

[7]) Council Directive 91/308/EEC of 10 June 1991 on prevention of the use of the financial system for the purpose of money laundering (OJ L 166, 28. 6. 1991, p. 77).

3. The receipt of funds within the meaning of Article 1(3)(b)(ii) does not constitute a deposit or other repayable funds according to Article 3 of Directive 2000/12/EC, if the funds received are immediately exchanged for electronic money.

Article 3
Redeemability

1. A bearer of electronic money may, during the period of validity, ask the issuer to redeem it at par value in coins and bank notes or by a transfer to an account free of charges other than those strictly necessary to carry out that operation.

2. The contract between the issuer and the bearer shall clearly state the conditions of redemption.

3. The contract may stipulate a minimum threshold for redemption. The threshold may not exceed EUR 10.

Article 4
Initial capital and ongoing own funds requirements

1. Electronic money institutions shall have an initial capital, as defined in Article 34(2), subparagraphs (1) and (2) of Directive 2000/12/EC, of not less than EUR 1 million. Notwithstanding paragraphs 2 and 3, their own funds, as defined in Directive 2000/12/EC, shall not fall below that amount.

2. Electronic money institutions shall have at all times own funds which are equal to or above 2% of the higher of the current amount or the average of the preceding six months' total amount of their financial liabilities related to outstanding electronic money.

3. Where an electronic money institution has not completed a six months' period of business, including the day it

starts up, it shall have own funds which are equal to or above 2% of the higher of the current amount or the six months' target total amount of its financial liabilities related to outstanding electronic money. The six months' target total amount of the institution's financial liabilities related to outstanding electronic money shall be evidenced by its business plan subject to any adjustment to that plan having been required by the competent authorities.

Article 5
Limitations of investments

1. Electronic money institutions shall have investments of an amount of no less than their financial liabilities related to outstanding electronic money in the following assets only:

(a) asset items which according to Article 43(1)(a) (1), (2), (3) and (4) and Article 44(1) of Directive 2000/12/EC attract a zero credit risk weighting and which are sufficiently liquid;

(b) sight deposits held with Zone A credit institutions as defined in Directive 2000/12/EC; and

(c) debt instruments which are:

(i) sufficiently liquid;

(ii) not covered by paragraph 1(a);

(iii) recognised by competent authorities as qualifying items within the meaning of Article 2(12) of Directive 93/6/EEC; and

(iv) issued by undertakings other than undertakings which have a qualifying holding, as defined in Article 1 of Directive 2000/12/EC, in the electronic money institution concerned or which must be included in those undertakings' consolidated accounts.

2. Investments referred to in paragraph 1(b) and (c) may not exceed 20 times the own funds of the electronic money institution concerned and shall be subject to limitations which are at least as stringent as those applying to credit institutions in accordance with Title V, Chapter 2, Section III of Directive 2000/12/EC.

3. For the purpose of hedging market risks arising from the issuance of electronic money and from the investments referred to in paragraph 1, electronic money institutions may use sufficiently liquid interest-rate and foreign-exchange-related off balance-sheet items in the form of exchange-traded (i. e. not OTC) derivative instruments where they are subject to daily margin requirements or foreign exchange contracts with an original maturity of 14 calendar days or less. The use of derivative instruments according to the first sentence is permissible only if the full elimination of market risks is intended and, to the extent possible, achieved.

4. Member States shall impose appropriate limitations on the market risks electronic money institutions may incur from the investments referred to in paragraph 1.

5. For the purpose of applying paragraph 1, assets shall be valued at the lower of cost or market value.

6. If the value of the assets referred to in paragraph 1 falls below the amount of financial liabilities related to outstanding electronic money, the competent authorities shall ensure that the electronic money institution in question takes appropriate measures to remedy that situation promptly. To this end, and for a temporary period only, the competent authorities may allow the institution's financial liabilities related to outstanding electronic money to be backed by assets other than those referred to in paragraph 1 up to an

9

amount not exceeding the lower of 5% of these liabilities or the institution's total amount of own funds.

Article 6
Verification of specific requirements by the competent authorities

The competent authorities shall ensure that the calculations justifying compliance with Articles 4 and 5 are made, not less than twice each year, either by electronic money institutions themselves, which shall communicate them, and any component data required, to the competent authorities, or by competent authorities, using data supplied by the electronic money institutions.

Article 7
Sound and prudent operation

Electronic money institutions shall have sound and prudent management, administrative and accounting procedures and adequate internal control mechanisms. These should respond to the financial and non-financial risks to which the institution is exposed including technical and procedural risks as well as risks connected to its cooperation with any undertaking performing operational or other ancillary functions related to its business activities.

Article 8
Waiver

1. Member States may allow their competent authorities to waive the application of some or all of the provisions of this Directive and the application of Directive 2000/12/EC to electronic money institutions in cases where either:

(a) the total business activities of the type referred to in Article 1(3)(a) of this Directive of the institution generate a total amount of financial liabilities related to outstanding electronic money that normally does not exceed EUR 5 million and never exceeds EUR 6 million; or

(b) the electronic money issued by the institution is accepted as a means of payment only by any subsidiaries of the institution which perform operational or other ancillary functions related to electronic money issued or distributed by the institution, any parent undertaking of the institution or any other subsidiaries of that parent undertaking; or

(c) electronic money issued by the institution is accepted as payment only by a limited number of undertakings, which can be clearly distinguished by:

(i) their location in the same premises or other limited local area; or

(ii) their close financial or business relationship with the issuing institution, such as a common marketing or distribution scheme.

The underlying contractual arrangements must provide that the electronic storage device at the disposal of bearers for the purpose of making payments is subject to a maximum storage amount of not more than EUR 150.

2. An electronic money institution for which a waiver has been granted under paragraph 1 shall not benefit from the mutual recognition arrangements provided for in Directive 2000/12/EC.

3. Member States shall require that all electronic money institutions to which the application of this Directive and Directive 2000/12/EC has been waived report periodically on their activities including the total amount of financial liabilities related to electronic money.

Article 9
Grandfathering

Electronic money institutions subject to this Directive which have commenced their activity in accordance with the provisions in force in the Member State in which they have their head office before the date of entry into force of the provisions adopted in implementation of this Directive or the date referred to in Article 10(1), whichever date is earlier, shall be presumed to be authorised. The Member States shall oblige such electronic money institutions to submit all relevant information to the competent authorities in order to allow them to assess within six months from the date of entry into force of the provisions adopted in implementation of this Directive, whether the institutions comply with the requirements pursuant to this Directive, which measures need to be taken in order to ensure compliance, or whether a withdrawal of authorisation is appropriate. If compliance is not ensured within six months from the date referred to in Article 10(1), the electronic money institution shall not benefit from mutual recognition after that time.

Article 10
Implementation

1. Member States shall bring into force the laws, regulations and administrative provisions necessary to comply with this Directive not later than 27 April 2002. They shall immediately inform the Commission thereof.

When Member States adopt these measures, they shall contain a reference to this Directive or shall be accompanied by such reference on the occasion of their official publication. The methods of making such a reference shall be laid down by the Member States.

2. Member States shall communicate to the Commission the text of the main provisions of national law, which they adopt in the field covered by this Directive.

Article 11
Review

Not later than 27 April 2005 the Commission shall present a report to the European Parliament and the Council on the application of this Directive, in particular on:

– the measures to protect the bearers of electronic money, including the possible need to introduce a guarantee scheme,

– capital requirements,

– waivers, and

– the possible need to prohibit interest being paid on funds received in exchange for electronic money,

accompanied where appropriate by a proposal for its revision.

Article 12
Entry into force

This Directive shall enter into force on the day of its publication in the Official Journal of the European Communities.

Article 13

This Directive is addressed to the Member States.

10

2002 „eu." Domain Name Regulation
Regulation (EC) No 733/2002 of the European Parliament and of the Council of 22 April 2002 on the implementation of the .eu Top Level Domain

Text with EEA relevance
OJ L 113, 30. 4. 2002, p. 1

THE EUROPEAN PARLIAMENT AND THE COUNCIL OF THE EUROPEAN UNION,

Having regard to the Treaty establishing the European Community, and in particular Article 156 thereof,

Having regard to the proposal from the Commission[1]),

Having regard to the opinion of the Economic and Social Committee[2]),

Following consultation of the Committee of the Regions,

Acting in accordance with the procedure laid down in Article 251 of the Treaty[3]),

Whereas:

(1) The creation of the .eu Top Level Domain (TLD) is included as one of the targets to accelerate electronic commerce in the e-Europe initiative as endorsed by the European Council at

_____

[1]) OJ C 96 E, 27. 3. 2001, p. 333.
[2]) OJ C 155, 29. 5. 2001, p. 10.
[3]) Opinion of the European Parliament of 4 July 2001 (OJ C 65 E, 14. 3. 2002, p. 147), Council Common Position of 6 November 2001 (OJ C 45 E, 19. 2. 2002, p. 53) and Decision of the European Parliament of 28 February 2002 (not yet published in the Official Journal). Council Decision of 25 March 2002.

its meeting in Lisbon on 23 and 24 March 2000.

(2) The communication from the Commission to the Council and the European Parliament on the organisation and management of the Internet refers to the creation of the .eu TLD and the Council resolution of 3 October 2000 on the organisation and management of the Internet[4]) charges the Commission to encourage the coordination of policies in relation to the management of the Internet.

(3) TLDs are an integral part of the Internet infrastructure. They are an essential element of the global interoperability of the World Wide Web ('WWW' or 'the Web'). The connection and presence permitted by the allocation of domain names and the related addresses allow users to locate computers and websites on the Web. TLDs are also an integral part of every Internet e-mail address.

(4) The .eu TLD should promote the use of, and access to, the Internet networks and the virtual market place based on the Internet, in accordance with Article 154(2) of the Treaty, by providing a complementary registra-

_____

[4]) OJ C 293, 14. 10. 2000, p. 3.

10

tion domain to existing country code Top Level Domains (ccTLDs) or global registration in the generic Top Level Domains, and should in consequence increase choice and competition.

(5) The .eu TLD should improve the interoperability of trans-European networks, in accordance with Articles 154 and 155 of the Treaty, by ensuring the availability of .eu name servers in the Community. This will affect the topology and technical infrastructure of the Internet in Europe which will benefit from an additional set of name servers in the Community.

(6) Through the .eu TLD, the Internal market should acquire higher visibility in the virtual market place based on the Internet. The .eu TLD should provide a clearly identified link with the Community, the associated legal framework, and the European market place. It should enable undertakings, organisations and natural persons within the Community to register in a specific domain which will make this link obvious. As such, the .eu TLD will not only be a key building block for electronic commerce in Europe but will also support the objectives of Article 14 of the Treaty.

(7) The .eu TLD can accelerate the benefits of the information society in Europe as a whole, play a role in the integration of future Member States into the European Union, and help combat the risk of digital divide with neighbouring countries. It is therefore to be expected that this Regulation will be extended to the European Economic Area and that amendments may be sought to the existing arrangements between the European Union and European third countries, with a view to accommodating the requirements of the .eu TLD so that entities in those countries may participate in it.

(8) This Regulation is without prejudice to Community law in the field of personal data protection. This Regulation should be implemented in compliance with the principles relating to privacy and the protection of personal data.

(9) Internet management has generally been based on the principles of non-interference, self-management and self-regulation. To the extent possible and without prejudice to Community law, these principles should also apply to the .eu ccTLD. The implementation of the .eu TLD may take into consideration best practices in this regard and could be supported by voluntary guidelines or codes of conduct where appropriate.

(10) The establishment of the .eu TLD should contribute to the promotion of the European Union image on the global information networks and bring an added value to the Internet naming system in addition to the national ccTLDs.

(11) The objective of this Regulation is to establish the conditions of implementation of the .eu TLD, to provide for the designation of a Registry and establish the general policy framework within which the Registry will function. National ccTLDs are not covered by this Regulation.

(12) The Registry is the entity charged with the organisation, administration and management of the .eu TLD, including maintenance of the corresponding databases and the associated public query services, the accreditation of Registrars, the registration of domain names applied for by accredited Registrars, the operation of the TLD name servers and the dissemination of TLD zone files. Public query services associated with the TLD are re-

10

ferred to as 'Who is' queries. 'Who is'-type databases should be in conformity with Community law on data protection and privacy. Access to these databases provides information on a domain name holder and is an essential tool in boosting user confidence.

(13) After publishing a call for expressions of interest in the Official Journal of the European Communities, the Commission should, on the basis of an open, transparent and non-discriminatory selection procedure, designate a Registry. The Commission should enter into a contract with the selected Registry which should specify the conditions applying to the Registry for the organisation, administration and management of the .eu TLD and which should be limited in time and renewable.

(14) The Commission, acting on behalf of the Community, has requested the delegation of the EU code for the purpose of creating an Internet ccTLD. On 25 September 2000, the Internet Corporation for Assigned Names and Numbers (ICANN) issued a resolution providing that 'alpha-2 codes are delegable as ccTLDs only in cases where the ISO 3166 Maintenance Agency, on its exceptional reservation list, has reserved a reservation of the code that covers any application of ISO 3166-1 that needs a coded representation in the name of the country, territory or area involved'. Such conditions are met by the EU code which is therefore 'delegable' to the Community.

(15) ICANN is at present responsible for coordinating the delegation of codes representing ccTLD to Registries. The Council resolution of 3 October 2000 encourages the implementation of the principles applied to ccTLD Registries adopted by the Governmental Advisory Committee (GAC). The Reg-

istry should enter into a contract with ICANN respecting the GAC principles.

(16) The adoption of a public policy addressing speculative and abusive registration of domain names should provide that holders of prior rights recognised or established by national and/or Community law and public bodies will benefit from a specific period of time (a 'sunrise period') during which the registration of their domain names is exclusively reserved to such holders of prior rights recognised or established by national and/or Community law and public bodies.

(17) Domain names should not be revoked arbitrarily. A revocation may, however, be obtained in particular should a domain name be manifestly contrary to public order. The revocation policy should nevertheless provide for a timely and efficient mechanism.

(18) Rules should be adopted on the question of *bona vacantia* to address the status of domain names the registration of which is not renewed or which, for example because of succession law, are left without holder.

(19) The new .eu TLD registry should not be empowered to create second-level domains using alpha-2 codes representing countries.

(20) Within the framework established by this Regulation, the public policy rules concerning the implementation and functions of the .eu TLD and the public policy principles on registration, various options including the 'first come, first served' method should be considered when registration policy is formulated.

(21) When reference is made to interested parties, provision should be made for consultation encompassing, in particular, public authorities, undertakings, organisations and natural persons. The Registry could establish an

10

advisory body to organise such consultation.

(22) The measures necessary for the implementation of this Regulation, including criteria for the selection procedure of the Registry, the designation of the Registry, as well as the adoption of public policy rules, should be adopted in accordance with Council Decision 1999/468/EC of 28 June 1999 laying down the procedures for the exercise of implementing powers conferred on the Commission[5]).

(23) Since the objective of the proposed action, namely to implement the .eu TLD, cannot be sufficiently achieved by the Member States and can therefore, by reason of the scale and effects of the action, be better achieved at Community level, the Community may adopt measures, in accordance with the principle of subsidiarity as set out in Article 5 of the Treaty. In accordance with the principle of proportionality as set out in that Article, this Regulation does not go beyond what is necessary in order to achieve that objective,

HAVE ADOPTED THIS REGULATION:

Article 1
Objective and scope

1. The objective of this Regulation is to implement the .eu country code Top Level Domain (ccTLD) within the Community. The Regulation sets out the conditions for such implementation, including the designation of a Registry, and establishes the general policy framework within which the Registry will function.

2. This Regulation shall apply without prejudice to arrangements in Member States regarding national ccTLDs.

---

[5]) OJ L 184, 17. 7. 1999, p. 23.

Article 2
Definitions

For the purposes of this Regulation:

(a) 'Registry' means the entity entrusted with the organisation, administration and management of the .eu TLD including maintenance of the corresponding databases and the associated public query services, registration of domain names, operation of the Registry of domain names, operation of the Registry TLD name servers and dissemination of TLD zone files;

(b) 'Registrar' means a person or entity that, via contract with the Registry, provides domain name registration services to registrants.

Article 3
Characteristics of the Registry

1. The Commission shall:

(a) establish, in accordance with the procedure referred to in Article 6(3), the criteria and the procedure for the designation of the Registry;

(b) designate, in accordance with the procedure referred to in Article 6(2), the Registry after publishing a call for expressions of interest in the Official Journal of the European Communities and after the procedure for such call has been completed;

(c) enter into, in accordance with the procedure referred to in Article 6(2), a contract which shall specify the conditions according to which the Commission supervises the organisation, administration and management of the .eu TLD by the Registry. The contract between the Commission and the Registry shall be limited in time and renewable.

The Registry may not accept registrations until the registration policy is in place.

2. The Registry shall be a non-profit organisation, formed in accordance with the law of a Member State and having its registered office, central administration and principal place of business within the Community.

3. Having obtained the prior consent of the Commission, the Registry shall enter into the appropriate contract providing for the delegation of the .eu ccTLD code. To this effect the relevant principles adopted by the Governmental Advisory Committee shall be taken into account.

4. The .eu TLD Registry shall not act itself as Registrar.

Article 4
Obligations of the Registry

1. The Registry shall observe the rules, policies and procedures laid down in this Regulation and the contracts referred to in Article 3. The Registry shall observe transparent and non-discriminatory procedures.

2. The Registry shall:

(a) organise, administer and manage the .eu TLD in the general interest and on the basis of principles of quality, efficiency, reliability and accessibility;

(b) register domain names in the .eu TLD through any accredited .eu Registrar requested by any:

(i) undertaking having its registered office, central administration or principal place of business within the Community, or

(ii) organisation established within the Community without prejudice to the application of national law, or

(iii) natural person resident within the Community;

(c) impose fees directly related to costs incurred;

(d) implement the extra-judicial settlement of conflicts policy based on recovery of costs and a procedure to resolve promptly disputes between domain name holders regarding rights relating to names including intellectual property rights as well as disputes in relation to individual decisions by the Registry. This policy shall be adopted in accordance with Article 5(1) and take into consideration the recommendations of the World Intellectual Property Organisation. The policy shall provide adequate procedural guaranties for the parties concerned, and shall apply without prejudice to any court proceeding;

(e) adopt procedures for, and carry out, accreditation of .eu Registrars and ensure effective and fair conditions of competition among .eu Registrars;

(f) ensure the integrity of the databases of domain names.

Article 5
Policy framework

1. After consulting the Registry and following the procedure referred to in Article 6(3), the Commission shall adopt public policy rules concerning the implementation and functions of the .eu TLD and the public policy principles on registration. Public policy shall include:

(a) an extra-judicial settlement of conflicts policy;

(b) public policy on speculative and abusive registration of domain names including the possibility of registrations of domain names in a phased manner to ensure appropriate temporary opportunities for the holders of prior rights recognised or established by national and/or Community law and for public bodies to register their names;

111

10

(c) policy on possible revocation of domain names, including the question of *bona vacantia,*

(d) issues of language and geographical concepts;

(e) treatment of intellectual property and other rights.

2. Within three months of the entry into force of this Regulation, Member States may notify to the Commission and to the other Member States a limited list of broadly-recognised names with regard to geographical and/or geopolitical concepts which affect their political or territorial organisation that may either:

(a) not be registered, or

(b) be registered only under a second level domain according to the public policy rules.

The Commission shall notify to the Registry without delay the list of notified names to which such criteria apply. The Commission shall publish the list at the same time as it notifies the Registry.

Where a Member State or the Commission within 30 days of publication raises an objection to an item included in a notified list, the Commission shall take measures, in accordance with the procedure referred to in Article 6(3), to remedy the situation.

3. Before starting registration operations, the Registry shall adopt the initial registration policy for the .eu TLD in consultation with the Commission and other interested parties. The Registry shall implement in the registration policy the public policy rules adopted pursuant to paragraph 1 taking into account the exception lists referred to in paragraph 2.

4. The Commission shall periodically inform the Committee referred to in Article 6 on the activities referred to in paragraph 3 of this Article.

Article 6
Committee

1. The Commission shall be assisted by the Communications Committee established by Article 22(1) of Directive 2002/21/EC of the European Parliament and of the Council of 7 March 2002 on a common regulatory framework for electronic communications networks and services (Framework Directive)[6]. Until the Communications Committee is established pursuant to Decision 1999/468/EC, the Commission shall be assisted by the Committee established by Article 9 of Council Directive 90/387/EEC of 28 June 1990 on the establishment of the internal market for telecommunication services through the implementation of open network provision[7]).

2. Where reference is made to this paragraph, Articles 3 and 7 of Decision 1999/468/EC shall apply, having regard to the provisions of Article 8 thereof.

3. Where reference is made to this paragraph, Articles 5 and 7 of Decision 1999/468/EC shall apply, having regard to the provisions of Article 8 thereof.

The period laid down in Article 5(6) of Decision 1999/468/EC shall be set at three months.

4. The Committee shall adopt its rules of procedure.

Article 7
Reservation of rights

The Community shall retain all rights relating to the .eu TLD including, in particular, intellectual property rights and other rights to the Registry

---

[6]) OJ L 108, 24. 4. 2002, p. 33.

[7]) OJ L 192, 24. 7. 1990, p. 1. Directive as last amended by Directive 97/51/EC of the European Parliament and of the Council (OJ L 295, 29. 10. 1997, p. 23).

10

databases required to ensure the implementation of this Regulation and the right to re-designate the Registry.

Article 8
Implementation report

The Commission shall submit a report to the European Parliament and the Council on the implementation, effectiveness and functioning of the .eu TLD one year after the adoption of this Regulation and thereafter every two years.

Article 9
Entry into force

This Regulation shall enter into force on the day of its publication in the Official Journal of the European Communities.

This Regulation shall be binding in its entirety and directly applicable in all Member States.

11

2004 „.eu" Domain Name Regulation
Commission Regulation (EC) No 874/2004 of 28 April 2004 laying down public policy rules concerning the implementation and functions of the .eu Top Level Domain and the principles governing registration

Text with EEA relevance
OJ L 162, 30. 4. 2004, p. 40, amended by OJ L 266, 11. 10. 2005, p. 35,
OJ L 282, 26. 10. 2007, p. 16

THE COMMISSION OF THE EUROPEAN COMMUNITIES,

Having regard to the Treaty establishing the European Community,

Having regard to Regulation (EC) No 733/2002 of the European Parliament and of the Council of 22 April 2002 on the implementation of the .eu Top Level Domain[1]), and in particular Article 5(1) thereof,

Having consulted the Registry in accordance with Article 5(1) of Regulation (EC) No 733/2002,

Whereas:

(1) The initial implementation stages of the .eu Top Level Domain (TLD), to be created pursuant to Regulation (EC) No 733/2002, have been completed by designating a legal entity, established within the Community to administer and manage the .eu TLD Registry function. The Registry, designated by Commission Decision 2003/375/EC[2]), is required to be a non-profit organisation that should operate

and provide services on a cost covering basis and at an affordable price.

(2) Requesting a domain name should be possible through electronic means in a simple, speedy and efficient procedure, in all official languages of the Community, through accredited registrars.

(3) Accreditation of registrars should be carried out by the Registry following a procedure that ensures fair and open competition between Registrars. The accreditation process should be objective, transparent and non-discriminatory. Only parties who meet certain basic technical requirements to be determined by the Registry should be eligible for accreditation.

(4) Registrars should only accept applications for the registration of domain names filed after their accreditation and should forward them in the chronological order in which they were received.

(5) To ensure better protection of consumers' rights, and without prejudice to any Community rules concerning jurisdiction and applicable law, the applicable law in disputes between registrars and registrants on matters con-

---
[1]) OJ L 113, 30. 4. 2002, p. 1.
[2]) OJ L 128, 24. 5. 2003, p. 29.

11

cerning Community titles should be the law of one of the Member States.

(6) Registrars should require accurate contact information from their clients, such as full name, address of domicile, telephone number and electronic mail, as well as information concerning a natural or legal person responsible for the technical operation of the domain name.

(7) The Registry policy should promote the use of all the official languages of the Community.

(8) Pursuant to Regulation (EC) No 733/2002, Member States may request that their official name and the name under which they are commonly known should not be registered directly under .eu TLD otherwise than by their national government. Countries that are expected to join the European Union later than May 2004 should be enabled to block their official names and the names under which they are commonly known, so that they can be registered at a later date.

(9) A Member State should be authorised to designate an operator that will register as a domain name its official name and the name under which it is commonly known. Similarly, the Commission should be authorised to select domain names for use by the institutions of the Community, and to designate the operator of those domain names. The Registry should be empowered to reserve a number of specified domain names for its operational functions.

(10) In accordance with Article 5(2) of Regulation (EC) No 733/2002, a number of Member States have notified to the Commission and to other Member States a limited list of broadly-recognised names with regard to geographical and/or geopolitical concepts which affect their political or territorial organisation. Such lists include names that could either not be registered or which could be registered only under the second level domain in accordance with the public policy rules. The names included in these lists are not subject to the first-come first-served principle.

(11) The principle of first-come-first-served should be the basic principle for resolving a dispute between holders of prior rights during the phased registration. After the termination of the phased registration the principle of first come first served should apply in the allocation of domain names.

(12) In order to safeguard prior rights recognised by Community or national law, a procedure for phased registration should be put in place. Phased registration should take place in two phases, with the aim of ensuring that holders of prior rights have appropriate opportunities to register the names on which they hold prior rights. The Registry should ensure that validation of the rights is performed by appointed validation agents. On the basis of evidence provided by the applicants, validation agents should assess the right which is claimed for a particular name. Allocation of that name should then take place on a first-come, first-served basis if there are two or more applicants for a domain name, each having a prior right.

(13) The Registry should enter into an appropriate escrow agreement to ensure continuity of service, and in particular to ensure that in the event of re-delegation or other unforeseen circumstances it is possible to continue to provide services to the local Internet community with minimum disruption. The Registry should also comply with the relevant data protection rules, prin-

ciples, guidelines and best practices, notably concerning the amount and type of data displayed in the WHOIS database. Domain names considered by a Member State court to be defamatory, racist or contrary to public policy should be blocked and eventually revoked once the court decision becomes final. Such domain names should be blocked from future registrations.

(14) In the event of the death or insolvency of a domain name holder, if no transfer has been initiated at the expiry of the registration period, the domain name should be suspended for 40 calendar days. If the heirs or administrators concerned have not registered the name during that period it should become available for general registration.

(15) Domain names should be open to revocation by the Registry on a limited number of specified grounds, after giving the domain name holder concerned an opportunity to take appropriate measures. Domain names should also be capable of revocation through an alternative dispute resolution (ADR) procedure.

(16) The Registry should provide for an ADR procedure which takes into account the international best practices in this area and in particular the relevant World Intellectual Property Organization (WIPO) recommendations, to ensure that speculative and abusive registrations are avoided as far as possible.

(17) The Registry should select service providers that have appropriate expertise on the basis of objective, transparent and non-discriminatory criteria. ADR should respect a minimum of uniform procedural rules, similar to the ones set out in the Uniform Dispute Resolution Policy adopted by the Internet Corporation

of Assigned Names and Numbers (ICANN).

(18) In view of the impending enlargement of the Union it is imperative that the system of public policy rules set up by this Regulation enter into force without delay.

(19) The measures provided for in this Regulation are in accordance with the opinion of the Communications Committee established by Article 22(1) of Directive 2002/21/EC of the European Parliament and of the Council[3]),

HAS ADOPTED THIS REGULATION:

CHAPTER I
SUBJECT MATTER
Article 1
Subject matter

This Regulation sets out the public policy rules concerning the implementation and functions of the .eu Top Level Domain (TLD) and the public policy principles on registration referred to in Article 5(1) of Regulation (EC) No 733/2002.

CHAPTER II
PRINCIPLES ON REGISTRATION
Article 2
Eligibility and general principles for registration

An eligible party, as listed in Article 4(2)(b) of Regulation (EC) No 733/2002, may register one or more domain names under .eu TLD.

Without prejudice to Chapter IV, a specific domain name shall be allocated for use to the eligible party whose request has been received first by the Reg-

---

[3]) OJ L 108, 24. 4. 2002, p. 33.

istry in the technically correct manner and in accordance with this Regulation. For the purposes of this Regulation, this criterion of first receipt shall be referred to as the "first-come-first-served" principle.

Once a domain name is registered it shall become unavailable for further registration until the registration expires without renewal, or until the domain name is revoked.

Unless otherwise specified in this Regulation, domain names shall be registered directly under the .eu TLD.

Domain name registration shall be valid only after the appropriate fee has been paid by the requesting party.

Domain names registered under the .eu TLD shall only be transferable to parties that are eligible for registration of .eu domain names.

Article 3
Requests for domain name registration

The request for domain name registration shall include all of the following:

(a) the name and address of the requesting party;

(b) a confirmation by electronic means from the requesting party that it satisfies the general eligibility criteria set out in Article 4(2)(b) of Regulation (EC) No 733/2002;

(c) an affirmation by electronic means from the requesting party that to its knowledge the request for domain name registration is made in good faith and does not infringe any rights of a third party;

(d) an undertaking by electronic means from the requesting party that it shall abide by all the terms and conditions for registration, including the policy on the extra-judicial settlement of conflicts set out in Chapter VI.

Any material inaccuracy in the elements set out in points (a) to (d) shall constitute a breach of the terms of registration.

Any verification by the Registry of the validity of registration applications shall take place subsequently to the registration at the initiative of the Registry or pursuant to a dispute for the registration of the domain name in question, except for applications filed in the course of the phased registration procedure under Articles 10, 12, and 14.

Article 4
Accreditation of registrars

Only registrars accredited by the Registry shall be permitted to offer registration services for names under the .eu TLD.

The procedure for the accreditation of registrars shall be determined by the Registry and shall be reasonable, transparent and non-discriminatory, and shall ensure effective and fair conditions of competition.

Registrars are required to access and use the Registry's automated registration systems. The Registry may set further basic technical requirements for the accreditation of registrars.

The Registry may ask registrars for advance payment of registration fees, to be set annually by the Registry based on a reasonable market estimate.

The procedure, terms of accreditation of registrars and the list of accredited registrars shall be made publicly available by the Registry in readily accessible form.

Each registrar shall be bound by contract with the Registry to observe the terms of accreditation and in particular to comply with the public policy principles set out in this Regulation.

Article 5
provisions for registrars

Without prejudice to any rule governing jurisdiction and applicable law, agreements between the Registrar and the registrant of a domain name cannot designate, as applicable law, a law other than the law of one of the Member States, nor can they designate a dispute-resolution body, unless selected by the Registry pursuant to Article 23, nor an arbitration court or a court located outside the Community.

A registrar who receives more than one registration request for the same name shall forward those requests to the Registry in the chronological order in which they were received.

Only applications received after the date of accreditation shall be forwarded to the Registry.

Registrars shall require all applicants to submit accurate and reliable contact details of at least one natural or legal person responsible for the technical operation of the domain name that is requested.

Registrars may develop label, authentication and trustmark schemes in order to promote consumer confidence in the reliability of information that is available under a domain name that is registered by them, in accordance with applicable national and Community law.

CHAPTER III
LANGUAGES AND GEOGRAPHICAL CONCEPTS

Article 6
Languages

registrations of .eu domain names shall start only after the Registry has informed the Commission that the filing of applications for the registration of .eu domain names and communications of decisions concerning registration is possible in all official languages of the Community, hereinafter referred to as 'official languages'.

For any communication by the Registry that affects the rights of a party in conjunction with a registration, such as the grant, transfer, cancellation or revocation of a domain, the Registry shall ensure that these communications are possible in all official languages.

The Registry shall perform the registration of domain names in all the alphabetic characters of the official languages when adequate international standards become available.

The Registry shall not be required to perform functions using languages other than the official languages.

Article 7
Procedure for reserved geographical and geopolitical names

For the procedure of raising objections to the lists of broadly recognised names in accordance with the third subparagraph of Article 5(2) of Regulation (EC) No 733/2002, objections shall be notified to the members of the Communications Committee established by Article 22(1) of Directive 2002/21/EC and to the Director-General of the Commission's Directorate-General Information Society. The members of the Communications Committee and the Director-General may designate other contact points for these notifications.

Objections and designations of contact points shall be notified in the form of electronic mail, delivery by courier or in person, or by postal delivery effected by way of registered letter and acknowledgement of receipt.

Upon the resolution of any objections, the Registry shall publish on its web site two lists of names. The one list shall contain the list of names that the Commission shall have notified as 'not registrable'. The other list shall contain the list of names that the Commission shall have notified to the Registry as 'registrable only under a second level domain'.

Article 8
Reservation of names by countries and alpha-2 codes representing countries

1. The list of names set out in the Annex to this Regulation shall only be reserved or registered as second level domain names directly under the .eu TLD by the countries indicated in the list.

2. Alpha-2 codes representing countries shall not be registered as second level domain names directly under the .eu TLD.

Article 9
Second level domain name for geographical and geopolitical names

Registration of geographical and geopolitical concepts as domain names in accordance with Article 5(2)(b) of Regulation (EC) No 733/2002 may be provided for by a Member State that has notified the names. This may be done under any domain name that has been registered by that Member State.

The Commission may ask the Registry to introduce domain names directly under the .eu TLD for use by the Community institutions and bodies. After the entry into force of this Regulation

and not later than a week before the beginning of the phased registration period provided for in Chapter IV, the Commission shall notify the Registry of the names that are to be reserved and the bodies that represent the Community institutions and bodies in registering the names.

CHAPTER IV
PHASED REGISTRATION
Article 10
Eligible parties and the names they can register

1. Holders of prior rights recognised or established by national and/or Community law and public bodies shall be eligible to apply to register domain names during a period of phased registration before general registration of. eu domain starts.

'Prior rights' shall be understood to include, *inter alia*, registered national and community trademarks, geographical indications or designations of origin, and, in as far as they are protected under national law in the Member-State where they are held: unregistered trademarks, trade names, business identifiers, company names, family names, and distinctive titles of protected literary and artistic works.

'Public bodies' shall include: institutions and bodies of the Community, national and local governments, governmental bodies, authorities, organisations and bodies governed by public law, and international and intergovernmental organisations.

2. The registration on the basis of a prior right shall consist of the registration of the complete name for which the prior right exists, as written in the documentation which proves that such a right exists.

3. The registration by a public body may consist of the complete name of the public body or the acronym that is generally used. Public bodies that are responsible for governing a particular geographic territory may also register the complete name of the territory for which they are responsible, and the name under which the territory is commonly known.

Article 11
Special characters

As far as the registration of complete names is concerned, where such names comprise a space between the textual or word elements, identicality shall be deemed to exist between such complete names and the same names written with a hyphen between the word elements or combined in one word in the domain name applied for.

Where the name for which prior rights are claimed contains special characters, spaces, or punctuations, these shall be eliminated entirely from the corresponding domain name, replaced with hyphens, or, if possible, rewritten.

Special character and punctuations as referred to in the second paragraph shall include the following:
~ @ # $ % ^ & * ( ) + = <> { } [ ] | \ / : ; ' , . ?

Without prejudice to the third paragraph of Article 6, if the prior right name contains letters which have additional elements that cannot be reproduced in ASCII code, such as ä, é or ñ, the letters concerned shall be reproduced without these elements (such as a, e, n), or shall be replaced by conventionally accepted spellings (such as ae). In all other respects, the domain name shall be identical to the textual or word elements of the prior right name.

Article 12
Principles for phased registration

1. Phased registration shall not start before the requirement of the first paragraph of Article 6 is fulfilled.

The Registry shall publish the date on which phased registration shall start at least two months in advance and shall inform all accredited Registrars accordingly.

The Registry shall publish on its website two months before the beginning of the phased registration a detailed description of all the technical and administrative measures that it shall use to ensure a proper, fair and technically sound administration of the phased registration period.

2. The duration of the phased registration period shall be four months. General registration of domain names shall not start prior to the completion of the phased registration period.

Phased registration shall be comprised of two parts of two months each.

During the first part of phased registration, only registered national and Community trademarks, geographical indications, and the names and acronyms referred to in Article 10(3), may be applied for as domain names by holders or licensees of prior rights and by the public bodies mentioned in Article 10(1).

During the second part of phased registration, the names that can be registered in the first part as well as names based on all other prior rights can be applied for as domain names by holders of prior rights on those names.

3. The request to register a domain name based on a prior right under Article 10(1) and (2) shall include a reference to the legal basis in national or Community law for the right to the name, as well as other relevant infor-

11

mation, such as trademark registration number, information concerning publication in an official journal or government gazette, registration information at professional or business associations and chambers of commerce.

4. The Registry may make the requests for domain name registration subject to payment of additional fees, provided that these serve merely to cover the costs generated by the application of this Chapter. The Registry may charge differential fees depending upon the complexity of the process required to validate prior rights.

5. At the end of the phased registration an independent audit shall be performed at the expense of the Registry and shall report its findings to the Commission. The auditor shall be appointed by the Registry after consulting the Commission. The purpose of the audit shall be to confirm the fair, appropriate and sound operational and technical administration of the phased registration period by the Registry.

6. To resolve a dispute over a domain name the rules provided in Chapter VI shall apply.

Article 13
Selection of validation agents

Validation agents shall be legal persons established within the territory of the Community. Validation agents shall be reputable bodies with appropriate expertise. The Registry shall select the validation agents in an objective, transparent and non-discriminatory manner, ensuring the widest possible geographical diversity. The Registry shall require the validation agent to execute the validation in an objective, transparent and non-discriminatory manner.

Member States shall provide for validation concerning the names mentioned in Article 10(3). To that end, the Member States shall send to the Commission within two months following entry into force of this Regulation, a clear indication of the addresses to which documentary evidence is to be sent for verification. The Commission shall notify the Registry of these addresses.

The Registry shall publish information about the validation agents at its website.

Article 14
Validation and registration of applications received during phased registration

All claims for prior rights under Article 10(1) and (2) must be verifiable by documentary evidence which demonstrates the right under the law by virtue of which it exists.

The Registry, upon receipt of the application, shall block the domain name in question until validation has taken place or until the deadline passes for receipt of documentation. If the Registry receives more than one claim for the same domain during the phased registration period, applications shall be dealt with in strict chronological order.

The Registry shall make available a database containing information about the domain names applied for under the procedure for phased registration, the applicants, the Registrar that submitted the application, the deadline for submission of validation documents, and subsequent claims on the names.

Every applicant shall submit documentary evidence that shows that he or she is the holder of the prior right claimed on the name in question. The documentary evidence shall be submitted to a validation agent indicated by the Registry. The applicant shall submit the evidence in such a way that it shall be received by the validation agent within forty days from the submission of the application for the domain name. If the documentary evidence has not been received by this deadline, the application for the domain name shall be rejected.

Validation agents shall time-stamp documentary evidence upon receipt.

Validation agents shall examine applications for any particular domain name in the order in which the application was received at the Registry.

The relevant validation agent shall examine whether the applicant that is first in line to be assessed for a domain name and that has submitted the documentary evidence before the deadline has prior rights on the name. If the documentary evidence has not been received in time or if the validation agent finds that the documentary evidence does not substantiate a prior right, he shall notify the Registry of this.

If the validation agent finds that prior rights exist regarding the application for a particular domain name that is first in line, he shall notify the Registry accordingly.

This examination of each claim in chronological order of receipt shall be followed until a claim is found for which prior rights on the name in question are confirmed by a validation agent.

The Registry shall register the domain name, on the first come first served basis, if it finds that the applicant has demonstrated a prior right in accordance with the procedure set out in the second, third and fourth paragraphs.

CHAPTER V
RESERVATIONS, WHOIS DATA AND IMPROPER REGISTRATIONS
Article 15
Escrow agreement

1. The Registry shall, at its own expense, enter into an agreement with a reputable trustee or other escrow agent established within the territory of the Community designating the Commission as the beneficiary of the escrow agreement. The Commission shall give its consent to that agreement before it is concluded. The Registry shall submit to the escrow agent on a daily basis an electronic copy of the current content of the .eu database.

2. The agreement shall provide that the data shall be held by the escrow agent on the following terms and conditions:

(a) the data shall be received and held in escrow, undergoing no procedure other than verification that it is complete, consistent, and in proper format, until it is released to the Commission;

(b) the data shall be released from escrow upon expiration without renewal or upon termination of the contract between the Registry and the Commission for any of the reasons described therein and irrespectively of any disputes or litigation between the Commission and the Registry;

(c) in the event that the escrow is released, the Commission shall have the exclusive, irrevocable, royalty-free right to exercise or to have exercised all rights necessary to re-designate the Registry;

(d) if the contract with the Registry is terminated the Commission, with the cooperation of the Registry, shall take all necessary steps to transfer the administrative and operational responsibility for the .eu TLD and any reserve funds to such party as the Commission may designate: in that event, the Registry shall make all efforts to avoid disruption of the service and shall in particular continue to update the information that is subject to the escrow until the time of completion of the transfer.

Article 16
WHOIS database

The purpose of the WHOIS database shall be to provide reasonably accurate and up to date information about the technical and administrative points of contact administering the domain names under the .eu TLD.

The WHOIS database shall contain information about the holder of a domain name that is relevant and not excessive in relation to the purpose of the database. In as far as the information is not strictly necessary in relation to the purpose of the database, and if the domain name holder is a natural person, the information that is to be made publicly available shall be subject to the unambiguous consent of the domain name holder. The deliberate submission of inaccurate information, shall constitute grounds for considering the domain name registration to have been in breach of the terms of registration.

Article 17
Names reserved by the Registry

The following names shall be reserved for the operational functions of the Registry:
eurid.eu, registry.eu, nic.eu, dns.eu, internic.eu, whois.eu, das.eu, coc.eu, eurethix.eu, eurethics.eu, euthics.eu

Article 18
Improper registrations

Where a domain name is considered by a Court of a Member State to be defamatory, racist or contrary to public policy, it shall be blocked by the Registry upon notification of a Court decision and shall be revoked upon notification of a final court decision. The Registry shall block from future registration those names which have been subject to such a court order for as long as such order remains valid.

Article 19
Death and winding up

1. If the domain name holder dies during the registration period of the domain name, the executors of his or her estate, or his or her legal heirs, may request transfer of the name to the heirs along with submission of the appropriate documentation. If, on expiry of the registration period, no transfer has been initiated, the domain name shall be suspended for a period of 40 calendar days and shall be published on the Registry's website. During this period the executors or the legal heirs may apply to register the name along with submission of the appropriate documentation. If the heirs have not registered the name during that 40-day period, the domain name shall thereafter become available for general registration.

2. If the domain name holder is an undertaking, a legal or natural person, or an organisation that becomes subject to insolvency proceedings, winding up, cessation of trading, winding up by court order or any similar proceeding provided for by national law, during the registration period of the domain name, then the legally appointed ad-

ministrator of the domain name holder may request transfer to the purchaser of the domain name holders assets along with submission of the appropriate documentation. If, on expiry of the registration period, no transfer has been initiated, the domain name shall be suspended for a period of forty calendar days and shall be published on the registry's website. During this period the administrator may apply to register the name along with submission of appropriate documentation. If the administrator has not registered the name during that 40-day period, the domain name shall thereafter become available for general registration.

CHAPTER VI
REVOCATION AND
SETTLEMENT OF CONFLICTS

Article 20
Revocation of domain names

The Registry may revoke a domain name at its own initiative and without submitting the dispute to any extrajudicial settlement of conflicts, exclusively on the following grounds:

(a) outstanding unpaid debts owed to the Registry;

(b) holder's non-fulfilment of the general eligibility criteria pursuant to Article 4(2)(b) of Regulation (EC) 733/2002;

(c) holder's breach of the terms of registration under Article 3.

The Registry shall lay down a procedure in accordance with which it may revoke domain names on these grounds. This procedure shall include a notice to the domain name holder and shall afford him an opportunity to take appropriate measures.

Revocation of a domain name, and where necessary its subsequent trans-

fer, may also be effected in accordance with a decision issued by an extrajudicial settlement body.

Article 21
Speculative and abusive registrations

1. A registered domain name shall be subject to revocation, using an appropriate extra-judicial or judicial procedure, where that name is identical or confusingly similar to a name in respect of which a right is recognised or established by national and/or Community law, such as the rights mentioned in Article 10(1), and where it:

(a) has been registered by its holder without rights or legitimate interest in the name; or

(b) has been registered or is being used in bad faith.

2. A legitimate interest within the meaning of point (a) of paragraph 1 may be demonstrated where:

(a) prior to any notice of an alternative dispute resolution (ADR) procedure, the holder of a domain name has used the domain name or a name corresponding to the domain name in connection with the offering of goods or services or has made demonstrable preparation to do so;

(b) the holder of a domain name, being an undertaking, organisation or natural person, has been commonly known by the domain name, even in the absence of a right recognised or established by national and/or Community law;

(c) the holder of a domain name is making a legitimate and non-commercial or fair use of the domain name, without intent to mislead consumers or harm the reputation of a name on which a right is recognised or established by national and/or Community law.

3. Bad faith, within the meaning of point (b) of paragraph 1 may be demonstrated, where:

(a) circumstances indicate that the domain name was registered or acquired primarily for the purpose of selling, renting, or otherwise transferring the domain name to the holder of a name in respect of which a right is recognised or established by national and/or Community law or to a public body; or

(b) the domain name has been registered in order to prevent the holder of such a name in respect of which a right is recognised or established by national and/or Community law, or a public body, from reflecting this name in a corresponding domain name, provided that:

(i) a pattern of such conduct by the registrant can be demonstrated; or

(ii) the domain name has not been used in a relevant way for at least two years from the date of registration; or

(iii) in circumstances where, at the time the ADR procedure was initiated, the holder of a domain name in respect of which a right is recognised or established by national and/or Community law or the holder of a domain name of a public body has declared his/its intention to use the domain name in a relevant way but fails to do so within six months of the day on which the ADR procedure was initiated;

(c) the domain name was registered primarily for the purpose of disrupting the professional activities of a competitor; or

(d) the domain name was intentionally used to attract Internet users, for commercial gain, to the holder of a domain name website or other on-line

location, by creating a likelihood of confusion with a name on which a right is recognised or established by national and/or Community law or a name of a public body, such likelihood arising as to the source, sponsorship, affiliation or endorsement of the website or location or of a product or service on the website or location of the holder of a domain name; or

(e) the domain name registered is a personal name for which no demonstrable link exists between the domain name holder and the domain name registered.

4. The provisions in paragraphs 1, 2 and 3 may not be invoked so as to obstruct claims under national law.

Article 22
Alternative dispute resolution (ADR) procedure

1. An ADR procedure may be initiated by any party where:

(a) the registration is speculative or abusive within the meaning of Article 21; or

(b) a decision taken by the Registry conflicts with this Regulation or with Regulation (EC) No 733/2002.

2. Participation in the ADR procedure shall be compulsory for the holder of a domain name and the Registry.

3. A fee for the ADR shall be paid by the complainant.

4. Unless otherwise agreed by the parties, or specified otherwise in the registration agreement between registrar and domain name holder, the language of the administrative proceeding shall be the language of that agreement. This rule shall be subject to the authority of the panel to determine otherwise, having regard to the circumstances of the case.

11

5. The complaints and the responses to those complaints must be submitted to an ADR provider chosen by the complainant from the list referred to in the first paragraph of Article 23. That submission shall be made in accordance with this Regulation and the published supplementary procedures of the ADR provider.

6. As soon as a request for ADR is properly filed with the ADR provider and the appropriate fee is paid, the ADR provider shall inform the Registry of the identity of the complainant and the domain name involved. The Registry shall suspend the domain name involved from cancellation or transfer until the dispute resolution proceedings or subsequent legal proceedings are complete and the decision has been notified to the Registry.

7. The ADR provider shall examine the complaint for compliance with its rules of procedure, with the provisions of this Regulation and with Regulation (EC) No 733/2002, and, unless non-compliance is established, shall forward the complaint to the respondent within five working days following receipt of the fees to be paid by the complainant.

8. Within 30 working days of the date of receipt of the complaint the respondent shall submit a response to the provider.

9. Any written communication to a complainant or respondent shall be made by the preferred means stated by the complainant or respondent, respectively, or in the absence of such specification electronically via the Internet, provided that a record of transmission is available.

All communications concerning the ADR procedure to the holder of a domain name that is subject to an ADR procedure shall be sent to the address information that is available to the Registrar that maintains the registration of the domain name in accordance with the terms and conditions of registration.

10. Failure of any of the parties involved in an ADR procedure to respond within the given deadlines or appear to a panel hearing may be considered as grounds to accept the claims of the counterparty.

11. In the case of a procedure against a domain name holder, the ADR panel shall decide that the domain name shall be revoked, if it finds that the registration is speculative or abusive as defined in Article 21. The domain name shall be transferred to the complainant if the complainant applies for this domain name and satisfies the general eligibility criteria set out in Article 4(2)(b) of Regulation (EC) No 733/2002.

In the case of a procedure against the Registry, the ADR panel shall decide whether a decision taken by the Registry conflicts with this Regulation or with Regulation (EC) No 733/2002. The ADR panel shall decide that the decision shall be annulled and may decide in appropriate cases that the domain name in question shall be transferred, revoked or attributed, provided that, where necessary, the general eligibility criteria set out in Article 4(2)(b) of Regulation (EC) No 733/2002 are fulfilled.

The decision of the ADR panel shall state the date for implementation of the decision.

Decisions of the panel are taken by simple majority. The alternative dispute panel shall issue its decision within one month from the date of receipt of the response by the ADR provider. The decision shall be duly motivated. The decisions of the panel shall be published.

11

12. Within three working days after receiving the decision from the panel, the provider shall notify the full text of the decision to each party, the concerned registrar(s) and the Registry. The decision shall be notified to the Registry and the complainant by registered post or other equivalent electronic means.

13. The results of ADR shall be binding on the parties and the Registry unless court proceedings are initiated within 30 calendar days of the notification of the result of the ADR procedure to the parties.

Article 23
Selection of providers and panellists for alternative dispute resolution

1. The Registry may select ADR providers, who shall be reputable bodies with appropriate expertise in an objective, transparent and non-discriminatory manner. A list of the ADR providers shall be published on the Registry's website.

2. A dispute which is submitted to the ADR procedure shall be examined by arbitrators appointed to a panel of one or three members.

The panellists shall be selected in accordance to the internal procedures of the selected ADR providers. They shall have appropriate expertise and shall be selected in an objective, transparent and non-discriminatory manner. Each provider shall maintain a publicly available list of panellists and their qualifications.

A panellist shall be impartial and independent and shall have, before accepting appointment, disclosed to the provider any circumstances giving rise to justifiable doubt as to their impartiality or independence. If, at any stage during the administrative proceedings, new circumstances arise that could give rise to justifiable doubt as to the impartiality or independence of the panellist, that panellist shall promptly disclose such circumstances to the provider.

In such event, the provider shall appoint a substitute panellist.

CHAPTER VII
FINAL PROVISIONS

Article 24
Entry into force

This Regulation shall enter into force on the day of its publication in the Official Journal of the European Union.

This Regulation shall be binding in its entirety and directly applicable in all Member States.

ANNEX

[not printed]

12

Directive on Privacy and Electronic Communications Directive 2002/58/EC of the European Parliament and of the Council of 12 July 2002 concerning the processing of personal data and the protection of privacy in the electronic communications sector (Directive on privacy and electronic communications)

OJ L 201, 31. 7. 2002, p. 37, amended by OJ L 105, 13. 4. 2006, p. 54

THE EUROPEAN PARLIAMENT AND THE COUNCIL OF THE EUROPEAN UNION,

Having regard to the Treaty establishing the European Community, and in particular Article 95 thereof,

Having regard to the proposal from the Commission[1]),

Having regard to the opinion of the Economic and Social Committee[2]),

Having consulted the Committee of the Regions,

Acting in accordance with the procedure laid down in Article 251 of the Treaty[3]),

Whereas:

(1) Directive 95/46/EC of the European Parliament and of the Council of 24 October 1995 on the protection of individuals with regard to the process-

ing of personal data and on the free movement of such data[4]) requires Member States to ensure the rights and freedoms of natural persons with regard to the processing of personal data, and in particular their right to privacy, in order to ensure the free flow of personal data in the Community.

(2) This Directive seeks to respect the fundamental rights and observes the principles recognised in particular by the Charter of fundamental rights of the European Union. In particular, this Directive seeks to ensure full respect for the rights set out in Articles 7 and 8 of that Charter.

(3) Confidentiality of communications is guaranteed in accordance with the international instruments relating to human rights, in particular the European Convention for the Protection of Human Rights and Fundamental Freedoms, and the constitutions of the Member States.

(4) Directive 97/66/EC of the European Parliament and of the Council of 15 December 1997 concerning the processing of personal data and the protection of privacy in the telecommunica-

---

[1]) OJ C 365 E, 19. 12. 2000, p. 223.
[2]) OJ C 123, 25. 4. 2001, p. 53.
[3]) Opinion of the European Parliament of 13 November 2001 (not yet published in the Official Journal), Council Common Position of 28 January 2002 (OJ C 113 E, 14. 5. 2002, p. 39) and Decision of the European Parliament of 30 May 2002 (not yet published in the Official Journal). Council Decision of 25 June 2002.

[4]) OJ L 281, 23. 11. 1995, p. 31.

tions sector[5]) translated the principles set out in Directive 95/46/EC into specific rules for the telecommunications sector. Directive 97/66/EC has to be adapted to developments in the markets and technologies for electronic communications services in order to provide an equal level of protection of personal data and privacy for users of publicly available electronic communications services, regardless of the technologies used. That Directive should therefore be repealed and replaced by this Directive.

(5) New advanced digital technologies are currently being introduced in public communications networks in the Community, which give rise to specific requirements concerning the protection of personal data and privacy of the user. The development of the information society is characterised by the introduction of new electronic communications services. Access to digital mobile networks has become available and affordable for a large public. These digital networks have large capacities and possibilities for processing personal data. The successful cross-border development of these services is partly dependent on the confidence of users that their privacy will not be at risk.

(6) The Internet is overturning traditional market structures by providing a common, global infrastructure for the delivery of a wide range of electronic communications services. Publicly available electronic communications services over the Internet open new possibilities for users but also new risks for their personal data and privacy.

(7) In the case of public communications networks, specific legal, regulatory and technical provisions should be

5) OJ L 24, 30. 1. 1998, p. 1.

made in order to protect fundamental rights and freedoms of natural persons and legitimate interests of legal persons, in particular with regard to the increasing capacity for automated storage and processing of data relating to subscribers and users.

(8) Legal, regulatory and technical provisions adopted by the Member States concerning the protection of personal data, privacy and the legitimate interest of legal persons, in the electronic communication sector, should be harmonised in order to avoid obstacles to the internal market for electronic communication in accordance with Article 14 of the Treaty. Harmonisation should be limited to requirements necessary to guarantee that the promotion and development of new electronic communications services and networks between Member States are not hindered.

(9) The Member States, providers and users concerned, together with the competent Community bodies, should cooperate in introducing and developing the relevant technologies where this is necessary to apply the guarantees provided for by this Directive and taking particular account of the objectives of minimising the processing of personal data and of using anonymous or pseudonymous data where possible.

(10) In the electronic communications sector, Directive 95/46/EC applies in particular to all matters concerning protection of fundamental rights and freedoms, which are not specifically covered by the provisions of this Directive, including the obligations on the controller and the rights of individuals. Directive 95/46/EC applies to non-public communications services.

(11) Like Directive 95/46/EC, this Directive does not address issues of protection of fundamental rights and

freedoms related to activities which are not governed by Community law. Therefore it does not alter the existing balance between the individual's right to privacy and the possibility for Member States to take the measures referred to in Article 15(1) of this Directive, necessary for the protection of public security, defence, State security (including the economic well-being of the State when the activities relate to State security matters) and the enforcement of criminal law. Consequently, this Directive does not affect the ability of Member States to carry out lawful interception of electronic communications, or take other measures, if necessary for any of these purposes and in accordance with the European Convention for the Protection of Human Rights and Fundamental Freedoms, as interpreted by the rulings of the European Court of Human Rights. Such measures must be appropriate, strictly proportionate to the intended purpose and necessary within a democratic society and should be subject to adequate safeguards in accordance with the European Convention for the Protection of Human Rights and Fundamental Freedoms.

(12) Subscribers to a publicly available electronic communications service may be natural or legal persons. By supplementing Directive 95/46/EC, this Directive is aimed at protecting the fundamental rights of natural persons and particularly their right to privacy, as well as the legitimate interests of legal persons. This Directive does not entail an obligation for Member States to extend the application of Directive 95/46/EC to the protection of the legitimate interests of legal persons, which is ensured within the framework of the applicable Community and national legislation.

(13) The contractual relation between a subscriber and a service provider may entail a periodic or a one-off payment for the service provided or to be provided. Prepaid cards are also considered as a contract.

(14) Location data may refer to the latitude, longitude and altitude of the user's terminal equipment, to the direction of travel, to the level of accuracy of the location information, to the identification of the network cell in which the terminal equipment is located at a certain point in time and to the time the location information was recorded.

(15) A communication may include any naming, numbering or addressing information provided by the sender of a communication or the user of a connection to carry out the communication. Traffic data may include any translation of this information by the network over which the communication is transmitted for the purpose of carrying out the transmission. Traffic data may, *inter alia,* consist of data referring to the routing, duration, time or volume of a communication, to the protocol used, to the location of the terminal equipment of the sender or recipient, to the network on which the communication originates or terminates, to the beginning, end or duration of a connection. They may also consist of the format in which the communication is conveyed by the network.

(16) Information that is part of a broadcasting service provided over a public communications network is intended for a potentially unlimited audience and does not constitute a communication in the sense of this Directive. However, in cases where the individual subscriber or user receiving such information can be identified, for example with video-on-demand services, the in-

formation conveyed is covered within the meaning of a communication for the purposes of this Directive.

(17) For the purposes of this Directive, consent of a user or subscriber, regardless of whether the latter is a natural or a legal person, should have the same meaning as the data subject's consent as defined and further specified in Directive 95/46/EC. Consent may be given by any appropriate method enabling a freely given specific and informed indication of the user's wishes, including by ticking a box when visiting an Internet website.

(18) Value added services may, for example, consist of advice on least expensive tariff packages, route guidance, traffic information, weather forecasts and tourist information.

(19) The application of certain requirements relating to presentation and restriction of calling and connected line identification and to automatic call forwarding to subscriber lines connected to analogue exchanges should not be made mandatory in specific cases where such application would prove to be technically impossible or would require a disproportionate economic effort. It is important for interested parties to be informed of such cases and the Member States should therefore notify them to the Commission.

(20) Service providers should take appropriate measures to safeguard the security of their services, if necessary in conjunction with the provider of the network, and inform subscribers of any special risks of a breach of the security of the network. Such risks may especially occur for electronic communications services over an open network such as the Internet or analogue mobile telephony. It is particularly important for subscribers and users of such ser-

vices to be fully informed by their service provider of the existing security risks which lie outside the scope of possible remedies by the service provider. Service providers who offer publicly available electronic communications services over the Internet should inform users and subscribers of measures they can take to protect the security of their communications for instance by using specific types of software or encryption technologies. The requirement to inform subscribers of particular security risks does not discharge a service provider from the obligation to take, at its own costs, appropriate and immediate measures to remedy any new, unforeseen security risks and restore the normal security level of the service. The provision of information about security risks to the subscriber should be free of charge except for any nominal costs which the subscriber may incur while receiving or collecting the information, for instance by downloading an electronic mail message. Security is appraised in the light of Article 17 of Directive 95/46/EC.

(21) Measures should be taken to prevent unauthorised access to communications in order to protect the confidentiality of communications, including both the contents and any data related to such communications, by means of public communications networks and publicly available electronic communications services. National legislation in some Member States only prohibits intentional unauthorised access to communications.

(22) The prohibition of storage of communications and the related traffic data by persons other than the users or without their consent is not intended to prohibit any automatic, intermediate and transient storage of this informa-

tion in so far as this takes place for the sole purpose of carrying out the transmission in the electronic communications network and provided that the information is not stored for any period longer than is necessary for the transmission and for traffic management purposes, and that during the period of storage the confidentiality remains guaranteed. Where this is necessary for making more efficient the onward transmission of any publicly accessible information to other recipients of the service upon their request, this Directive should not prevent such information from being further stored, provided that this information would in any case be accessible to the public without restriction and that any data referring to the individual subscribers or users requesting such information are erased.

(23) Confidentiality of communications should also be ensured in the course of lawful business practice. Where necessary and legally authorised, communications can be recorded for the purpose of providing evidence of a commercial transaction. Directive 95/46/EC applies to such processing. Parties to the communications should be informed prior to the recording about the recording, its purpose and the duration of its storage. The recorded communication should be erased as soon as possible and in any case at the latest by the end of the period during which the transaction can be lawfully challenged.

(24) Terminal equipment of users of electronic communications networks and any information stored on such equipment are part of the private sphere of the users requiring protection under the European Convention for the Protection of Human Rights and Fundamental Freedoms. So-called spy-

ware, web bugs, hidden identifiers and other similar devices can enter the user's terminal without their knowledge in order to gain access to information, to store hidden information or to trace the activities of the user and may seriously intrude upon the privacy of these users. The use of such devices should be allowed only for legitimate purposes, with the knowledge of the users concerned.

(25) However, such devices, for instance so-called 'cookies', can be a legitimate and useful tool, for example, in analysing the effectiveness of website design and advertising, and in verifying the identity of users engaged in on-line transactions. Where such devices, for instance cookies, are intended for a legitimate purpose, such as to facilitate the provision of information society services, their use should be allowed on condition that users are provided with clear and precise information in accordance with Directive 95/46/EC about the purposes of cookies or similar devices so as to ensure that users are made aware of information being placed on the terminal equipment they are using. Users should have the opportunity to refuse to have a cookie or similar device stored on their terminal equipment. This is particularly important where users other than the original user have access to the terminal equipment and thereby to any data containing privacy-sensitive information stored on such equipment. Information and the right to refuse may be offered once for the use of various devices to be installed on the user's terminal equipment during the same connection and also covering any further use that may be made of those devices during subsequent connections. The methods for giving information, offering a right to refuse or requesting consent should

be made as user-friendly as possible. Access to specific website content may still be made conditional on the well-informed acceptance of a cookie or similar device, if it is used for a legitimate purpose.

(26) The data relating to subscribers processed within electronic communications networks to establish connections and to transmit information contain information on the private life of natural persons and concern the right to respect for their correspondence or concern the legitimate interests of legal persons. Such data may only be stored to the extent that is necessary for the provision of the service for the purpose of billing and for interconnection payments, and for a limited time. Any further processing of such data which the provider of the publicly available electronic communications services may want to perform, for the marketing of electronic communications services or for the provision of value added services, may only be allowed if the subscriber has agreed to this on the basis of accurate and full information given by the provider of the publicly available electronic communications services about the types of further processing it intends to perform and about the subscriber's right not to give or to withdraw his/her consent to such processing. Traffic data used for marketing communications services or for the provision of value added services should also be erased or made anonymous after the provision of the service. Service providers should always keep subscribers informed of the types of data they are processing and the purposes and duration for which this is done.

(27) The exact moment of the completion of the transmission of a communication, after which traffic data should be erased except for billing purposes, may depend on the type of electronic communications service that is provided. For instance for a voice telephony call the transmission will be completed as soon as either of the users terminates the connection. For electronic mail the transmission is completed as soon as the addressee collects the message, typically from the server of his service provider.

(28) The obligation to erase traffic data or to make such data anonymous when it is no longer needed for the purpose of the transmission of a communication does not conflict with such procedures on the Internet as the caching in the domain name system of IP addresses or the caching of IP addresses to physical address bindings or the use of log-in information to control the right of access to networks or services.

(29) The service provider may process traffic data relating to subscribers and users where necessary in individual cases in order to detect technical failure or errors in the transmission of communications. Traffic data necessary for billing purposes may also be processed by the provider in order to detect and stop fraud consisting of unpaid use of the electronic communications service.

(30) Systems for the provision of electronic communications networks and services should be designed to limit the amount of personal data necessary to a strict minimum. Any activities related to the provision of the electronic communications service that go beyond the transmission of a communication and the billing thereof should be based on aggregated, traffic data that cannot be related to subscribers or users. Where such activities cannot be based on aggregated data, they should be considered as value added services for which the consent of the subscriber is required.

(31) Whether the consent to be obtained for the processing of personal data with a view to providing a particular value added service should be that of the user or of the subscriber, will depend on the data to be processed and on the type of service to be provided and on whether it is technically, procedurally and contractually possible to distinguish the individual using an electronic communications service from the legal or natural person having subscribed to it.

(32) Where the provider of an electronic communications service or of a value added service subcontracts the processing of personal data necessary for the provision of these services to another entity, such subcontracting and subsequent data processing should be in full compliance with the requirements regarding controllers and processors of personal data as set out in Directive 95/46/EC. Where the provision of a value added service requires that traffic or location data are forwarded from an electronic communications service provider to a provider of value added services, the subscribers or users to whom the data are related should also be fully informed of this forwarding before giving their consent for the processing of the data.

(33) The introduction of itemised bills has improved the possibilities for the subscriber to check the accuracy of the fees charged by the service provider but, at the same time, it may jeopardise the privacy of the users of publicly available electronic communications services. Therefore, in order to preserve the privacy of the user, Member States should encourage the development of electronic communication service options such as alternative payment facilities which allow anonymous or strictly private access to publicly available electronic communications services, for example calling cards and facilities for payment by credit card. To the same end, Member States may ask the operators to offer their subscribers a different type of detailed bill in which a certain number of digits of the called number have been deleted.

(34) It is necessary, as regards calling line identification, to protect the right of the calling party to withhold the presentation of the identification of the line from which the call is being made and the right of the called party to reject calls from unidentified lines. There is justification for overriding the elimination of calling line identification presentation in specific cases. Certain subscribers, in particular help lines and similar organisations, have an interest in guaranteeing the anonymity of their callers. It is necessary, as regards connected line identification, to protect the right and the legitimate interest of the called party to withhold the presentation of the identification of the line to which the calling party is actually connected, in particular in the case of forwarded calls. The providers of publicly available electronic communications services should inform their subscribers of the existence of calling and connected line identification in the network and of all services which are offered on the basis of calling and connected line identification as well as the privacy options which are available. This will allow the subscribers to make an informed choice about the privacy facilities they may want to use. The privacy options which are offered on a per-line basis do not necessarily have to be available as an automatic network service but may be obtainable through a simple request to the provider of the publicly available electronic communications service.

(35) In digital mobile networks, location data giving the geographic position of the terminal equipment of the mobile user are processed to enable the transmission of communications. Such data are traffic data covered by Article 6 of this Directive. However, in addition, digital mobile networks may have the capacity to process location data which are more precise than is necessary for the transmission of communications and which are used for the provision of value added services such as services providing individualised traffic information and guidance to drivers. The processing of such data for value added services should only be allowed where subscribers have given their consent. Even in cases where subscribers have given their consent, they should have a simple means to temporarily deny the processing of location data, free of charge.

(36) Member States may restrict the users' and subscribers' rights to privacy with regard to calling line identification where this is necessary to trace nuisance calls and with regard to calling line identification and location data where this is necessary to allow emergency services to carry out their tasks as effectively as possible. For these purposes, Member States may adopt specific provisions to entitle providers of electronic communications services to provide access to calling line identification and location data without the prior consent of the users or subscribers concerned.

(37) Safeguards should be provided for subscribers against the nuisance which may be caused by automatic call forwarding by others. Moreover, in such cases, it must be possible for subscribers to stop the forwarded calls being passed on to their terminals by simple request to the provider of the publicly available electronic communications service.

(38) Directories of subscribers to electronic communications services are widely distributed and public. The right to privacy of natural persons and the legitimate interest of legal persons require that subscribers are able to determine whether their personal data are published in a directory and if so, which. Providers of public directories should inform the subscribers to be included in such directories of the purposes of the directory and of any particular usage which may be made of electronic versions of public directories especially through search functions embedded in the software, such as reverse search functions enabling users of the directory to discover the name and address of the subscriber on the basis of a telephone number only.

(39) The obligation to inform subscribers of the purpose(s) of public directories in which their personal data are to be included should be imposed on the party collecting the data for such inclusion. Where the data may be transmitted to one or more third parties, the subscriber should be informed of this possibility and of the recipient or the categories of possible recipients. Any transmission should be subject to the condition that the data may not be used for other purposes than those for which they were collected. If the party collecting the data from the subscriber or any third party to whom the data have been transmitted wishes to use the data for an additional purpose, the renewed consent of the subscriber is to be obtained either by the initial party collecting the data or by the third party to whom the data have been transmitted.

(40) Safeguards should be provided for subscribers against intrusion of their privacy by unsolicited com-

munications for direct marketing purposes in particular by means of automated calling machines, telefaxes, and e-mails, including SMS messages. These forms of unsolicited commercial communications may on the one hand be relatively easy and cheap to send and on the other may impose a burden and/ or cost on the recipient. Moreover, in some cases their volume may also cause difficulties for electronic communications networks and terminal equipment. For such forms of unsolicited communications for direct marketing, it is justified to require that prior explicit consent of the recipients is obtained before such communications are addressed to them. The single market requires a harmonised approach to ensure simple, Community-wide rules for businesses and users.

(41) Within the context of an existing customer relationship, it is reasonable to allow the use of electronic contact details for the offering of similar products or services, but only by the same company that has obtained the electronic contact details in accordance with Directive 95/46/EC. When electronic contact details are obtained, the customer should be informed about their further use for direct marketing in a clear and distinct manner, and be given the opportunity to refuse such usage. This opportunity should continue to be offered with each subsequent direct marketing message, free of charge, except for any costs for the transmission of this refusal.

(42) Other forms of direct marketing that are more costly for the sender and impose no financial costs on subscribers and users, such as person-to-person voice telephony calls, may justify the maintenance of a system giving subscribers or users the possibility to indicate that they do not want to re-

ceive such calls. Nevertheless, in order not to decrease existing levels of privacy protection, Member States should be entitled to uphold national systems, only allowing such calls to subscribers and users who have given their prior consent.

(43) To facilitate effective enforcement of Community rules on unsolicited messages for direct marketing, it is necessary to prohibit the use of false identities or false return addresses or numbers while sending unsolicited messages for direct marketing purposes.

(44) Certain electronic mail systems allow subscribers to view the sender and subject line of an electronic mail, and also to delete the message, without having to download the rest of the electronic mail's content or any attachments, thereby reducing costs which could arise from downloading unsolicited electronic mails or attachments. These arrangements may continue to be useful in certain cases as an additional tool to the general obligations established in this Directive.

(45) This Directive is without prejudice to the arrangements which Member States make to protect the legitimate interests of legal persons with regard to unsolicited communications for direct marketing purposes. Where Member States establish an opt-out register for such communications to legal persons, mostly business users, the provisions of Article 7 of Directive 2000/31/EC of the European Parliament and of the Council of 8 June 2000 on certain legal aspects of information society services, in particular electronic commerce, in the internal market (Directive on electronic commerce)[6] are fully applicable.

---

[6] OJ L 178, 17. 7. 2000, p. 1.

(46) The functionalities for the provision of electronic communications services may be integrated in the network or in any part of the terminal equipment of the user, including the software. The protection of the personal data and the privacy of the user of publicly available electronic communications services should be independent of the configuration of the various components necessary to provide the service and of the distribution of the necessary functionalities between these components. Directive 95/46/EC covers any form of processing of personal data regardless of the technology used. The existence of specific rules for electronic communications services alongside general rules for other components necessary for the provision of such services may not facilitate the protection of personal data and privacy in a technologically neutral way. It may therefore be necessary to adopt measures requiring manufacturers of certain types of equipment used for electronic communications services to construct their product in such a way as to incorporate safeguards to ensure that the personal data and privacy of the user and subscriber are protected. The adoption of such measures in accordance with Directive 1999/5/EC of the European Parliament and of the Council of 9 March 1999 on radio equipment and telecommunications terminal equipment and the mutual recognition of their conformity[7]) will ensure that the introduction of technical features of electronic communication equipment including software for data protection purposes is harmonised in order to be compatible with the implementation of the internal market.

---

[7]) OJ L 91, 7. 4. 1999, p. 10.

(47) Where the rights of the users and subscribers are not respected, national legislation should provide for judicial remedies. Penalties should be imposed on any person, whether governed by private or public law, who fails to comply with the national measures taken under this Directive.

(48) It is useful, in the field of application of this Directive, to draw on the experience of the Working Party on the Protection of Individuals with regard to the Processing of Personal Data composed of representatives of the supervisory authorities of the Member States, set up by Article 29 of Directive 95/46/EC.

(49) To facilitate compliance with the provisions of this Directive, certain specific arrangements are needed for processing of data already under way on the date that national implementing legislation pursuant to this Directive enters into force,

HAVE ADOPTED THIS DIRECTIVE:

Article 1
Scope and aim

1. This Directive harmonises the provisions of the Member States required to ensure an equivalent level of protection of fundamental rights and freedoms, and in particular the right to privacy, with respect to the processing of personal data in the electronic communication sector and to ensure the free movement of such data and of electronic communication equipment and services in the Community.

2. The provisions of this Directive particularise and complement Directive 95/46/EC for the purposes mentioned in paragraph 1. Moreover, they provide for protection of the legitimate interests of subscribers who are legal persons.

12

3. This Directive shall not apply to activities which fall outside the scope of the Treaty establishing the European Community, such as those covered by Titles V and VI of the Treaty on European Union, and in any case to activities concerning public security, defence, State security (including the economic well-being of the State when the activities relate to State security matters) and the activities of the State in areas of criminal law.

Article 2
Definitions

Save as otherwise provided, the definitions in Directive 95/46/EC and in Directive 2002/21/EC of the European Parliament and of the Council of 7 March 2002 on a common regulatory framework for electronic communications networks and services (Framework Directive)[8] shall apply.

The following definitions shall also apply:

(a) 'user' means any natural person using a publicly available electronic communications service, for private or business purposes, without necessarily having subscribed to this service;

(b) 'traffic data' means any data processed for the purpose of the conveyance of a communication on an electronic communications network or for the billing thereof;

(c) 'location data' means any data processed in an electronic communications network, indicating the geographic position of the terminal equipment of a user of a publicly available electronic communications service;

(d) 'communication' means any information exchanged or conveyed between a finite number of parties by

---

[8] OJ L 108, 24. 4. 2002, p. 33.

means of a publicly available electronic communications service. This does not include any information conveyed as part of a broadcasting service to the public over an electronic communications network except to the extent that the information can be related to the identifiable subscriber or user receiving the information;

(e) 'call' means a connection established by means of a publicly available telephone service allowing two-way communication in real time;

(f) 'consent' by a user or subscriber corresponds to the data subject's consent in Directive 95/46/EC;

(g) 'value added service' means any service which requires the processing of traffic data or location data other than traffic data beyond what is necessary for the transmission of a communication or the billing thereof;

(h) 'electronic mail' means any text, voice, sound or image message sent over a public communications network which can be stored in the network or in the recipient's terminal equipment until it is collected by the recipient.

Article 3
Services concerned

1. This Directive shall apply to the processing of personal data in connection with the provision of publicly available electronic communications services in public communications networks in the Community.

2. Articles 8, 10 and 11 shall apply to subscriber lines connected to digital exchanges and, where technically possible and if it does not require a disproportionate economic effort, to subscriber lines connected to analogue exchanges.

3. Cases where it would be technically impossible or require a disproportionate economic effort to fulfil the requirements of Articles 8, 10 and 11 shall be notified to the Commission by the Member States.

Article 4
Security

1. The provider of a publicly available electronic communications service must take appropriate technical and organisational measures to safeguard security of its services, if necessary in conjunction with the provider of the public communications network with respect to network security. Having regard to the state of the art and the cost of their implementation, these measures shall ensure a level of security appropriate to the risk presented.

2. In case of a particular risk of a breach of the security of the network, the provider of a publicly available electronic communications service must inform the subscribers concerning such risk and, where the risk lies outside the scope of the measures to be taken by the service provider, of any possible remedies, including an indication of the likely costs involved.

Article 5
Confidentiality of the communications

1. Member States shall ensure the confidentiality of communications and the related traffic data by means of a public communications network and publicly available electronic communications services, through national legislation. In particular, they shall prohibit listening, tapping, storage or other kinds of interception or surveillance of communications and the related traffic

data by persons other than users, without the consent of the users concerned, except when legally authorised to do so in accordance with Article 15(1). This paragraph shall not prevent technical storage which is necessary for the conveyance of a communication without prejudice to the principle of confidentiality.

2. Paragraph 1 shall not affect any legally authorised recording of communications and the related traffic data when carried out in the course of lawful business practice for the purpose of providing evidence of a commercial transaction or of any other business communication.

3. Member States shall ensure that the use of electronic communications networks to store information or to gain access to information stored in the terminal equipment of a subscriber or user is only allowed on condition that the subscriber or user concerned is provided with clear and comprehensive information in accordance with Directive 95/46/EC, inter alia about the purposes of the processing, and is offered the right to refuse such processing by the data controller. This shall not prevent any technical storage or access for the sole purpose of carrying out or facilitating the transmission of a communication over an electronic communications network, or as strictly necessary in order to provide an information society service explicitly requested by the subscriber or user.

Article 6
Traffic data

1. Traffic data relating to subscribers and users processed and stored by the provider of a public communications network or publicly available electronic communications service

must be erased or made anonymous when it is no longer needed for the purpose of the transmission of a communication without prejudice to paragraphs 2, 3 and 5 of this Article and Article 15(1).

2. Traffic data necessary for the purposes of subscriber billing and interconnection payments may be processed. Such processing is permissible only up to the end of the period during which the bill may lawfully be challenged or payment pursued.

3. For the purpose of marketing electronic communications services or for the provision of value added services, the provider of a publicly available electronic communications service may process the data referred to in paragraph 1 to the extent and for the duration necessary for such services or marketing, if the subscriber or user to whom the data relate has given his/her consent. Users or subscribers shall be given the possibility to withdraw their consent for the processing of traffic data at any time.

4. The service provider must inform the subscriber or user of the types of traffic data which are processed and of the duration of such processing for the purposes mentioned in paragraph 2 and, prior to obtaining consent, for the purposes mentioned in paragraph 3.

5. Processing of traffic data, in accordance with paragraphs 1, 2, 3 and 4, must be restricted to persons acting under the authority of providers of the public communications networks and publicly available electronic communications services handling billing or traffic management, customer enquiries, fraud detection, marketing electronic communications services or providing a value added service, and must be restricted to what is necessary for the purposes of such activities.

6. Paragraphs 1, 2, 3 and 5 shall apply without prejudice to the possibility for competent bodies to be informed of traffic data in conformity with applicable legislation with a view to settling disputes, in particular interconnection or billing disputes.

Article 7
Itemised billing

1. Subscribers shall have the right to receive non-itemised bills.

2. Member States shall apply national provisions in order to reconcile the rights of subscribers receiving itemised bills with the right to privacy of calling users and called subscribers, for example by ensuring that sufficient alternative privacy enhancing methods of communications or payments are available to such users and subscribers.

Article 8
Presentation and restriction of calling and connected line identification

1. Where presentation of calling line identification is offered, the service provider must offer the calling user the possibility, using a simple means and free of charge, of preventing the presentation of the calling line identification on a per-call basis. The calling subscriber must have this possibility on a per-line basis.

2. Where presentation of calling line identification is offered, the service provider must offer the called subscriber the possibility, using a simple means and free of charge for reasonable use of this function, of preventing the presentation of the calling line identification of incoming calls.

3. Where presentation of calling line identification is offered and where

the calling line identification is presented prior to the call being established, the service provider must offer the called subscriber the possibility, using a simple means, of rejecting incoming calls where the presentation of the calling line identification has been prevented by the calling user or subscriber.

4. Where presentation of connected line identification is offered, the service provider must offer the called subscriber the possibility, using a simple means and free of charge, of preventing the presentation of the connected line identification to the calling user.

5. Paragraph 1 shall also apply with regard to calls to third countries originating in the Community. Paragraphs 2, 3 and 4 shall also apply to incoming calls originating in third countries.

6. Member States shall ensure that where presentation of calling and/or connected line identification is offered, the providers of publicly available electronic communications services inform the public thereof and of the possibilities set out in paragraphs 1, 2, 3 and 4.

Article 9
Location data other than traffic data

1. Where location data other than traffic data, relating to users or subscribers of public communications networks or publicly available electronic communications services, can be processed, such data may only be processed when they are made anonymous, or with the consent of the users or subscribers to the extent and for the duration necessary for the provision of a value added service. The service provider must inform the users or subscribers, prior to obtaining their con-

sent, of the type of location data other than traffic data which will be processed, of the purposes and duration of the processing and whether the data will be transmitted to a third party for the purpose of providing the value added service. Users or subscribers shall be given the possibility to withdraw their consent for the processing of location data other than traffic data at any time.

2. Where consent of the users or subscribers has been obtained for the processing of location data other than traffic data, the user or subscriber must continue to have the possibility, using a simple means and free of charge, of temporarily refusing the processing of such data for each connection to the network or for each transmission of a communication.

3. Processing of location data other than traffic data in accordance with paragraphs 1 and 2 must be restricted to persons acting under the authority of the provider of the public communications network or publicly available communications service or of the third party providing the value added service, and must be restricted to what is necessary for the purposes of providing the value added service.

Article 10
Exceptions

Member States shall ensure that there are transparent procedures governing the way in which a provider of a public communications network and/or a publicly available electronic communications service may override:

(a) the elimination of the presentation of calling line identification, on a temporary basis, upon application of a subscriber requesting the tracing of malicious or nuisance calls. In this case,

141

in accordance with national law, the data containing the identification of the calling subscriber will be stored and be made available by the provider of a public communications network and/or publicly available electronic communications service;

(b) the elimination of the presentation of calling line identification and the temporary denial or absence of consent of a subscriber or user for the processing of location data, on a per-line basis for organisations dealing with emergency calls and recognised as such by a Member State, including law enforcement agencies, ambulance services and fire brigades, for the purpose of responding to such calls.

Article 11
Automatic call forwarding

Member States shall ensure that any subscriber has the possibility, using a simple means and free of charge, of stopping automatic call forwarding by a third party to the subscriber's terminal.

Article 12
Directories of subscribers

1. Member States shall ensure that subscribers are informed, free of charge and before they are included in the directory, about the purpose(s) of a printed or electronic directory of subscribers available to the public or obtainable through directory enquiry services, in which their personal data can be included and of any further usage possibilities based on search functions embedded in electronic versions of the directory.

2. Member States shall ensure that subscribers are given the opportunity to determine whether their personal

data are included in a public directory, and if so, which, to the extent that such data are relevant for the purpose of the directory as determined by the provider of the directory, and to verify, correct or withdraw such data. Not being included in a public subscriber directory, verifying, correcting or withdrawing personal data from it shall be free of charge.

3. Member States may require that for any purpose of a public directory other than the search of contact details of persons on the basis of their name and, where necessary, a minimum of other identifiers, additional consent be asked of the subscribers.

4. Paragraphs 1 and 2 shall apply to subscribers who are natural persons. Member States shall also ensure, in the framework of Community law and applicable national legislation, that the legitimate interests of subscribers other than natural persons with regard to their entry in public directories are sufficiently protected.

Article 13
Unsolicited communications

1. The use of automated calling systems without human intervention (automatic calling machines), facsimile machines (fax) or electronic mail for the purposes of direct marketing may only be allowed in respect of subscribers who have given their prior consent.

2. Notwithstanding paragraph 1, where a natural or legal person obtains from its customers their electronic contact details for electronic mail, in the context of the sale of a product or a service, in accordance with Directive 95/46/EC, the same natural or legal person may use these electronic contact details for direct marketing of its own similar

products or services provided that customers clearly and distinctly are given the opportunity to object, free of charge and in an easy manner, to such use of electronic contact details when they are collected and on the occasion of each message in case the customer has not initially refused such use.

3. Member States shall take appropriate measures to ensure that, free of charge, unsolicited communications for purposes of direct marketing, in cases other than those referred to in paragraphs 1 and 2, are not allowed either without the consent of the subscribers concerned or in respect of subscribers who do not wish to receive these communications, the choice between these options to be determined by national legislation.

4. In any event, the practice of sending electronic mail for purposes of direct marketing disguising or concealing the identity of the sender on whose behalf the communication is made, or without a valid address to which the recipient may send a request that such communications cease, shall be prohibited.

5. Paragraphs 1 and 3 shall apply to subscribers who are natural persons. Member States shall also ensure, in the framework of Community law and applicable national legislation, that the legitimate interests of subscribers other than natural persons with regard to unsolicited communications are sufficiently protected.

Article 14
Technical features and standardisation

1. In implementing the provisions of this Directive, Member States shall ensure, subject to paragraphs 2 and 3, that no mandatory requirements for specific technical features are imposed on terminal or other electronic communication equipment which could impede the placing of equipment on the market and the free circulation of such equipment in and between Member States.

2. Where provisions of this Directive can be implemented only by requiring specific technical features in electronic communications networks, Member States shall inform the Commission in accordance with the procedure provided for by Directive 98/34/EC of the European Parliament and of the Council of 22 June 1998 laying down a procedure for the provision of information in the field of technical standards and regulations and of rules on information society services[9]).

3. Where required, measures may be adopted to ensure that terminal equipment is constructed in a way that is compatible with the right of users to protect and control the use of their personal data, in accordance with Directive 1999/5/EC and Council Decision 87/95/EEC of 22 December 1986 on standardisation in the field of information technology and communications[10]).

Article 15
Application of certain provisions of Directive 95/46/EC

1. Member States may adopt legislative measures to restrict the scope of the rights and obligations provided for in Article 5, Article 6, Article 8(1), (2), (3) and (4), and Article 9 of this Direc-

---

[9]) OJ L 204, 21. 7. 1998, p. 37. Directive as amended by Directive 98/48/EC (OJ L 217, 5. 8. 1998, p. 18).
[10]) OJ L 36, 7. 2. 1987, p. 31. Decision as last amended by the 1994 Act of Accession.

12

tive when such restriction constitutes a necessary, appropriate and proportionate measure within a democratic society to safeguard national security (i. e. State security), defence, public security, and the prevention, investigation, detection and prosecution of criminal offences or of unauthorised use of the electronic communication system, as referred to in Article 13(1) of Directive 95/46/EC. To this end, Member States may, *inter alia,* adopt legislative measures providing for the retention of data for a limited period justified on the grounds laid down in this paragraph. All the measures referred to in this paragraph shall be in accordance with the general principles of Community law, including those referred to in Article 6(1) and (2) of the Treaty on European Union.

1 a. Paragraph 1 shall not apply to data specifically required by Directive 2006/24/EC of the European Parliament and of the Council of 15 March 2006 on the retention of data generated or processed in connection with the provision of publicly available electronic communications services or of public communications networks[11]) to be retained for the purposes referred to in Article 1(1) of that Directive.

2. The provisions of Chapter III on judicial remedies, liability and sanctions of Directive 95/46/EC shall apply with regard to national provisions adopted pursuant to this Directive and with regard to the individual rights derived from this Directive.

3. The Working Party on the Protection of Individuals with regard to the Processing of Personal Data instituted by Article 29 of Directive 95/46/EC shall also carry out the tasks laid down

in Article 30 of that Directive with regard to matters covered by this Directive, namely the protection of fundamental rights and freedoms and of legitimate interests in the electronic communications sector.

Article 16
Transitional arrangements

1. Article 12 shall not apply to editions of directories already produced or placed on the market in printed or off-line electronic form before the national provisions adopted pursuant to this Directive enter into force.

2. Where the personal data of subscribers to fixed or mobile public voice telephony services have been included in a public subscriber directory in conformity with the provisions of Directive 95/46/EC and of Article 11 of Directive 97/66/EC before the national provisions adopted in pursuance of this Directive enter into force, the personal data of such subscribers may remain included in this public directory in its printed or electronic versions, including versions with reverse search functions, unless subscribers indicate otherwise, after having received complete information about purposes and options in accordance with Article 12 of this Directive.

Article 17
Transposition

1. Before 31 October 2003 Member States shall bring into force the provisions necessary to comply with this Directive. They shall forthwith inform the Commission thereof.

When Member States adopt those provisions, they shall contain a reference to this Directive or be accompanied by such a reference on the occa-

---

[11]) OJ L 105, 13. 4. 2006, p. 54.

sion of their official publication. The methods of making such reference shall be laid down by the Member States.

2. Member States shall communicate to the Commission the text of the provisions of national law which they adopt in the field governed by this Directive and of any subsequent amendments to those provisions.

Article 18
Review

The Commission shall submit to the European Parliament and the Council, not later than three years after the date referred to in Article 17(1), a report on the application of this Directive and its impact on economic operators and consumers, in particular as regards the provisions on unsolicited communications, taking into account the international environment. For this purpose, the Commission may request information from the Member States, which shall be supplied without undue delay. Where appropriate, the Commission shall submit proposals to amend this Directive, taking account of the results of that report, any changes in the sector and any other proposal it may deem necessary in order to improve the effectiveness of this Directive.

Article 19
Repeal

Directive 97/66/EC is hereby repealed with effect from the date referred to in Article 17(1).

References made to the repealed Directive shall be construed as being made to this Directive.

Article 20
Entry into force

This Directive shall enter into force on the day of its publication in the Official Journal of the European Communities.

Article 21
Addressees

This Directive is addressed to the Member States.

13

Data Retention Directive
Directive 2006/24/EC of the European Parliament and of the Council of 15 March 2006 on the retention of data generated or processed in connection with the provision of publicly available electronic communications services or of public communications networks and amending Directive 2002/58/EC

OJ L 105, 13. 4. 2006, p. 54

THE EUROPEAN PARLIAMENT AND THE COUNCIL OF THE EUROPEAN UNION,

Having regard to the Treaty establishing the European Community, and in particular Article 95 thereof,

Having regard to the proposal from the Commission,

Having regard to the Opinion of the European Economic and Social Committee[1]),

Acting in accordance with the procedure laid down in Article 251 of the Treaty[2]),

Whereas:

(1) Directive 95/46/EC of the European Parliament and of the Council of 24 October 1995 on the protection of individuals with regard to the processing of personal data and on the free movement of such data[3]) requires Member States to protect the rights and freedoms of natural persons with regard to the processing of personal data, and in particular their right to privacy, in order to ensure the free flow of personal data in the Community.

(2) Directive 2002/58/EC of the European Parliament and of the Council of 12 July 2002 concerning the processing of personal data and the protection of privacy in the electronic communications sector (Directive on privacy and electronic communications)[4]) translates the principles set out in Directive 95/46/EC into specific rules for the electronic communications sector.

(3) Articles 5, 6 and 9 of Directive 2002/58/EC lay down the rules applicable to the processing by network and service providers of traffic and location data generated by using electronic communications services. Such data must be erased or made anonymous when no longer needed for the purpose of the transmission of a communication, except for the data necessary for billing or interconnection payments. Subject to consent, certain data may

---

[1]) Opinion delivered on 19 January 2006 (not yet published in the Official Journal).

[2]) Opinion of the European Parliament of 14 December 2005 (not yet published in the Official Journal) and Council Decision of 21 February 2006.

[3]) OJ L 281, 23. 11. 1995, p. 31. Directive as amended by Regulation (EC) No 1882/2003 (OJ L 284, 31. 10. 2003, p. 1).

[4]) OJ L 201, 31. 7. 2002, p. 37.

also be processed for marketing purposes and the provision of value-added services.

(4) Article 15(1) of Directive 2002/58/EC sets out the conditions under which Member States may restrict the scope of the rights and obligations provided for in Article 5, Article 6, Article 8(1), (2), (3) and (4), and Article 9 of that Directive. Any such restrictions must be necessary, appropriate and proportionate within a democratic society for specific public order purposes, i.e. to safeguard national security (i.e. State security), defence, public security or the prevention, investigation, detection and prosecution of criminal offences or of unauthorised use of the electronic communications systems.

(5) Several Member States have adopted legislation providing for the retention of data by service providers for the prevention, investigation, detection, and prosecution of criminal offences. Those national provisions vary considerably.

(6) The legal and technical differences between national provisions concerning the retention of data for the purpose of prevention, investigation, detection and prosecution of criminal offences present obstacles to the internal market for electronic communications, since service providers are faced with different requirements regarding the types of traffic and location data to be retained and the conditions and periods of retention.

(7) The Conclusions of the Justice and Home Affairs Council of 19 December 2002 underline that, because of the significant growth in the possibilities afforded by electronic communications, data relating to the use of electronic communications are particularly important and therefore a valuable tool in the prevention, investigation, detection and prosecution of criminal offences, in particular organised crime.

(8) The Declaration on Combating Terrorism adopted by the European Council on 25 March 2004 instructed the Council to examine measures for establishing rules on the retention of communications traffic data by service providers.

(9) Under Article 8 of the European Convention for the Protection of Human Rights and Fundamental Freedoms (ECHR), everyone has the right to respect for his private life and his correspondence. Public authorities may interfere with the exercise of that right only in accordance with the law and where necessary in a democratic society, *inter alia,* in the interests of national security or public safety, for the prevention of disorder or crime, or for the protection of the rights and freedoms of others. Because retention of data has proved to be such a necessary and effective investigative tool for law enforcement in several Member States, and in particular concerning serious matters such as organised crime and terrorism, it is necessary to ensure that retained data are made available to law enforcement authorities for a certain period, subject to the conditions provided for in this Directive. The adoption of an instrument on data retention that complies with the requirements of Article 8 of the ECHR is therefore a necessary measure.

(10) On 13 July 2005, the Council reaffirmed in its declaration condemning the terrorist attacks on London the need to adopt common measures on the retention of telecommunications data as soon as possible.

(11) Given the importance of traffic and location data for the investigation, detection, and prosecution of criminal

offences, as demonstrated by research and the practical experience of several Member States, there is a need to ensure at European level that data that are generated or processed, in the course of the supply of communications services, by providers of publicly available electronic communications services or of a public communications network are retained for a certain period, subject to the conditions provided for in this Directive.

(12) Article 15(1) of Directive 2002/58/EC continues to apply to data, including data relating to unsuccessful call attempts, the retention of which is not specifically required under this Directive and which therefore fall outside the scope thereof, and to retention for purposes, including judicial purposes, other than those covered by this Directive.

(13) This Directive relates only to data generated or processed as a consequence of a communication or a communication service and does not relate to data that are the content of the information communicated. Data should be retained in such a way as to avoid their being retained more than once. Data generated or processed when supplying the communications services concerned refers to data which are accessible. In particular, as regards the retention of data relating to Internet e-mail and Internet telephony, the obligation to retain data may apply only in respect of data from the providers' or the network providers' own services.

(14) Technologies relating to electronic communications are changing rapidly and the legitimate requirements of the competent authorities may evolve. In order to obtain advice and encourage the sharing of experience of best practice in these matters, the Commission intends to establish a group composed of Member States' law enforcement authorities, associations of the electronic communications industry, representatives of the European Parliament and data protection authorities, including the European Data Protection Supervisor.

(15) Directive 95/46/EC and Directive 2002/58/EC are fully applicable to the data retained in accordance with this Directive. Article 30(1)(c) of Directive 95/46/EC requires the consultation of the Working Party on the Protection of Individuals with regard to the Processing of Personal Data established under Article 29 of that Directive.

(16) The obligations incumbent on service providers concerning measures to ensure data quality, which derive from Article 6 of Directive 95/46/EC, and their obligations concerning measures to ensure confidentiality and security of processing of data, which derive from Articles 16 and 17 of that Directive, apply in full to data being retained within the meaning of this Directive.

(17) It is essential that Member States adopt legislative measures to ensure that data retained under this Directive are provided to the competent national authorities only in accordance with national legislation in full respect of the fundamental rights of the persons concerned.

(18) In this context, Article 24 of Directive 95/46/EC imposes an obligation on Member States to lay down sanctions for infringements of the provisions adopted pursuant to that Directive. Article 15(2) of Directive 2002/58/EC imposes the same requirement in relation to national provisions adopted pursuant to Directive 2002/58/EC. Council Framework Decision 2005/222/JHA of 24 February 2005 on at-

tacks against information systems[5]) provides that the intentional illegal access to information systems, including to data retained therein, is to be made punishable as a criminal offence.

(19) The right of any person who has suffered damage as a result of an unlawful processing operation or of any act incompatible with national provisions adopted pursuant to Directive 95/46/EC to receive compensation, which derives from Article 23 of that Directive, applies also in relation to the unlawful processing of any personal data pursuant to this Directive.

(20) The 2001 Council of Europe Convention on Cybercrime and the 1981 Council of Europe Convention for the Protection of Individuals with Regard to Automatic Processing of Personal Data also cover data being retained within the meaning of this Directive.

(21) Since the objectives of this Directive, namely to harmonise the obligations on providers to retain certain data and to ensure that those data are available for the purpose of the investigation, detection and prosecution of serious crime, as defined by each Member State in its national law, cannot be sufficiently achieved by the Member States and can therefore, by reason of the scale and effects of this Directive, be better achieved at Community level, the Community may adopt measures, in accordance with the principle of subsidiarity as set out in Article 5 of the Treaty. In accordance with the principle of proportionality, as set out in that Article, this Directive does not go beyond what is necessary in order to achieve those objectives.

(22) This Directive respects the fundamental rights and observes the principles recognised, in particular, by the Charter of Fundamental Rights of the European Union. In particular, this Directive, together with Directive 2002/58/EC, seeks to ensure full compliance with citizens' fundamental rights to respect for private life and communications and to the protection of their personal data, as enshrined in Articles 7 and 8 of the Charter.

(23) Given that the obligations on providers of electronic communications services should be proportionate, this Directive requires that they retain only such data as are generated or processed in the process of supplying their communications services. To the extent that such data are not generated or processed by those providers, there is no obligation to retain them. This Directive is not intended to harmonise the technology for retaining data, the choice of which is a matter to be resolved at national level.

(24) In accordance with paragraph 34 of the Interinstitutional agreement on better law-making[6]), Member States are encouraged to draw up, for themselves and in the interests of the Community, their own tables illustrating, as far as possible, the correlation between this Directive and the transposition measures, and to make them public.

(25) This Directive is without prejudice to the power of Member States to adopt legislative measures concerning the right of access to, and use of, data by national authorities, as designated by them. Issues of access to data retained pursuant to this Directive by national authorities for such activities as are referred to in the first indent of Article 3(2) of Directive 95/46/EC fall

---

[5]) OJ L 69, 16. 3. 2005, p. 67.

[6]) OJ C 321, 31. 12. 2003, p. 1.

outside the scope of Community law. However, they may be subject to national law or action pursuant to Title VI of the Treaty on European Union. Such laws or action must fully respect fundamental rights as they result from the common constitutional traditions of the Member States and as guaranteed by the ECHR. Under Article 8 of the ECHR, as interpreted by the European Court of Human Rights, interference by public authorities with privacy rights must meet the requirements of necessity and proportionality and must therefore serve specified, explicit and legitimate purposes and be exercised in a manner that is adequate, relevant and not excessive in relation to the purpose of the interference,

HAVE ADOPTED THIS DIRECTIVE:

Article 1
Subject matter and scope

1. This Directive aims to harmonise Member States' provisions concerning the obligations of the providers of publicly available electronic communications services or of public communications networks with respect to the retention of certain data which are generated or processed by them, in order to ensure that the data are available for the purpose of the investigation, detection and prosecution of serious crime, as defined by each Member State in its national law.

2. This Directive shall apply to traffic and location data on both legal entities and natural persons and to the related data necessary to identify the subscriber or registered user. It shall not apply to the content of electronic communications, including information consulted using an electronic communications network.

Article 2
Definitions

1. For the purpose of this Directive, the definitions in Directive 95/46/EC, in Directive 2002/21/EC of the European Parliament and of the Council of 7 March 2002 on a common regulatory framework for electronic communications networks and services (Framework Directive)[7]), and in Directive 2002/58/EC shall apply.

2. For the purpose of this Directive:

(a) 'data' means traffic data and location data and the related data necessary to identify the subscriber or user;

(b) 'user' means any legal entity or natural person using a publicly available electronic communications service, for private or business purposes, without necessarily having subscribed to that service;

(c) 'telephone service' means calls (including voice, voicemail and conference and data calls), supplementary services (including call forwarding and call transfer) and messaging and multimedia services (including short message services, enhanced media services and multi-media services);

(d) 'user ID' means a unique identifier allocated to persons when they subscribe to or register with an Internet access service or Internet communications service;

(e) 'cell ID' means the identity of the cell from which a mobile telephony call originated or in which it terminated;

(f) 'unsuccessful call attempt' means a communication where a telephone call has been successfully connected but not answered or there has been a network management intervention.

---

[7]) OJ L 108, 24. 4. 2002, p. 33.

Article 3
Obligation to retain data

1. By way of derogation from Articles 5, 6 and 9 of Directive 2002/58/EC, Member States shall adopt measures to ensure that the data specified in Article 5 of this Directive are retained in accordance with the provisions thereof, to the extent that those data are generated or processed by providers of publicly available electronic communications services or of a public communications network within their jurisdiction in the process of supplying the communications services concerned.

2. The obligation to retain data provided for in paragraph 1 shall include the retention of the data specified in Article 5 relating to unsuccessful call attempts where those data are generated or processed, and stored (as regards telephony data) or logged (as regards Internet data), by providers of publicly available electronic communications services or of a public communications network within the jurisdiction of the Member State concerned in the process of supplying the communication services concerned. This Directive shall not require data relating to unconnected calls to be retained.

Article 4
Access to data

Member States shall adopt measures to ensure that data retained in accordance with this Directive are provided only to the competent national authorities in specific cases and in accordance with national law. The procedures to be followed and the conditions to be fulfilled in order to gain access to retained data in accordance with necessity and proportionality requirements shall be defined by each Member State in its national law, subject to the relevant provisions of European Union law or public international law, and in particular the ECHR as interpreted by the European Court of Human Rights.

Article 5
Categories of data to be retained

1. Member States shall ensure that the following categories of data are retained under this Directive:

(a) data necessary to trace and identify the source of a communication:

(1) concerning fixed network telephony and mobile telephony:

(i) the calling telephone number;

(ii) the name and address of the subscriber or registered user;

(2) concerning Internet access, Internet e-mail and Internet telephony:

(i) the user ID(s) allocated;

(ii) the user ID and telephone number allocated to any communication entering the public telephone network;

(iii) the name and address of the subscriber or registered user to whom an Internet Protocol (IP) address, user ID or telephone number was allocated at the time of the communication;

(b) data necessary to identify the destination of a communication:

(1) concerning fixed network telephony and mobile telephony:

(i) the number(s) dialled (the telephone number(s) called), and, in cases involving supplementary services such as call forwarding or call transfer, the number or numbers to which the call is routed;

(ii) the name(s) and address(es) of the subscriber(s) or registered user(s);

(2) concerning Internet e-mail and Internet telephony:

13

(i) the user ID or telephone number of the intended recipient(s) of an Internet telephony call;

(ii) the name(s) and address(es) of the subscriber(s) or registered user(s) and user ID of the intended recipient of the communication;

(c) data necessary to identify the date, time and duration of a communication:

(1) concerning fixed network telephony and mobile telephony, the date and time of the start and end of the communication;

(2) concerning Internet access, Internet e-mail and Internet telephony:

(i) the date and time of the log-in and log-off of the Internet access service, based on a certain time zone, together with the IP address, whether dynamic or static, allocated by the Internet access service provider to a communication, and the user ID of the subscriber or registered user;

(ii) the date and time of the log-in and log-off of the Internet e-mail service or Internet telephony service, based on a certain time zone;

(d) data necessary to identify the type of communication:

(1) concerning fixed network telephony and mobile telephony: the telephone service used;

(2) concerning Internet e-mail and Internet telephony: the Internet service used;

(e) data necessary to identify users' communication equipment or what purports to be their equipment:

(1) concerning fixed network telephony, the calling and called telephone numbers;

(2) concerning mobile telephony:

(i) the calling and called telephone numbers;

(ii) the International Mobile Subscriber Identity (IMSI) of the calling party;

(iii) the International Mobile Equipment Identity (IMEI) of the calling party;

(iv) the IMSI of the called party;

(v) the IMEI of the called party;

(vi) in the case of pre-paid anonymous services, the date and time of the initial activation of the service and the location label (Cell ID) from which the service was activated;

(3) concerning Internet access, Internet e-mail and Internet telephony:

(i) the calling telephone number for dial-up access;

(ii) the digital subscriber line (DSL) or other end point of the originator of the communication;

(f) data necessary to identify the location of mobile communication equipment:

(1) the location label (Cell ID) at the start of the communication;

(2) data identifying the geographic location of cells by reference to their location labels (Cell ID) during the period for which communications data are retained.

2. No data revealing the content of the communication may be retained pursuant to this Directive.

Article 6
Periods of retention

Member States shall ensure that the categories of data specified in Article 5 are retained for periods of not less than six months and not more than two years from the date of the communication.

Article 7
Data protection and data security

Without prejudice to the provisions adopted pursuant to Directive 95/46/

13

EC and Directive 2002/58/EC, each Member State shall ensure that providers of publicly available electronic communications services or of a public communications network respect, as a minimum, the following data security principles with respect to data retained in accordance with this Directive:

(a) the retained data shall be of the same quality and subject to the same security and protection as those data on the network;

(b) the data shall be subject to appropriate technical and organisational measures to protect the data against accidental or unlawful destruction, accidental loss or alteration, or unauthorised or unlawful storage, processing, access or disclosure;

(c) the data shall be subject to appropriate technical and organisational measures to ensure that they can be accessed by specially authorised personnel only;

and

(d) the data, except those that have been accessed and preserved, shall be destroyed at the end of the period of retention.

Article 8
Storage requirements for retained data

Member States shall ensure that the data specified in Article 5 are retained in accordance with this Directive in such a way that the data retained and any other necessary information relating to such data can be transmitted upon request to the competent authorities without undue delay.

Article 9
Supervisory authority

1. Each Member State shall designate one or more public authorities to be responsible for monitoring the application within its territory of the provisions adopted by the Member States pursuant to Article 7 regarding the security of the stored data. Those authorities may be the same authorities as those referred to in Article 28 of Directive 95/46/EC.

2. The authorities referred to in paragraph 1 shall act with complete independence in carrying out the monitoring referred to in that paragraph.

Article 10
Statistics

1. Member States shall ensure that the Commission is provided on a yearly basis with statistics on the retention of data generated or processed in connection with the provision of publicly available electronic communications services or a public communications network. Such statistics shall include:

– the cases in which information was provided to the competent authorities in accordance with applicable national law,

– the time elapsed between the date on which the data were retained and the date on which the competent authority requested the transmission of the data,

– the cases where requests for data could not be met.

2. Such statistics shall not contain personal data.

Article 11
Amendment of Directive 2002/58/EC

The following paragraph shall be inserted in Article 15 of Directive 2002/58/EC:

"1 a. Paragraph 1 shall not apply to data specifically required by Directive

2006/24/EC of the European Parliament and of the Council of 15 March 2006 on the retention of data generated or processed in connection with the provision of publicly available electronic communications services or of public communications networks[8]) to be retained for the purposes referred to in Article 1(1) of that Directive."

Article 12
Future measures

1. A Member State facing particular circumstances that warrant an extension for a limited period of the maximum retention period referred to in Article 6 may take the necessary measures. That Member State shall immediately notify the Commission and inform the other Member States of the measures taken under this Article and shall state the grounds for introducing them.

2. The Commission shall, within a period of six months after the notification referred to in paragraph 1, approve or reject the national measures concerned, after having examined whether they are a means of arbitrary discrimination or a disguised restriction of trade between Member States and whether they constitute an obstacle to the functioning of the internal market. In the absence of a decision by the Commission within that period the national measures shall be deemed to have been approved.

3. Where, pursuant to paragraph 2, the national measures of a Member State derogating from the provisions of this Directive are approved, the Commission may consider whether to propose an amendment to this Directive.

---

[8]) OJ L 105, 13. 4. 2006, p. 54.

Article 13
Remedies, liability and penalties

1. Each Member State shall take the necessary measures to ensure that the national measures implementing Chapter III of Directive 95/46/EC providing for judicial remedies, liability and sanctions are fully implemented with respect to the processing of data under this Directive.

2. Each Member State shall, in particular, take the necessary measures to ensure that any intentional access to, or transfer of, data retained in accordance with this Directive that is not permitted under national law adopted pursuant to this Directive is punishable by penalties, including administrative or criminal penalties, that are effective, proportionate and dissuasive.

Article 14
Evaluation

1. No later than 15 September 2010, the Commission shall submit to the European Parliament and the Council an evaluation of the application of this Directive and its impact on economic operators and consumers, taking into account further developments in electronic communications technology and the statistics provided to the Commission pursuant to Article 10 with a view to determining whether it is necessary to amend the provisions of this Directive, in particular with regard to the list of data in Article 5 and the periods of retention provided for in Article 6. The results of the evaluation shall be made public.

2. To that end, the Commission shall examine all observations communicated to it by the Member States or by the Working Party established under Article 29 of Directive 95/46/EC.

Article 15
Transposition

1. Member States shall bring into force the laws, regulations and administrative provisions necessary to comply with this Directive by no later than 15 September 2007. They shall forthwith inform the Commission thereof. When Member States adopt those measures, they shall contain a reference to this Directive or shall be accompanied by such reference on the occasion of their official publication. The methods of making such reference shall be laid down by Member States.

2. Member States shall communicate to the Commission the text of the main provisions of national law which they adopt in the field covered by this Directive.

3. Until 15 March 2009, each Member State may postpone application of this Directive to the retention of communications data relating to Internet Access, Internet telephony and Internet e-mail. Any Member State that intends to make use of this paragraph shall, upon adoption of this Directive, notify the Council and the Commission to that effect by way of a declaration. The declaration shall be published in the *Official Journal of the European Union*.

Article 16
Entry into force

This Directive shall enter into force on the twentieth day following that of its publication in the *Official Journal of the European Union*.

Article 17
Addressees

This Directive is addressed to the Member States.

Declaration by the Netherlands pursuant to Article 15(3) of Directive 2006/24/EC

Regarding the Directive of the European Parliament and of the Council on the retention of data processed in connection with the provision of publicly available electronic communications services and amending Directive 2002/58/EC, the Netherlands will be making use of the option of postponing application of the Directive to the retention of communications data relating to Internet access, Internet telephony and Internet e-mail, for a period not exceeding 18 months following the date of entry into force of the Directive.

Declaration by Austria pursuant to Article 15(3) of Directive 2006/24/EC

Austria declares that it will be postponing application of this Directive to the retention of communications data relating to Internet access, Internet telephony and Internet e-mail, for a period of 18 months following the date specified in Article 15(1).

Declaration by Estonia pursuant to Article 15(3) of Directive 2006/24/EC

In accordance with Article 15(3) of the Directive of the European Parliament and of the Council on the retention of data generated or processed in connection with the provision of publicly available electronic communications services or of public communications networks and amending Directive 2002/58/EC, Estonia hereby states its intention to make use of use that paragraph and to postpone application of the Directive to retention of communications data relating to Internet access,

13

Internet telephony and Internet e-mail until 36 months after the date of adoption of the Directive.

Declaration by the United Kingdom
pursuant to Article 15(3) of Directive 2006/24/EC

The United Kingdom declares in accordance with Article 15(3) of the Directive on the retention of data generated or processed in connection with the provision of publicly available electronic communications services or of public communications networks and amending Directive 2002/58/EC that it will postpone application of that Directive to the retention of communications data relating to Internet access, Internet telephony and Internet e-mail.

Declaration by the Republic of Cyprus
pursuant to Article 15(3) of Directive 2006/24/EC

The Republic of Cyprus declares that it is postponing application of the Directive in respect of the retention of communications data relating to Internet access, Internet telephony and Internet e-mail until the date fixed in Article 15(3).

Declaration by the Hellenic Republic
pursuant to Article 15(3) of Directive 2006/24/EC

Greece declares that, pursuant to Article 15(3), it will postpone application of this Directive in respect of the retention of communications data relating to Internet access, Internet telephony and Internet e-mail until 18 months after expiry of the period provided for in Article 15(1).

Declaration by the Grand Duchy of Luxembourg
pursuant to Article 15(3) of Directive 2006/24/EC

Pursuant to Article 15(3) of the Directive of the European Parliament and of the Council on the retention of data generated or processed in connection with the provision of publicly available electronic communications services or of public communications networks and amending Directive 2002/58/EC, the Government of the Grand Duchy of Luxembourg declares that it intends to make use of Article 15(3) of the Directive in order to have the option of postponing application of the Directive to the retention of communications data relating to Internet access, Internet telephony and Internet e-mail.

Declaration by Slovenia
pursuant to Article 15(3) of Directive 2006/24/EC

Slovenia is joining the group of Member States which have made a declaration under Article 15(3) of the Directive of the European Parliament and the Council on the retention of data generated or processed in connection with the provision of publicly available electronic communications services or of public communications networks, for the 18 months postponement of the application of the Directive to the retention of communication data relating to Internet, Internet telephony and Internet e-mail.

Declaration by Sweden
pursuant to Article 15(3) of Directive 2006/24/EC

Pursuant to Article 15(3), Sweden wishes to have the option of postpon-

13

156

ing application of this Directive to the retention of communications data relating to Internet access, Internet telephony and Internet e-mail.

Declaration by the Republic of Lithuania pursuant to Article 15(3) of Directive 2006/24/EC

Pursuant to Article 15(3) of the draft Directive of the European Parliament and of the Council on the retention of data generated or processed in connection with the provision of publicly available electronic communications services or public communications networks and amending Directive 2002/58/EC (hereafter the 'Directive'), the Republic of Lithuania declares that once the Directive has been adopted it will postpone the application thereof to the retention of communications data relating to Internet access, Internet telephony and Internet e-mail for the period provided for in Article 15(3).

Declaration by the Republic of Latvia pursuant to Article 15(3) of Directive 2006/24/EC

Latvia states in accordance with Article 15(3) of Directive 2006/24/EC of 15 March 2006 on the retention of data generated or processed in connection with the provision of publicly available electronic communications services or of public communications networks and amending Directive 2002/58/EC that it is postponing application of the Directive to the retention of communications data relating to Internet access, Internet telephony and Internet e-mail until 15 March 2009.

Declaration by the Czech Republic pursuant to Article 15(3) of Directive 2006/24/EC

Pursuant to Article 15(3), the Czech Republic hereby declares that it is postponing application of this Directive to the retention of communications data relating to Internet access, Internet telephony and Internet e-mail until 36 months after the date of adoption thereof.

Declaration by Belgium pursuant to Article 15(3) of Directive 2006/24/EC

Belgium declares that, taking up the option available under Article 15(3), it will postpone application of this Directive, for a period of 36 months after its adoption, to the retention of communications data relating to Internet access, Internet telephony and Internet e-mail.

Declaration by the Republic of Poland pursuant to Article 15(3) of Directive 2006/24/EC

Poland hereby declares that it intends to make use of the option provided for under Article 15(3) of the Directive of the European Parliament and of the Council on the retention of data processed in connection with the provision of publicly available electronic communications services and amending Directive 2002/58/EC and postpone application of the Directive to the retention of communications data relating to Internet access, Internet telephony and Internet e-mail for a period of 18 months following the date specified in Article 15(1).

13

Declaration by Finland
pursuant to Article 15(3)
of Directive 2006/24/EC

Finland declares in accordance with Article 15(3) of the Directive on the retention of data generated or processed in connection with the provision of publicly available electronic communications services or of public communications networks and amending Directive 2002/58/EC that it will postpone application of that Directive to the retention of communications data relating to Internet access, Internet telephony and Internet e-mail.

Declaration by Germany
pursuant to Article 15(3)
of Directive 2006/24/EC

Germany reserves the right to postpone application of this Directive to the retention of communications data relating to Internet access, Internet telephony and Internet e-mail for a period of 18 months following the date specified in the first sentence of Article 15(1).

14

Data Protection Directive
Directive 95/46/EC of the European Parliament and of the Council of 24 October 1995 on the protection of individuals with regard to the processing of personal data and on the free movement of such data

OJ L 281, 23. 11. 1995, p. 31, amended by OJ L 284, 31. 10. 2003, p. 1

THE EUROPEAN PARLIAMENT AND THE COUNCIL OF THE EUROPEAN UNION,

Having regard to the Treaty establishing the European Community, and in particular Article 100 a thereof,

Having regard to the proposal from the Commission[1]),

Having regard to the opinion of the Economic and Social Committee[2]),

Acting in accordance with the procedure referred to in Article 189 b of the Treaty[3]),

(1) Whereas the objectives of the Community, as laid down in the Treaty, as amended by the Treaty on European Union, include creating an ever closer union among the peoples of Europe, fostering closer relations between the States belonging to the Community, ensuring economic and social progress by common action to eliminate the barriers which divide Europe, encouraging the constant improvement of the living conditions of its peoples, preserving and strengthening peace and liberty and promoting democracy on the basis of the fundamental rights recognized in the constitution and laws of the Member States and in the European Convention for the Protection of Human Rights and Fundamental Freedoms;

(2) Whereas data-processing systems are designed to serve man; whereas they must, whatever the nationality or residence of natural persons, respect their fundamental rights and freedoms, notably the right to privacy, and contribute to economic and social progress, trade expansion and the well-being of individuals;

(3) Whereas the establishment and functioning of an internal market in which, in accordance with Article 7 a of the Treaty, the free movement of goods, persons, services and capital is ensured require not only that personal data should be able to flow freely from one Member State to another, but also that the fundamental rights of individuals should be safeguarded;

(4) Whereas increasingly frequent recourse is being had in the Commu-

---

[1]) OJ No C 277, 5. 11. 1990, p. 3 and OJ No C 311, 27. 11. 1992, p. 30.

[2]) OJ No C 159, 17. 6. 1991, p 38.

[3]) Opinion of the European Parliament of 11 March 1992 (OJ No C 94, 13. 4. 1992, p. 198), confirmed on 2 December 1993 (OJ No C 342, 20. 12. 1993, p. 30); Council common position of 20 February 1995 (OJ No C 93, 13. 4. 1995, p. 1) and Decision of the European Parliament of 15 June 1995 (OJ No C 166, 3. 7. 1995).

14

nity to the processing of personal data in the various spheres of economic and social activity; whereas the progress made in information technology is making the processing and exchange of such data considerably easier;

(5) Whereas the economic and social integration resulting from the establishment and functioning of the internal market within the meaning of Article 7a of the Treaty will necessarily lead to a substantial increase in cross-border flows of personal data between all those involved in a private or public capacity in economic and social activity in the Member States; whereas the exchange of personal data between undertakings in different Member States is set to increase; whereas the national authorities in the various Member States are being called upon by virtue of Community law to collaborate and exchange personal data so as to be able to perform their duties or carry out tasks on behalf of an authority in another Member State within the context of the area without internal frontiers as constituted by the internal market;

(6) Whereas, furthermore, the increase in scientific and technical cooperation and the coordinated introduction of new telecommunications networks in the Community necessitate and facilitate cross-border flows of personal data;

(7) Whereas the difference in levels of protection of the rights and freedoms of individuals, notably the right to privacy, with regard to the processing of personal data afforded in the Member States may prevent the transmission of such data from the territory of one Member State to that of another Member State; whereas this difference may therefore constitute an obstacle to the pursuit of a number of economic activities at Community level, distort competition and impede authorities in the discharge of their responsibilities under Community law; whereas this difference in levels of protection is due to the existence of a wide variety of national laws, regulations and administrative provisions;

(8) Whereas, in order to remove the obstacles to flows of personal data, the level of protection of the rights and freedoms of individuals with regard to the processing of such data must be equivalent in all Member States; whereas this objective is vital to the internal market but cannot be achieved by the Member States alone, especially in view of the scale of the divergences which currently exist between the relevant laws in the Member States and the need to coordinate the laws of the Member States so as to ensure that the cross-border flow of personal data is regulated in a consistent manner that is in keeping with the objective of the internal market as provided for in Article 7a of the Treaty; whereas Community action to approximate those laws is therefore needed;

(9) Whereas, given the equivalent protection resulting from the approximation of national laws, the Member States will no longer be able to inhibit the free movement between them of personal data on grounds relating to protection of the rights and freedoms of individuals, and in particular the right to privacy; whereas Member States will be left a margin for manoeuvre, which may, in the context of implementation of the Directive, also be exercised by the business and social partners; whereas Member States will therefore be able to specify in their national law the general conditions governing the lawfulness of data processing; whereas in doing so the Member States shall strive to improve the pro-

14

tection currently provided by their legislation; whereas, within the limits of this margin for manoeuvre and in accordance with Community law, disparities could arise in the implementation of the Directive, and this could have an effect on the movement of data within a Member State as well as within the Community;

(10) Whereas the object of the national laws on the processing of personal data is to protect fundamental rights and freedoms, notably the right to privacy, which is recognized both in Article 8 of the European Convention for the Protection of Human Rights and Fundamental Freedoms and in the general principles of Community law; whereas, for that reason, the approximation of those laws must not result in any lessening of the protection they afford but must, on the contrary, seek to ensure a high level of protection in the Community;

(11) Whereas the principles of the protection of the rights and freedoms of individuals, notably the right to privacy, which are contained in this Directive, give substance to and amplify those contained in the Council of Europe Convention of 28 January 1981 for the Protection of Individuals with regard to Automatic Processing of Personal Data;

(12) Whereas the protection principles must apply to all processing of personal data by any person whose activities are governed by Community law; whereas there should be excluded the processing of data carried out by a natural person in the exercise of activities which are exclusively personal or domestic, such as correspondence and the holding of records of addresses;

(13) Whereas the acitivities referred to in Titles V and VI of the Treaty on European Union regarding public

safety, defence, State security or the activities of the State in the area of criminal laws fall outside the scope of Community law, without prejudice to the obligations incumbent upon Member States under Article 56 (2), Article 57 or Article 100 a of the Treaty establishing the European Community; whereas the processing of personal data that is necessary to safeguard the economic well-being of the State does not fall within the scope of this Directive where such processing relates to State security matters;

(14) Whereas, given the importance of the developments under way, in the framework of the information society, of the techniques used to capture, transmit, manipulate, record, store or communicate sound and image data relating to natural persons, this Directive should be applicable to processing involving such data;

(15) Whereas the processing of such data is covered by this Directive only if it is automated or if the data processed are contained or are intended to be contained in a filing system structured according to specific criteria relating to individuals, so as to permit easy access to the personal data in question;

(16) Whereas the processing of sound and image data, such as in cases of video surveillance, does not come within the scope of this Directive if it is carried out for the purposes of public security, defence, national security or in the course of State activities relating to the area of criminal law or of other activities which do not come within the scope of Community law;

(17) Whereas, as far as the processing of sound and image data carried out for purposes of journalism or the purposes of literary or artistic expression is concerned, in particular in the audio-

visual field, the principles of the Directive are to apply in a restricted manner according to the provisions laid down in Article 9;

(18) Whereas, in order to ensure that individuals are not deprived of the protection to which they are entitled under this Directive, any processing of personal data in the Community must be carried out in accordance with the law of one of the Member States; whereas, in this connection, processing carried out under the responsibility of a controller who is established in a Member State should be governed by the law of that State;

(19) Whereas establishment on the territory of a Member State implies the effective and real exercise of activity through stable arrangements; whereas the legal form of such an establishment, whether simply branch or a subsidiary with a legal personality, is not the determining factor in this respect; whereas, when a single controller is established on the territory of several Member States, particularly by means of subsidiaries, he must ensure, in order to avoid any circumvention of national rules, that each of the establishments fulfils the obligations imposed by the national law applicable to its activities;

(20) Whereas the fact that the processing of data is carried out by a person established in a third country must not stand in the way of the protection of individuals provided for in this Directive; whereas in these cases, the processing should be governed by the law of the Member State in which the means used are located, and there should be guarantees to ensure that the rights and obligations provided for in this Directive are respected in practice;

(21) Whereas this Directive is without prejudice to the rules of territoriality applicable in criminal matters;

(22) Whereas Member States shall more precisely define in the laws they enact or when bringing into force the measures taken under this Directive the general circumstances in which processing is lawful; whereas in particular Article 5, in conjunction with Articles 7 and 8, allows Member States, independently of general rules, to provide for special processing conditions for specific sectors and for the various categories of data covered by Article 8;

(23) Whereas Member States are empowered to ensure the implementation of the protection of individuals both by means of a general law on the protection of individuals as regards the processing of personal data and by sectorial laws such as those relating, for example, to statistical institutes;

(24) Whereas the legislation concerning the protection of legal persons with regard to the processing data which concerns them is not affected by this Directive;

(25) Whereas the principles of protection must be reflected, on the one hand, in the obligations imposed on persons, public authorities, enterprises, agencies or other bodies responsible for processing, in particular regarding data quality, technical security, notification to the supervisory authority, and the circumstances under which processing can be carried out, and, on the other hand, in the right conferred on individuals, the data on whom are the subject of processing, to be informed that processing is taking place, to consult the data, to request corrections and even to object to processing in certain circumstances;

(26) Whereas the principles of protection must apply to any information concerning an identified or identifiable person; whereas, to determine whether a person is identifiable, account should

be taken of all the means likely reasonably to be used either by the controller or by any other person to identify the said person; whereas the principles of protection shall not apply to data rendered anonymous in such a way that the data subject is no longer identifiable; whereas codes of conduct within the meaning of Article 27 may be a useful instrument for providing guidance as to the ways in which data may be rendered anonymous and retained in a form in which identification of the data subject is no longer possible;

(27) Whereas the protection of individuals must apply as much to automatic processing of data as to manual processing; whereas the scope of this protection must not in effect depend on the techniques used, otherwise this would create a serious risk of circumvention; whereas, nonetheless, as regards manual processing, this Directive covers only filing systems, not unstructured files; whereas, in particular, the content of a filing system must be structured according to specific criteria relating to individuals allowing easy access to the personal data; whereas, in line with the definition in Article 2 (c), the different criteria for determining the constituents of a structured set of personal data, and the different criteria governing access to such a set, may be laid down by each Member State; whereas files or sets of files as well as their cover pages, which are not structured according to specific criteria, shall under no circumstances fall within the scope of this Directive;

(28) Whereas any processing of personal data must be lawful and fair to the individuals concerned; whereas, in particular, the data must be adequate, relevant and not excessive in relation to the purposes for which they are processed; whereas such purposes must be explicit and legitimate and must be determined at the time of collection of the data; whereas the purposes of processing further to collection shall not be incompatible with the purposes as they were originally specified;

(29) Whereas the further processing of personal data for historical, statistical or scientific purposes is not generally to be considered incompatible with the purposes for which the data have previously been collected provided that Member States furnish suitable safeguards; whereas these safeguards must in particular rule out the use of the data in support of measures or decisions regarding any particular individual;

(30) Whereas, in order to be lawful, the processing of personal data must in addition be carried out with the consent of the data subject or be necessary for the conclusion or performance of a contract binding on the data subject, or as a legal requirement, or for the performance of a task carried out in the public interest or in the exercise of official authority, or in the legitimate interests of a natural or legal person, provided that the interests or the rights and freedoms of the data subject are not overriding; whereas, in particular, in order to maintain a balance between the interests involved while guaranteeing effective competition, Member States may determine the circumstances in which personal data may be used or disclosed to a third party in the context of the legitimate ordinary business activities of companies and other bodies; whereas Member States may similarly specify the conditions under which personal data may be disclosed to a third party for the purposes of marketing whether carried out commercially or by a charitable organization or by any other association or foundation,

of a political nature for example, subject to the provisions allowing a data subject to object to the processing of data regarding him, at no cost and without having to state his reasons;

(31) Whereas the processing of personal data must equally be regarded as lawful where it is carried out in order to protect an interest which is essential for the data subject's life;

(32) Whereas it is for national legislation to determine whether the controller performing a task carried out in the public interest or in the exercise of official authority should be a public administration or another natural or legal person governed by public law, or by private law such as a professional association;

(33) Whereas data which are capable by their nature of infringing fundamental freedoms or privacy should not be processed unless the data subject gives his explicit consent; whereas, however, derogations from this prohibition must be explicitly provided for in respect of specific needs, in particular where the processing of these data is carried out for certain health-related purposes by persons subject to a legal obligation of professional secrecy or in the course of legitimate activities by certain associations or foundations the purpose of which is to permit the exercise of fundamental freedoms;

(34) Whereas Member States must also be authorized, when justified by grounds of important public interest, to derogate from the prohibition on processing sensitive categories of data where important reasons of public interest so justify in areas such as public health and social protection – especially in order to ensure the quality and cost-effectiveness of the procedures used for settling claims for benefits and services in the health insurance system – scientific research and government statistics; whereas it is incumbent on them, however, to provide specific and suitable safeguards so as to protect the fundamental rights and the privacy of individuals;

(35) Whereas, moreover, the processing of personal data by official authorities for achieving aims, laid down in constitutional law or international public law, of officially recognized religious associations is carried out on important grounds of public interest;

(36) Whereas where, in the course of electoral activities, the operation of the democratic system requires in certain Member States that political parties compile data on people's political opinion, the processing of such data may be permitted for reasons of important public interest, provided that appropriate safeguards are established;

(37) Whereas the processing of personal data for purposes of journalism or for purposes of literary of artistic expression, in particular in the audiovisual field, should qualify for exemption from the requirements of certain provisions of this Directive in so far as this is necessary to reconcile the fundamental rights of individuals with freedom of information and notably the right to receive and impart information, as guaranteed in particular in Article 10 of the European Convention for the Protection of Human Rights and Fundamental Freedoms; whereas Member States should therefore lay down exemptions and derogations necessary for the purpose of balance between fundamental rights as regards general measures on the legitimacy of data processing, measures on the transfer of data to third countries and the power of the supervisory authority; whereas this should not, however, lead Member

States to lay down exemptions from the measures to ensure security of processing; whereas at least the supervisory authority responsible for this sector should also be provided with certain ex-post powers, e. g. to publish a regular report or to refer matters to the judicial authorities;

(38) Whereas, if the processing of data is to be fair, the data subject must be in a position to learn of the existence of a processing operation and, where data are collected from him, must be given accurate and full information, bearing in mind the circumstances of the collection;

(39) Whereas certain processing operations involve data which the controller has not collected directly from the data subject; whereas, furthermore, data can be legitimately disclosed to a third party, even if the disclosure was not anticipated at the time the data were collected from the data subject; whereas, in all these cases, the data subject should be informed when the data are recorded or at the latest when the data are first disclosed to a third party;

(40) Whereas, however, it is not necessary to impose this obligation of the data subject already has the information; whereas, moreover, there will be no such obligation if the recording or disclosure are expressly provided for by law or if the provision of information to the data subject proves impossible or would involve disproportionate efforts, which could be the case where processing is for historical, statistical or scientific purposes; whereas, in this regard, the number of data subjects, the age of the data, and any compensatory measures adopted may be taken into consideration;

(41) Whereas any person must be able to exercise the right of access to data relating to him which are being processed, in order to verify in particular the accuracy of the data and the lawfulness of the processing; whereas, for the same reasons, every data subject must also have the right to know the logic involved in the automatic processing of data concerning him, at least in the case of the automated decisions referred to in Article 15 (1); whereas this right must not adversely affect trade secrets or intellectual property and in particular the copyright protecting the software; whereas these considerations must not, however, result in the data subject being refused all information;

(42) Whereas Member States may, in the interest of the data subject or so as to protect the rights and freedoms of others, restrict rights of access and information; whereas they may, for example, specify that access to medical data may be obtained only through a health professional;

(43) Whereas restrictions on the rights of access and information and on certain obligations of the controller may similarly be imposed by Member States in so far as they are necessary to safeguard, for example, national security, defence, public safety, or important economic or financial interests of a Member State or the Union, as well as criminal investigations and prosecutions and action in respect of breaches of ethics in the regulated professions; whereas the list of exceptions and limitations should include the tasks of monitoring, inspection or regulation necessary in the three last-mentioned areas concerning public security, economic or financial interests and crime prevention; whereas the listing of tasks in these three areas does not affect the legitimacy of exceptions or restrictions for reasons of State security or defence;

(44) Whereas Member States may also be led, by virtue of the provisions of Community law, to derogate from the provisions of this Directive concerning the right of access, the obligation to inform individuals, and the quality of data, in order to secure certain of the purposes referred to above;

(45) Whereas, in cases where data might lawfully be processed on grounds of public interest, official authority or the legitimate interests of a natural or legal person, any data subject should nevertheless be entitled, on legitimate and compelling grounds relating to his particular situation, to object to the processing of any data relating to himself; whereas Member States may nevertheless lay down national provisions to the contrary;

(46) Whereas the protection of the rights and freedoms of data subjects with regard to the processing of personal data requires that appropriate technical and organizational measures be taken, both at the time of the design of the processing system and at the time of the processing itself, particularly in order to maintain security and thereby to prevent any unauthorized processing; whereas it is incumbent on the Member States to ensure that controllers comply with these measures; whereas these measures must ensure an appropriate level of security, taking into account the state of the art and the costs of their implementation in relation to the risks inherent in the processing and the nature of the data to be protected;

(47) Whereas where a message containing personal data is transmitted by means of a telecommunications or electronic mail service, the sole purpose of which is the transmission of such messages, the controller in respect of the personal data contained in the message will normally be considered to be the person from whom the message originates, rather than the person offering the transmission services; whereas, nevertheless, those offering such services will normally be considered controllers in respect of the processing of the additional personal data necessary for the operation of the service;

(48) Whereas the procedures for notifying the supervisory authority are designed to ensure disclosure of the purposes and main features of any processing operation for the purpose of verification that the operation is in accordance with the national measures taken under this Directive;

(49) Whereas, in order to avoid unsuitable administrative formalities, exemptions from the obligation to notify and simplification of the notification required may be provided for by Member States in cases where processing is unlikely adversely to affect the rights and freedoms of data subjects, provided that it is in accordance with a measure taken by a Member State specifying its limits; whereas exemption or simplification may similarly be provided for by Member States where a person appointed by the controller ensures that the processing carried out is not likely adversely to affect the rights and freedoms of data subjects; whereas such a data protection official, whether or not an employee of the controller, must be in a position to exercise his functions in complete independence;

(50) Whereas exemption or simplification could be provided for in cases of processing operations whose sole purpose is the keeping of a register intended, according to national law, to provide information to the public and open to consultation by the public or by any person demonstrating a legitimate interest;

(51) Whereas, nevertheless, simplification or exemption from the obligation to notify shall not release the controller from any of the other obligations resulting from this Directive;

(52) Whereas, in this context, *ex post facto* verification by the competent authorities must in general be considered a sufficient measure;

(53) Whereas, however, certain processing operation are likely to pose specific risks to the rights and freedoms of data subjects by virtue of their nature, their scope or their purposes, such as that of excluding individuals from a right, benefit or a contract, or by virtue of the specific use of new technologies; whereas it is for Member States, if they so wish, to specify such risks in their legislation;

(54) Whereas with regard to all the processing undertaken in society, the amount posing such specific risks should be very limited; whereas Member States must provide that the supervisory authority, or the data protection official in cooperation with the authority, check such processing prior to it being carried out; whereas following this prior check, the supervisory authority may, according to its national law, give an opinion or an authorization regarding the processing; whereas such checking may equally take place in the course of the preparation either of a measure of the national parliament or of a measure based on such a legislative measure, which defines the nature of the processing and lays down appropriate safeguards;

(55) Whereas, if the controller fails to respect the rights of data subjects, national legislation must provide for a judicial remedy; whereas any damage which a person may suffer as a result of unlawful processing must be compensated for by the controller, who may be exempted from liability if he proves that he is not responsible for the damage, in particular in cases where he establishes fault on the part of the data subject or in case of *force majeure*; whereas sanctions must be imposed on any person, whether governed by private of public law, who fails to comply with the national measures taken under this Directive;

(56) Whereas cross-border flows of personal data are necessary to the expansion of international trade; whereas the protection of individuals guaranteed in the Community by this Directive does not stand in the way of transfers of personal data to third countries which ensure an adequate level of protection; whereas the adequacy of the level of protection afforded by a third country must be assessed in the light of all the circumstances surrounding the transfer operation or set of transfer operations;

(57) Whereas, on the other hand, the transfer of personal data to a third country which does not ensure an adequate level of protection must be prohibited;

(58) Whereas provisions should be made for exemptions from this prohibition in certain circumstances where the data subject has given his consent, where the transfer is necessary in relation to a contract or a legal claim, where protection of an important public interest so requires, for example in cases of international transfers of data between tax or customs administrations or between services competent for social security matters, or where the transfer is made from a register established by law and intended for consultation by the public or persons having a legitimate interest; whereas in this case such a transfer should not involve the entirety of the data or entire categories

14

of the data contained in the register and, when the register is intended for consultation by persons having a legitimate interest, the transfer should be made only at the request of those persons or if they are to be the recipients;

(59) Whereas particular measures may be taken to compensate for the lack of protection in a third country in cases where the controller offers appropriate safeguards; whereas, moreover, provision must be made for procedures for negotiations between the Community and such third countries;

(60) Whereas, in any event, transfers to third countries may be effected only in full compliance with the provisions adopted by the Member States pursuant to this Directive, and in particular Article 8 thereof;

(61) Whereas Member States and the Commission, in their respective spheres of competence, must encourage the trade associations and other representative organizations concerned to draw up codes of conduct so as to facilitate the application of this Directive, taking account of the specific characteristics of the processing carried out in certain sectors, and respecting the national provisions adopted for its implementation;

(62) Whereas the establishment in Member States of supervisory authorities, exercising their functions with complete independence, is an essential component of the protection of individuals with regard to the processing of personal data;

(63) Whereas such authorities must have the necessary means to perform their duties, including powers of investigation and intervention, particularly in cases of complaints from individuals, and powers to engage in legal proceedings; whereas such authorities must help to ensure transparency of processing in the Member States within whose jurisdiction they fall;

(64) Whereas the authorities in the different Member States will need to assist one another in performing their duties so as to ensure that the rules of protection are properly respected throughout the European Union;

(65) Whereas, at Community level, a Working Party on the Protection of Individuals with regard to the Processing of Personal Data must be set up and be completely independent in the performance of its functions; whereas, having regard to its specific nature, it must advise the Commission and, in particular, contribute to the uniform application of the national rules adopted pursuant to this Directive;

(66) Whereas, with regard to the transfer of data to third countries, the application of this Directive calls for the conferment of powers of implementation on the Commission and the establishment of a procedure as laid down in Council Decision 87/373/EEC[4]);

(67) Whereas an agreement on a *modus vivendi* between the European Parliament, the Council and the Commission concerning the implementing measures for acts adopted in accordance with the procedure laid down in Article 189b of the EC Treaty was reached on 20 December 1994;

(68) Whereas the principles set out in this Directive regarding the protection of the rights and freedoms of individuals, notably their right to privacy, with regard to the processing of personal data may be supplemented or clarified, in particular as far as certain sectors are concerned, by specific rules based on those principles;

---

[4]) OJ No L 197, 18. 7. 1987, p. 33.

14

(69) Whereas Member States should be allowed a period of not more than three years from the entry into force of the national measures transposing this Directive in which to apply such new national rules progressively to all processing operations already under way; whereas, in order to facilitate their cost-effective implementation, a further period expiring 12 years after the date on which this Directive is adopted will be allowed to Member States to ensure the conformity of existing manual filing systems with certain of the Directive's provisions; whereas, where data contained in such filing systems are manually processed during this extended transition period, those systems must be brought into conformity with these provisions at the time of such processing;

(70) Whereas it is not necessary for the data subject to give his consent again so as to allow the controller to continue to process, after the national provisions taken pursuant to this Directive enter into force, any sensitive data necessary for the performance of a contract concluded on the basis of free and informed consent before the entry into force of these provisions;

(71) Whereas this Directive does not stand in the way of a Member State's regulating marketing activities aimed at consumers residing in territory in so far as such regulation does not concern the protection of individuals with regard to the processing of personal data;

(72) Whereas this Directive allows the principle of public access to official documents to be taken into account when implementing the principles set out in this Directive,

HAVE ADOPTED THIS DIRECTIVE:

CHAPTER I
GENERAL PROVISIONS

Article 1
Object of the Directive

1. In accordance with this Directive, Member States shall protect the fundamental rights and freedoms of natural persons, and in particular their right to privacy with respect to the processing of personal data.

2. Member States shall neither restrict nor prohibit the free flow of personal data between Member States for reasons connected with the protection afforded under paragraph 1.

Article 2
Definitions

For the purposes of this Directive:

(a) 'personal data' shall mean any information relating to an identified or identifiable natural person ('data subject'); an identifiable person is one who can be identified, directly or indirectly, in particular by reference to an identification number or to one or more factors specific to his physical, physiological, mental, economic, cultural or social identity;

(b) 'processing of personal data' ('processing') shall mean any operation or set of operations which is performed upon personal data, whether or not by automatic means, such as collection, recording, organization, storage, adaptation or alteration, retrieval, consultation, use, disclosure by transmission, dissemination or otherwise making available, alignment or combination, blocking, erasure or destruction;

(c) 'personal data filing system' ('filing system') shall mean any structured set of personal data which are accessible according to specific criteria, whether centralized, decentralized or

14

dispersed on a functional or geographical basis;

(d) 'controller' shall mean the natural or legal person, public authority, agency or any other body which alone or jointly with others determines the purposes and means of the processing of personal data; where the purposes and means of processing are determined by national or Community laws or regulations, the controller or the specific criteria for his nomination may be designated by national or Community law;

(e) 'processor' shall mean a natural or legal person, public authority, agency or any other body which processes personal data on behalf of the controller;

(f) 'third party' shall mean any natural or legal person, public authority, agency or any other body other than the data subject, the controller, the processor and the persons who, under the direct authority of the controller or the processor, are authorized to process the data;

(g) 'recipient' shall mean a natural or legal person, public authority, agency or any other body to whom data are disclosed, whether a third party or not; however, authorities which may receive data in the framework of a particular inquiry shall not be regarded as recipients;

(h) 'the data subject's consent' shall mean any freely given specific and informed indication of his wishes by which the data subject signifies his agreement to personal data relating to him being processed.

Article 3
Scope

1. This Directive shall apply to the processing of personal data wholly or partly by automatic means, and to the processing otherwise than by automatic means of personal data which form part of a filing system or are intended to form part of a filing system.

2. This Directive shall not apply to the processing of personal data:

– in the course of an activity which falls outside the scope of Community law, such as those provided for by Titles V and VI of the Treaty on European Union and in any case to processing operations concerning public security, defence, State security (including the economic well-being of the State when the processing operation relates to State security matters) and the activities of the State in areas of criminal law,

– by a natural person in the course of a purely personal or household activity.

Article 4
National law applicable

1. Each Member State shall apply the national provisions it adopts pursuant to this Directive to the processing of personal data where:

(a) the processing is carried out in the context of the activities of an establishment of the controller on the territory of the Member State; when the same controller is established on the territory of several Member States, he must take the necessary measures to ensure that each of these establishments complies with the obligations laid down by the national law applicable;

(b) the controller is not established on the Member State's territory, but in a place where its national law applies by virtue of international public law;

(c) the controller is not established on Community territory and, for purposes of processing personal data makes use of equipment, automated or

14

otherwise, situated on the territory of the said Member State, unless such equipment is used only for purposes of transit through the territory of the Community.

2. In the circumstances referred to in paragraph 1 (c), the controller must designate a representative established in the territory of that Member State, without prejudice to legal actions which could be initiated against the controller himself.

CHAPTER II
GENERAL RULES ON THE LAWFULNESS OF THE PROCESSING OF PERSONAL DATA

Article 5

Member States shall, within the limits of the provisions of this Chapter, determine more precisely the conditions under which the processing of personal data is lawful.

SECTION I
PRINCIPLES RELATING TO DATA QUALITY

Article 6

1. Member States shall provide that personal data must be:

(a) processed fairly and lawfully;

(b) collected for specified, explicit and legitimate purposes and not further processed in a way incompatible with those purposes. Further processing of data for historical, statistical or scientific purposes shall not be considered as incompatible provided that Member States provide appropriate safeguards;

(c) adequate, relevant and not excessive in relation to the purposes for which they are collected and/or further processed;

(d) accurate and, where necessary, kept up to date; every reasonable step must be taken to ensure that data which are inaccurate or incomplete, having regard to the purposes for which they were collected or for which they are further processed, are erased or rectified;

(e) kept in a form which permits identification of data subjects for no longer than is necessary for the purposes for which the data were collected or for which they are further processed. Member States shall lay down appropriate safeguards for personal data stored for longer periods for historical, statistical or scientific use.

2. It shall be for the controller to ensure that paragraph 1 is complied with.

SECTION II
CRITERIA FOR MAKING DATA PROCESSING LEGITIMATE

Article 7

Member States shall provide that personal data may be processed only if:

(a) the data subject has unambiguously given his consent; or

(b) processing is necessary for the performance of a contract to which the data subject is party or in order to take steps at the request of the data subject prior to entering into a contract; or

(c) processing is necessary for compliance with a legal obligation to which the controller is subject; or

(d) processing is necessary in order to protect the vital interests of the data subject; or

(e) processing is necessary for the performance of a task carried out in the public interest or in the exercise of official authority vested in the controller or

14

in a third party to whom the data are disclosed; or

(f) processing is necessary for the purposes of the legitimate interests pursued by the controller or by the third party or parties to whom the data are disclosed, except where such interests are overridden by the interests for fundamental rights and freedoms of the data subject which require protection under Article 1 (1).

SECTION III
SPECIAL CATEGORIES OF PROCESSING

Article 8
The processing of special categories of data

1. Member States shall prohibit the processing of personal data revealing racial or ethnic origin, political opinions, religious or philosophical beliefs, trade-union membership, and the processing of data concerning health or sex life.

2. Paragraph 1 shall not apply where:

(a) the data subject has given his explicit consent to the processing of those data, except where the laws of the Member State provide that the prohibition referred to in paragraph 1 may not be lifted by the data subject's giving his consent; or

(b) processing is necessary for the purposes of carrying out the obligations and specific rights of the controller in the field of employment law in so far as it is authorized by national law providing for adequate safeguards; or

(c) processing is necessary to protect the vital interests of the data subject or of another person where the data subject is physically or legally incapable of giving his consent; or

(d) processing is carried out in the course of its legitimate activities with appropriate guarantees by a foundation, association or any other non-profit-seeking body with a political, philosophical, religious or trade-union aim and on condition that the processing relates solely to the members of the body or to persons who have regular contact with it in connection with its purposes and that the data are not disclosed to a third party without the consent of the data subjects; or

(e) the processing relates to data which are manifestly made public by the data subject or is necessary for the establishment, exercise or defence of legal claims.

3. Paragraph 1 shall not apply where processing of the data is required for the purposes of preventive medicine, medical diagnosis, the provision of care or treatment or the management of health-care services, and where those data are processed by a health professional subject under national law or rules established by national competent bodies to the obligation of professional secrecy or by another person also subject to an equivalent obligation of secrecy.

4. Subject to the provision of suitable safeguards, Member States may, for reasons of substantial public interest, lay down exemptions in addition to those laid down in paragraph 2 either by national law or by decision of the supervisory authority.

5. Processing of data relating to offences, criminal convictions or security measures may be carried out only under the control of official authority, or if suitable specific safeguards are provided under national law, subject to derogations which may be granted by the Member State under national provisions providing suitable specific safe-

guards. However, a complete register of criminal convictions may be kept only under the control of official authority.

Member States may provide that data relating to administrative sanctions or judgements in civil cases shall also be processed under the control of official authority.

6. Derogations from paragraph 1 provided for in paragraphs 4 and 5 shall be notified to the Commission.

7. Member States shall determine the conditions under which a national identification number or any other identifier of general application may be processed.

Article 9
Processing of personal data and freedom of expression

Member States shall provide for exemptions or derogations from the provisions of this Chapter, Chapter IV and Chapter VI for the processing of personal data carried out solely for journalistic purposes or the purpose of artistic or literary expression only if they are necessary to reconcile the right to privacy with the rules governing freedom of expression.

SECTION IV
INFORMATION TO BE GIVEN TO THE DATA SUBJECT
Article 10
Information in cases of collection of data from the data subject

Member States shall provide that the controller or his representative must provide a data subject from whom data relating to himself are collected with at least the following information, except where he already has it:

(a) the identity of the controller and of his representative, if any;

(b) the purposes of the processing for which the data are intended;

(c) any further information such as
– the recipients or categories of recipients of the data,
– whether replies to the questions are obligatory or voluntary, as well as the possible consequences of failure to reply,
– the existence of the right of access to and the right to rectify the data concerning him
in so far as such further information is necessary, having regard to the specific circumstances in which the data are collected, to guarantee fair processing in respect of the data subject.

Article 11
Information where the data have not been obtained from the data subject

1. Where the data have not been obtained from the data subject, Member States shall provide that the controller or his representative must at the time of undertaking the recording of personal data or if a disclosure to a third party is envisaged, no later than the time when the data are first disclosed provide the data subject with at least the following information, except where he already has it:

(a) the identity of the controller and of his representative, if any;

(b) the purposes of the processing;

(c) any further information such as
– the categories of data concerned,
– the recipients or categories of recipients,
– the existence of the right of access to and the right to rectify the data concerning him

in so far as such further information is necessary, having regard to the specific circumstances in which the data are processed, to guarantee fair processing in respect of the data subject.

2. Paragraph 1 shall not apply where, in particular for processing for statistical purposes or for the purposes of historical or scientific research, the provision of such information proves impossible or would involve a disproportionate effort or if recording or disclosure is expressly laid down by law. In these cases Member States shall provide appropriate safeguards.

SECTION V
THE DATA SUBJECT'S RIGHT OF ACCESS TO DATA

Article 12
Right of access

Member States shall guarantee every data subject the right to obtain from the controller:

(a) without constraint at reasonable intervals and without excessive delay or expense:

– confirmation as to whether or not data relating to him are being processed and information at least as to the purposes of the processing, the categories of data concerned, and the recipients or categories of recipients to whom the data are disclosed,

– communication to him in an intelligible form of the data undergoing processing and of any available information as to their source,

– knowledge of the logic involved in any automatic processing of data concerning him at least in the case of the automated decisions referred to in Article 15 (1);

(b) as appropriate the rectification, erasure or blocking of data the process-

ing of which does not comply with the provisions of this Directive, in particular because of the incomplete or inaccurate nature of the data;

(c) notification to third parties to whom the data have been disclosed of any rectification, erasure or blocking carried out in compliance with (b), unless this proves impossible or involves a disproportionate effort.

SECTION VI
EXEMPTIONS AND RESTRICTIONS

Article 13
Exemptions and restrictions

1. Member States may adopt legislative measures to restrict the scope of the obligations and rights provided for in Articles 6 (1), 10, 11 (1), 12 and 21 when such a restriction constitutes a necessary measures to safeguard:

(a) national security;

(b) defence;

(c) public security;

(d) the prevention, investigation, detection and prosecution of criminal offences, or of breaches of ethics for regulated professions;

(e) an important economic or financial interest of a Member State or of the European Union, including monetary, budgetary and taxation matters;

(f) a monitoring, inspection or regulatory function connected, even occasionally, with the exercise of official authority in cases referred to in (c), (d) and (e);

(g) the protection of the data subject or of the rights and freedoms of others.

2. Subject to adequate legal safeguards, in particular that the data are not used for taking measures or deci-

14

sions regarding any particular individual, Member States may, where there is clearly no risk of breaching the privacy of the data subject, restrict by a legislative measure the rights provided for in Article 12 when data are processed solely for purposes of scientific research or are kept in personal form for a period which does not exceed the period necessary for the sole purpose of creating statistics.

SECTION VII
THE DATA SUBJECT'S RIGHT TO OBJECT

Article 14
The data subject's right to object

Member States shall grant the data subject the right:

(a) at least in the cases referred to in Article 7 (e) and (f), to object at any time on compelling legitimate grounds relating to his particular situation to the processing of data relating to him, save where otherwise provided by national legislation. Where there is a justified objection, the processing instigated by the controller may no longer involve those data;

(b) to object, on request and free of charge, to the processing of personal data relating to him which the controller anticipates being processed for the purposes of direct marketing, or to be informed before personal data are disclosed for the first time to third parties or used on their behalf for the purposes of direct marketing, and to be expressly offered the right to object free of charge to such disclosures or uses.

Member States shall take the necessary measures to ensure that data subjects are aware of the existence of the right referred to in the first subparagraph of (b).

Article 15
Automated individual decisions

1. Member States shall grant the right to every person not to be subject to a decision which produces legal effects concerning him or significantly affects him and which is based solely on automated processing of data intended to evaluate certain personal aspects relating to him, such as his performance at work, creditworthiness, reliability, conduct, etc.

2. Subject to the other Articles of this Directive, Member States shall provide that a person may be subjected to a decision of the kind referred to in paragraph 1 if that decision:

(a) is taken in the course of the entering into or performance of a contract, provided the request for the entering into or the performance of the contract, lodged by the data subject, has been satisfied or that there are suitable measures to safeguard his legitimate interests, such as arrangements allowing him to put his point of view; or

(b) is authorized by a law which also lays down measures to safeguard the data subject's legitimate interests.

SECTION VIII
CONFIDENTIALITY AND SECURITY OF PROCESSING

Article 16
Confidentiality of processing

Any person acting under the authority of the controller or of the processor, including the processor himself, who has access to personal data must not process them except on instructions from the controller, unless he is required to do so by law.

Article 17
Security of processing

1. Member States shall provide that the controller must implement appropriate technical and organizational measures to protect personal data against accidental or unlawful destruction or accidental loss, alteration, unauthorized disclosure or access, in particular where the processing involves the transmission of data over a network, and against all other unlawful forms of processing.

Having regard to the state of the art and the cost of their implementation, such measures shall ensure a level of security appropriate to the risks represented by the processing and the nature of the data to be protected.

2. The Member States shall provide that the controller must, where processing is carried out on his behalf, choose a processor providing sufficient guarantees in respect of the technical security measures and organizational measures governing the processing to be carried out, and must ensure compliance with those measures.

3. The carrying out of processing by way of a processor must be governed by a contract or legal act binding the processor to the controller and stipulating in particular that:

– the processor shall act only on instructions from the controller,

– the obligations set out in paragraph 1, as defined by the law of the Member State in which the processor is established, shall also be incumbent on the processor.

4. For the purposes of keeping proof, the parts of the contract or the legal act relating to data protection and the requirements relating to the measures referred to in paragraph 1 shall be in writing or in another equivalent form.

SECTION IX
NOTIFICATION

Article 18
Obligation to notify
the supervisory authority

1. Member States shall provide that the controller or his representative, if any, must notify the supervisory authority referred to in Article 28 before carrying out any wholly or partly automatic processing operation or set of such operations intended to serve a single purpose or several related purposes.

2. Member States may provide for the simplification of or exemption from notification only in the following cases and under the following conditions:

– where, for categories of processing operations which are unlikely, taking account of the data to be processed, to affect adversely the rights and freedoms of data subjects, they specify the purposes of the processing, the data or categories of data undergoing processing, the category or categories of data subject, the recipients or categories of recipient to whom the data are to be disclosed and the length of time the data are to be stored, and/or

– where the controller, in compliance with the national law which governs him, appoints a personal data protection official, responsible in particular:

– for ensuring in an independent manner the internal application of the national provisions taken pursuant to this Directive

– for keeping the register of processing operations carried out by the controller, containing the items of information referred to in Article 21 (2),

thereby ensuring that the rights and freedoms of the data subjects are un-

14

likely to be adversely affected by the processing operations.

3. Member States may provide that paragraph 1 does not apply to processing whose sole purpose is the keeping of a register which according to laws or regulations is intended to provide information to the public and which is open to consultation either by the public in general or by any person demonstrating a legitimate interest.

4. Member States may provide for an exemption from the obligation to notify or a simplification of the notification in the case of processing operations referred to in Article 8 (2) (d).

5. Member States may stipulate that certain or all non-automatic processing operations involving personal data shall be notified, or provide for these processing operations to be subject to simplified notification.

Article 19
Contents of notification

1. Member States shall specify the information to be given in the notification. It shall include at least:

(a) the name and address of the controller and of his representative, if any;

(b) the purpose or purposes of the processing;

(c) a description of the category or categories of data subject and of the data or categories of data relating to them;

(d) the recipients or categories of recipient to whom the data might be disclosed;

(e) proposed transfers of data to third countries;

(f) a general description allowing a preliminary assessment to be made of the appropriateness of the measures taken pursuant to Article 17 to ensure security of processing.

2. Member States shall specify the procedures under which any change affecting the information referred to in paragraph 1 must be notified to the supervisory authority.

Article 20
Prior checking

1. Member States shall determine the processing operations likely to present specific risks to the rights and freedoms of data subjects and shall check that these processing operations are examined prior to the start thereof.

2. Such prior checks shall be carried out by the supervisory authority following receipt of a notification from the controller or by the data protection official, who, in cases of doubt, must consult the supervisory authority.

3. Member States may also carry out such checks in the context of preparation either of a measure of the national parliament or of a measure based on such a legislative measure, which define the nature of the processing and lay down appropriate safeguards.

Article 21
Publicizing of processing operations

1. Member States shall take measures to ensure that processing operations are publicized.

2. Member States shall provide that a register of processing operations notified in accordance with Article 18 shall be kept by the supervisory authority.

The register shall contain at least the information listed in Article 19 (1) (a) to (e).

The register may be inspected by any person.

3. Member States shall provide, in relation to processing operations not subject to notification, that controllers

or another body appointed by the Member States make available at least the information referred to in Article 19 (1) (a) to (e) in an appropriate form to any person on request.

Member States may provide that this provision does not apply to processing whose sole purpose is the keeping of a register which according to laws or regulations is intended to provide information to the public and which is open to consultation either by the public in general or by any person who can provide proof of a legitimate interest.

CHAPTER III
JUDICIAL REMEDIES, LIABILITY AND SANCTIONS

Article 22
Remedies

Without prejudice to any administrative remedy for which provision may be made, *inter alia* before the supervisory authority referred to in Article 28, prior to referral to the judicial authority, Member States shall provide for the right of every person to a judicial remedy for any breach of the rights guaranteed him by the national law applicable to the processing in question.

Article 23
Liability

1. Member States shall provide that any person who has suffered damage as a result of an unlawful processing operation or of any act incompatible with the national provisions adopted pursuant to this Directive is entitled to receive compensation from the controller for the damage suffered.

2. The controller may be exempted from this liability, in whole or in part, if he proves that he is not responsible for the event giving rise to the damage.

Article 24
Sanctions

The Member States shall adopt suitable measures to ensure the full implementation of the provisions of this Directive and shall in particular lay down the sanctions to be imposed in case of infringement of the provisions adopted pursuant to this Directive.

CHAPTER IV
TRANSFER OF PERSONAL DATA TO THIRD COUNTRIES

Article 25
Principles

1. The Member States shall provide that the transfer to a third country of personal data which are undergoing processing or are intended for processing after transfer may take place only if, without prejudice to compliance with the national provisions adopted pursuant to the other provisions of this Directive, the third country in question ensures an adequate level of protection.

2. The adequacy of the level of protection afforded by a third country shall be assessed in the light of all the circumstances surrounding a data transfer operation or set of data transfer operations; particular consideration shall be given to the nature of the data, the purpose and duration of the proposed processing operation or operations, the country of origin and country of final destination, the rules of law, both general and sectoral, in force in the third country in question and the professional rules and security measures which are complied with in that country.

3. The Member States and the Commission shall inform each other of cases where they consider that a third country does not ensure an adequate level of protection within the meaning of paragraph 2.

4. Where the Commission finds, under the procedure provided for in Article 31 (2), that a third country does not ensure an adequate level of protection within the meaning of paragraph 2 of this Article, Member States shall take the measures necessary to prevent any transfer of data of the same type to the third country in question.

5. At the appropriate time, the Commission shall enter into negotiations with a view to remedying the situation resulting from the finding made pursuant to paragraph 4.

6. The Commission may find, in accordance with the procedure referred to in Article 31 (2), that a third country ensures an adequate level of protection within the meaning of paragraph 2 of this Article, by reason of its domestic law or of the international commitments it has entered into, particularly upon conclusion of the negotiations referred to in paragraph 5, for the protection of the private lives and basic freedoms and rights of individuals.

Member States shall take the measures necessary to comply with the Commission's decision.

Article 26
Derogations

1. By way of derogation from Article 25 and save where otherwise provided by domestic law governing particular cases, Member States shall provide that a transfer or a set of transfers of personal data to a third country which does not ensure an adequate level of protection within the meaning

of Article 25 (2) may take place on condition that:

(a) the data subject has given his consent unambiguously to the proposed transfer; or

(b) the transfer is necessary for the performance of a contract between the data subject and the controller or the implementation of precontractual measures taken in response to the data subject's request; or

(c) the transfer is necessary for the conclusion or performance of a contract concluded in the interest of the data subject between the controller and a third party; or

(d) the transfer is necessary or legally required on important public interest grounds, or for the establishment, exercise or defence of legal claims; or

(e) the transfer is necessary in order to protect the vital interests of the data subject; or

(f) the transfer is made from a register which according to laws or regulations is intended to provide information to the public and which is open to consultation either by the public in general or by any person who can demonstrate legitimate interest, to the extent that the conditions laid down in law for consultation are fulfilled in the particular case.

2. Without prejudice to paragraph 1, a Member State may authorize a transfer or a set of transfers of personal data to a third country which does not ensure an adequate level of protection within the meaning of Article 25 (2), where the controller adduces adequate safeguards with respect to the protection of the privacy and fundamental rights and freedoms of individuals and as regards the exercise of the corresponding rights; such safeguards may in particular result from appropriate contractual clauses.

3. The Member State shall inform the Commission and the other Mem-

ber States of the authorizations it grants pursuant to paragraph 2.

If a Member State or the Commission objects on justified grounds involving the protection of the privacy and fundamental rights and freedoms of individuals, the Commission shall take appropriate measures in accordance with the procedure laid down in Article 31 (2).

Member States shall take the necessary measures to comply with the Commission's decision.

4. Where the Commission decides, in accordance with the procedure referred to in Article 31 (2), that certain standard contractual clauses offer sufficient safeguards as required by paragraph 2, Member States shall take the necessary measures to comply with the Commission's decision.

CHAPTER V
CODES OF CONDUCT
Article 27

1. The Member States and the Commission shall encourage the drawing up of codes of conduct intended to contribute to the proper implementation of the national provisions adopted by the Member States pursuant to this Directive, taking account of the specific features of the various sectors.

2. Member States shall make provision for trade associations and other bodies representing other categories of controllers which have drawn up draft national codes or which have the intention of amending or extending existing national codes to be able to submit them to the opinion of the national authority.

Member States shall make provision for this authority to ascertain, among

other things, whether the drafts submitted to it are in accordance with the national provisions adopted pursuant to this Directive. If it sees fit, the authority shall seek the views of data subjects or their representatives.

3. Draft Community codes, and amendments or extensions to existing Community codes, may be submitted to the Working Party referred to in Article 29. This Working Party shall determine, among other things, whether the drafts submitted to it are in accordance with the national provisions adopted pursuant to this Directive. If it sees fit, the authority shall seek the views of data subjects or their representatives. The Commission may ensure appropriate publicity for the codes which have been approved by the Working Party.

CHAPTER VI
SUPERVISORY AUTHORITY AND WORKING PARTY ON THE PROTECTION OF INDIVIDUALS WITH REGARD TO THE PROCESSING OF PERSONAL DATA
Article 28
Supervisory authority

1. Each Member State shall provide that one or more public authorities are responsible for monitoring the application within its territory of the provisions adopted by the Member States pursuant to this Directive.

These authorities shall act with complete independence in exercising the functions entrusted to them.

2. Each Member State shall provide that the supervisory authorities are consulted when drawing up administrative measures or regulations relating to the protection of individuals' rights

and freedoms with regard to the processing of personal data.

3. Each authority shall in particular be endowed with:

– investigative powers, such as powers of access to data forming the subject-matter of processing operations and powers to collect all the information necessary for the performance of its supervisory duties,

– effective powers of intervention, such as, for example, that of delivering opinions before processing operations are carried out, in accordance with Article 20, and ensuring appropriate publication of such opinions, of ordering the blocking, erasure or destruction of data, of imposing a temporary or definitive ban on processing, of warning or admonishing the controller, or that of referring the matter to national parliaments or other political institutions,

– the power to engage in legal proceedings where the national provisions adopted pursuant to this Directive have been violated or to bring these violations to the attention of the judicial authorities.

Decisions by the supervisory authority which give rise to complaints may be appealed against through the courts.

4. Each supervisory authority shall hear claims lodged by any person, or by an association representing that person, concerning the protection of his rights and freedoms in regard to the processing of personal data. The person concerned shall be informed of the outcome of the claim.

Each supervisory authority shall, in particular, hear claims for checks on the lawfulness of data processing lodged by any person when the national provisions adopted pursuant to Article 13 of this Directive apply. The person shall at any rate be informed that a check has taken place.

5. Each supervisory authority shall draw up a report on its activities at regular intervals. The report shall be made public.

6. Each supervisory authority is competent, whatever the national law applicable to the processing in question, to exercise, on the territory of its own Member State, the powers conferred on it in accordance with paragraph 3. Each authority may be requested to exercise its powers by an authority of another Member State.

The supervisory authorities shall cooperate with one another to the extent necessary for the performance of their duties, in particular by exchanging all useful information.

7. Member States shall provide that the members and staff of the supervisory authority, even after their employment has ended, are to be subject to a duty of professional secrecy with regard to confidential information to which they have access.

Article 29
Working Party on the Protection of Individuals with regard to the Processing of Personal Data

1. A Working Party on the Protection of Individuals with regard to the Processing of Personal Data, hereinafter referred to as 'the Working Party', is hereby set up.

It shall have advisory status and act independently.

2. The Working Party shall be composed of a representative of the supervisory authority or authorities designated by each Member State and of a representative of the authority or authorities established for the Community institutions and bodies, and of a representative of the Commission.

14

Each member of the Working Party shall be designated by the institution, authority or authorities which he represents. Where a Member State has designated more than one supervisory authority, they shall nominate a joint representative. The same shall apply to the authorities established for Community institutions and bodies.

3. The Working Party shall take decisions by a simple majority of the representatives of the supervisory authorities.

4. The Working Party shall elect its chairman. The chairman's term of office shall be two years. His appointment shall be renewable.

5. The Working Party's secretariat shall be provided by the Commission.

6. The Working Party shall adopt its own rules of procedure.

7. The Working Party shall consider items placed on its agenda by its chairman, either on his own initiative or at the request of a representative of the supervisory authorities or at the Commission's request.

Article 30

1. The Working Party shall:

(a) examine any question covering the application of the national measures adopted under this Directive in order to contribute to the uniform application of such measures;

(b) give the Commission an opinion on the level of protection in the Community and in third countries;

(c) advise the Commission on any proposed amendment of this Directive, on any additional or specific measures to safeguard the rights and freedoms of natural persons with regard to the processing of personal data and on any other proposed Community measures affecting such rights and freedoms;

(d) give an opinion on codes of conduct drawn up at Community level.

2. If the Working Party finds that divergences likely to affect the equivalence of protection for persons with regard to the processing of personal data in the Community are arising between the laws or practices of Member States, it shall inform the Commission accordingly.

3. The Working Party may, on its own initiative, make recommendations on all matters relating to the protection of persons with regard to the processing of personal data in the Community.

4. The Working Party's opinions and recommendations shall be forwarded to the Commission and to the committee referred to in Article 31.

5. The Commission shall inform the Working Party of the action it has taken in response to its opinions and recommendations. It shall do so in a report which shall also be forwarded to the European Parliament and the Council. The report shall be made public.

6. The Working Party shall draw up an annual report on the situation regarding the protection of natural persons with regard to the processing of personal data in the Community and in third countries, which it shall transmit to the Commission, the European Parliament and the Council. The report shall be made public.

CHAPTER VII
COMMUNITY IMPLEMENTING MEASURES

Article 31

1. The Commission shall be assisted by a committee.

2. Where reference is made to this Article, Articles 4 and 7 of Decision

1999/468/EC[5]) shall apply, having regard to the provisions of Article 8 thereof.

The period laid down in Article 4(3) of Decision 1999/468/EC shall be set at three months.

3. The Committee shall adopt its rules of procedure.

FINAL PROVISIONS

Article 32

1. Member States shall bring into force the laws, regulations and administrative provisions necessary to comply with this Directive at the latest at the end of a period of three years from the date of its adoption.

When Member States adopt these measures, they shall contain a reference to this Directive or be accompanied by such reference on the occasion of their official publication. The methods of making such reference shall be laid down by the Member States.

2. Member States shall ensure that processing already under way on the date the national provisions adopted pursuant to this Directive enter into force, is brought into conformity with these provisions within three years of this date.

By way of derogation from the preceding subparagraph, Member States may provide that the processing of data already held in manual filing systems on the date of entry into force of the national provisions adopted in implementation of this Directive shall be brought into conformity with Articles 6, 7 and 8 of this Directive within

12 years of the date on which it is adopted. Member States shall, however, grant the data subject the right to obtain, at his request and in particular at the time of exercising his right of access, the rectification, erasure or blocking of data which are incomplete, inaccurate or stored in a way incompatible with the legitimate purposes pursued by the controller.

3. By way of derogation from paragraph 2, Member States may provide, subject to suitable safeguards, that data kept for the sole purpose of historical research need not be brought into conformity with Articles 6, 7 and 8 of this Directive.

4. Member States shall communicate to the Commission the text of the provisions of domestic law which they adopt in the field covered by this Directive.

Article 33

The Commission shall report to the Council and the European Parliament at regular intervals, starting not later than three years after the date referred to in Article 32 (1), on the implementation of this Directive, attaching to its report, if necessary, suitable proposals for amendments. The report shall be made public.

The Commission shall examine, in particular, the application of this Directive to the data processing of sound and image data relating to natural persons and shall submit any appropriate proposals which prove to be necessary, taking account of developments in information technology and in the light of the state of progress in the information society.

Article 34

This Directive is addressed to the Member States.

---

[5]) Council Decision 1999/468/EC of 28 June 1999 laying down the procedures for the exercise of implementing powers conferred on the Commission (OJ L 184, 17. 7. 1999, p. 23).

14

15

Standard Contractual Clauses for the Transfer of Personal Data to Non-EU Member States Commission Decision 2001/497/EC of 15 June 2001 on standard contractual clauses for the transfer of personal data to third countries, under Directive 95/46/EC

OJ L 181, 4. 7. 2001, p. 19, corrected by OJ L 253, 21. 9. 2001, p. 34, and amended by OJ L 385, 29. 12. 2004, p. 74

THE COMMISSION OF THE EUROPEAN COMMUNITIES,

Having regard to the Treaty establishing the European Community,

Having regard to Directive 95/46/EC of the European Parliament and of the Council of 24 October 1995 on the protection of individuals with regard to the processing of personal data and on the free movement of such data[1]), and in particular Article 26(4) thereof,

Whereas:

(1) Pursuant to Directive 95/46/EC, Member States are required to provide that a transfer of personal data to a third country may only take place if the third country in question ensures an adequate level of data protection and the Member States' laws, which comply with the other provisions of the Directive, are respected prior to the transfer.

(2) However, Article 26(2) of Directive 95/46/EC provides that Member States may authorise, subject to certain safeguards, a transfer or a set of transfers of personal data to third countries which do not ensure an adequate level of protection. Such safeguards may in particular result from appropriate contractual clauses.

(3) Pursuant to Directive 95/46/EC, the level of data protection should be assessed in the light of all the circumstances surrounding the data transfer operation or set of data transfer operations. The Working Party on Protection of Individuals with regard to the processing of personal data established under that Directive[2]) has issued guidelines to aid with the assessment[3]).

---

[2]) The Internet address of the Working Party is: http://www.europa.eu.intlcomm/internal_market/en/medial/dataprot/wpdocs/index.htm.

[3]) WP 4 (5020/97) 'First orientations on transfers of personal data to third countries working document – possible ways forward in assessing adequacy', a discussion document adopted by the Working Party on 26 June 1997.

WP 7 (5057/97) 'Judging industry self regulation: when does it make a meaningful contribution to the level of data protection in a third country?', working document: adopted by the Working Party on 14 January 1998.

WP 9 (3005/98) 'Preliminary views on the use of contractual provisions in the context of transfers of personal data to third countries', working document: adopted by the Working Party on 22 April 1998.

---

[1]) OJ L 281, 23. 11. 1995, p. 31.

15

(4) Article 26(2) of Directive 95/46/EC, which provides flexibility for an organisation wishing to transfer data to third countries, and Article 26(4), which provides for standard contractual clauses, are essential for maintaining the necessary flow of personal data between the Community and third countries without unnecessary burdens for economic operators. Those Articles are particularly important in view of the fact that the Commission is unlikely to adopt adequacy findings under Article 25(6) for more than a limited number of countries in the short or even medium term.

(5) The standard contractual clauses are only one of several possibilities under Directive 95/46/EC, together with Article 25 and Article 26(1) and (2), for lawfully transferring personal data to a third country. It will be easier for organisations to transfer personal data to third countries by incorporating the standard contractual clauses in a contract. The standard contractual clauses relate only to data protection. The data exporter and the data importer are free to include any other clauses on business related issues, such as clauses on mutual assistance in cases of disputes with a data subject or a supervisory authority, which they consider as being pertinent for the contract as long as they do not contradict the standard contractual clauses.

(6) This Decision should be without prejudice to national authori-

sations Member States may grant in accordance with national provisions implementing Article 26(2) of Directive 95/46/EC. The circumstances of specific transfers may require that data controllers provide different safeguards within the meaning of Article 26(2). In any case, this Decision only has the effect of requiring the Member States not to refuse to recognise as providing adequate safeguards the contractual clauses described in it and does not therefore have any effect on other contractual clauses.

(7) The scope of this Decision is limited to establishing that the clauses in the Annex may be used by a controller established in the Community in order to adduce sufficient safeguards within the meaning of Article 26(2) of Directive 95/46/EC. The transfer of personal data to third countries is a processing operation in a Member State, the lawfulness of which is subject to national law. The data protection supervisory authorities of the Member States, in the exercise of their functions and powers under Article 28 of Directive 95/46/EC, should remain competent to assess whether the data exporter has complied with national legislation implementing the provisions of Directive 95/46/EC and, in particular, any specific rules as regards the obligation of providing information under that Directive.

(8) This Decision does not cover the transfer of personal data by controllers established in the Community to recipients established outside the territory of the Community who act only as processors. Those transfers do not require the same safeguards because the processor acts exclusively on behalf of the controller. The Commission intends to address that type of transfer in a subsequent decision.

WP 12: 'Transfers of personal data to third countries: applying Articles 25 and 26 of the EU data protection directive', working document adopted by the Working Party on 24 July 1998, available, in the web-working document site 'europa.eu.int/comm/internal_markt/en/media.dataprot/wpdocs/wp12/en' hosted by the European Commission.

(9) It is appropriate to lay down the minimum information that the parties must specify in the contract dealing with the transfer. Member States should retain the power to particularise the information the parties are required to provide. The operation of this Decision should be reviewed in the light of experience.

(10) The Commission will also consider in the future whether standard contractual clauses submitted by business organisations or other interested parties offer adequate safeguards in accordance with Directive 95/46/EC.

(11) While the parties should be free to agree on the substantive data protection rules to be complied with by the data importer, there are certain data protection principles which should apply in any event.

(12) Data should be processed and subsequently used or further communicated only for specified purposes and should not be kept longer than necessary.

(13) In accordance with Article 12 of Directive 95/46/EC, the data subject should have the right of access to all data relating to him and as appropriate to rectification, erasure or blocking of certain data.

(14) Further transfers of personal data to another controller established in a third country should be permitted only subject to certain conditions, in particular to ensure that data subjects are given proper information and have the opportunity to object, or in certain cases to withold their consent.

(15) In addition to assessing whether transfers to third countries are in accordance with national law, supervisory authorities should play a key role in this contractual mechanism in ensuring that personal data are adequately protected after the transfer. In specific circumstances, the supervisory authorities of the Member States should retain the power to prohibit or suspend a data transfer or a set of transfers based on the standard contractual clauses in those exceptional cases where it is established that a transfer on contractual basis is likely to have a substantial adverse effect on the guarantees providing adequate protection to the data subject.

(16) The standard contractual clauses should be enforceable not only by the organisations which are parties to the contract, but also by the data subjects, in particular, where the data subjects suffer damage as a consequence of a breach of the contract.

(17) The governing law of the contract should be the law of the Member State in which the data exporter is established, enabling a third-party beneficiary to enforce a contract. Data subjects should be allowed to be represented by associations or other bodies if they so wish and if authorised by national law.

(18) To reduce practical difficulties which data subjects could experience when trying to enforce their rights under the standard contractual clauses, the data exporter and the data importer should be jointly and severally liable for damages resulting from any violation of those provisions which are covered by the third-party beneficiary clause.

(19) The Data Subject is entitled to take action and receive compensation from the Data Exporter, the Data Importer or from both for any damage resulting from any act incompatible with the obligations contained in the standard contractual clauses. Both parties may be exempted from that liability if they prove that neither of them was responsible.

15

(20) Joint and several liability does not extend to those provisions not covered by the third-party beneficiary clause and does not need to leave one party paying for the damage resulting from the unlawful processing of the other party. Although mutual indemnification between the parties is not a requirement for the adequacy of the protection for the data subjects and may therefore be deleted, it is included in the standard contractual clauses for the sake of clarification and to avoid the need for the parties to negotiate indemnification clauses individually.

(21) In the event of a dispute between the parties and the data subject which is not amicably resolved and where the data subject invokes the third-party beneficiary clause, the parties agree to provide the data subject with the choice between mediation, arbitration or litigation. The extent to which the data subject will have an effective choice will depend on the availability of reliable and recognised systems of mediation and arbitration. Mediation by the supervisory authorities of a Member State should be an option where they provide such a service.

(22) The Working Party on the protection of individuals with regard to the processing of personal data established under Article 29 of Directive 95/46/EC has delivered an opinion on the level of protection provided under the standard contractual clauses annexed to this Decision, which has been taken into account in the preparation of this Decision[4]).

---

4) Opinion No 1/2001 adopted by the Working Party on 26 January 2001 (DG MARKT 5102/00 WP 38), available on the website 'Europa' hosted by the European Commission.

(23) The measures provided for in this Decision are in accordance with the opinion of the Committee established under Article 31 of Directive 95/46/EC,

HAS ADOPTED THIS DECISION:

Article 1

The standard contractual clauses set out in the Annex are considered as offering adequate safeguards with respect to the protection of the privacy and fundamental rights and freedoms of individuals and as regards the exercise of the corresponding rights as required by Article 26(2) of Directive 9/46/EC.

Data controllers may choose either of the sets I or II in the Annex. However, they may not amend the clauses nor combine individual clauses or the sets.

Article 2

This Decision concerns only the adequacy of protection provided by the standard contractual clauses for the transfer of personal data set out in the Annex. It does not affect the application of other national provisions implementing Directive 95/46/EC that pertain to the processing of personal data within the Member States.

This Decision shall not apply to the transfer of personal data by controllers established in the Community to recipients established outside the territory of the Community who act only as processors.

Article 3
For the purposes of this Decision:

(a) the definitions in Directive 95/46/EC shall apply;
(b) 'special categories of data' means the data referred to in Article 8 of that Directive;

15

(c) 'supervisory authority' means the authority referred to in Article 28 of that Directive;

(d) 'data exporter' means the controller who transfers the personal data;

(e) 'data importer' means the controller who agrees to receive from the data exporter personal data for further processing in accordance with the terms of this Decision.

Article 4

1. Without prejudice to their powers to take action to ensure compliance with national provisions adopted pursuant to chapters II, III, V and VI of Directive 95/46/EC, the competent authorities in the Member States may exercise their existing powers to prohibit or suspend data flows to third countries in order to protect individuals with regard to the processing of their personal data in cases where:

(a) it is established that the law to which the data importer is subject imposes upon him requirements to derogate from the relevant data protection rules which go beyond the restrictions necessary in a democratic society as provided for in Article 13 of Directive 95/46/EC where those requirements are likely to have a substantial adverse effect on the guarantees provided by the standard contractual clauses; or

(b) a competent authority has established that the data importer has not respected the contractual clauses; or

(c) there is a substantial likelihood that the standard contractual clauses in the Annex are not being or will not be complied with and the continuation of transfer would create an imminent risk of grave harm to the data subjects.

2. For the purposes of paragraph 1, where the data controller adduces adequate safeguards on the basis of the standard contractual clauses contained in set II in the Annex, the competent data protection authorities are entitled to exercise their existing powers to prohibit or suspend data flows in either of the following cases:

(a) refusal of the data importer to cooperate in good faith with the data protection authorities, or to comply with their clear obligations under the contract;

(b) refusal of the data exporter to take appropriate steps to enforce the contract against the data importer within the normal period of one month after notice by the competent data protection authority to the data exporter.

For the purposes of the first subparagraph, refusal in bad faith or refusal to enforce the contract by the data importer shall not include cases in which cooperation or enforcement would conflict with mandatory requirements of the national legislation applicable to the data importer which do not go beyond what is necessary in a democratic society on the basis of one of the interests listed in Article 13(1) of Directive 95/46/EC, in particular sanctions as laid down in international and/or national instruments, tax-reporting requirements or anti-money-laundering reporting requirements.

For the purposes of point (a) of the first subparagraph cooperation may include, in particular, the submission of the data importer's data processing facilities for audit or the obligation to abide by the advice of the data protection supervisory authority in the Community.

3. The prohibition or suspension pursuant to paragraphs 1 and 2 shall be lifted as soon as the reasons for the prohibition or suspension no longer exist.

4. When Member States adopt measures pursuant to paragraphs 1, 2

15

and 3, they shall without delay inform the Commission which will forward the information to the other Member States.

Article 5

The Commission shall evaluate the operation of this Decision on the basis of available information three years after its notification and the notification of any amendment thereto to the Member States. It shall submit a report on the endings to the Committee established under Article 31 of Directive 95/46/EC. It shall include any evidence that could affect the evaluation concerning the adequacy of the standard contractual clauses in the Annex and any evidence that this Decision is being applied in a discriminatory way.

Article 6

This Decision shall apply from 3 September 2001.

Article 7

This Decision is addressed to the Member States.

ANNEX
SET I

STANDARD CONTRACTUAL CLAUSES

for the purposes of Article 26(2) of Directive 95/46/EC for the transfer of personal data to third countries wich do not ensure an adequate level of protection

Name of the data exporting organisation: . . . .

. . . .

Address: . . . .

Tel.: . . . .   fax: . . . .   e-mail: . . . .

Other information needed to identify the organisation: . . . .

('the data **exporter**')

and

Name of the data importing organisation: . . . .

. . . .

Address: . . . .

Tel.: . . . .   fax: . . . .   e-mail: . . . .

Other information needed to identify the organisation: . . . .

('the data **importer**')

HAVE AGREED on the following contractual clauses ('the Clauses') in order to adduce adequate safeguards with respect to the protection of privacy and fundamental rights and freedoms of individuals for the transfer by the data exporter to the data importer of the personal data specified in Appendix 1:

Clause 1

Definitions

For the purposes of the Clauses:

a) **'personal data'**, **'special categories of data'**, **'process/processing'**, **'controller'**, **'processor'**, **'data subject'** and **'supervisory authority'** shall have the same meaning as in Directive 95/46/EC of the European Parliament and of the Council of 24 October 1995 on the protection of individuals with regard to the processing of personal data and on the free movement of such data ('hereinafter the Directive');

b) the **'data exporter'** shall mean the controller who transfers the personal data;

c) the **'data importer'** shall mean the controller who agrees to receive from the data exporter personal data for further processing in accordance with the terms of these clauses and who is not subject to a third country's system ensuring adequate protection.

Clause 2

Details of the transfer

The details of the transfer, and in particular the categories of personal data and the purposes for which they are transferred, are specified in Appendix 1 wich forms an integral part of the Clauses.

Clause 3

Third-party beneficiary clause

The data subjects can enforce this Clause, Clause 4(b), (c) and (d), Clause 5(a), (b), (c) and (e), Clause 6(1) and (2), and Clauses 7, 9 and 11 as third-party beneficaries. The parties do not object to the data subjects being represented by an association or other bodies if they so wish and if permitted by national law.

Clause 4

Obligations of the data exporter

The data exporter agrees and warrants:

(a) that the processing, including the transfer itself, of the personal data by him has been and, up to the moment of the transfer, will continue to be carried out in accordance with the relevant provisions of the Member State in wich the data exporter is established (and where applicable has been notified to the relevant authorities of the State) and does not violate the relevant provisions of that State;

(b) that if the transfer involves special categories of data the data subject has been informed or will be informed before the transfer that this data could be transmitted to a third country not providing adequate protection;

(c) to make available to the data subjects upon request a copy of the Clauses; and

(d) to respond in a reasonable time and to the extent reasonably possible to enquires from the supervisory authority on the processing of the relevant personal data by the data importer and to any enquiries from the data subject concerning the processing of this personal data by the data importer.

Clause 5

Obligations of the data importer

The data importer agrees and warrants:

(a) that he has no reason to believe that the legislation applicable to him prevents him from fulfilling his obligations under the contract and that in the event of a change in that legislation wich is likely to have a substantial adverse effect on the guarantees provided by the Clauses, he will notify the change to the data exporter and to the supervisory authority

15

where the data exporter is established, in wich case the data exporter is entitled to suspend the transfer of data and/or terminate the contract;
(b) to process the personal data in accordance with the mandatory data protection principles set out in Appendix 2;
or, if explicitly agreed by the parties by ticking below and subject to compliance with the mandatory data protection principles set out in Appendix 3, to process in all other respects the data in accordance with:
 – the relevant provisions of national law (attached to these Clauses) protecting the fundamental rights and freedoms of natural persons, and in particular their right to privacy with respect to the processing of personal data applicable to a data controller in the country in wich the data exporter is established, or
 – the relevant provisions of any Commission Decision under Article 25(6) of Directive 95/46/EC finding that a third country provides adequate protection in certain sectors of activity only, if the data importer is based in that third country and is not covered by those provisions , in so far as those provisions are of a nature wich makes them applicable in the sector of the transfer;
(c) to deal promptly and properly with all reasonable inquires from the data exporter or the data subject relating to his processing of the personal data subject to the transfer and to cooperate with the competent supervisory authority in the course of all its inquiries and abide by the advice of the supervisory authority with regard to the processing of the data transferred;
(d) at the request of the data exporter to submit its data processing facilities for audit wich shall be carried out by the data exporter or an inspection body composed of independent members and in possession of the required professional qualifications, selected by the data exporter, where applicable, in agreement with the supervisory authority;
(e) to make available to the data subject upon request a copy of the Clauses and indicate the office wich handles complaints.

Clause 6

Liability

1. The parties agree that a data subject who has suffered damage as a result of any violation of the provisions referred to in Clause 3 is entitled to receive compensation from the damage suffered. The parties agree that they may be exempted from this liability only if they prove that neither of them is responsible for the violation of those provisions.
2. The data exporter and the data importer agree that they will be jointly and severally liable for damage to the data subject resulting from any violation referred to in paragraph 1. In the event of such a violation, the data exporter or the data importer or both.
3. The parties agree that if one party is held liable for a violation referred to in paragraph 1 by the other party, the latter will, to the extent to wich is liable, indemnify the first party for any cost, charge, damages, expenses or loss it has incurred. (*).

Clause 7

Mediation und jurisdiction

1. The parties agree that if there is a dispute between a data subject and either party wich is not amicably resolved and the data subject invokes the third-party beneficiary provision in clause 3, they accept the decision of the data subject:
(a) to refer the dispute to mediation by an independent person or, where applicable, by the supervisory authority;
(b) to refer the dispute to the courts in the Member State in wich the data exporter is established.

(*) Paragraph 3 is optional.

15

2. The parties agree that by agreement between a data subject and the relevant party a dispute can be referred to an arbitration body, if that party is established in a country which has ratified the New York convention on enforcement of arbitration awards.

3. The parties agree that paragraphs 1 and 2 apply without prejudice to the data subject's substantitve or procedural rights to seek remedies in accordance with other provisions of national or international law.

Clause 8

Cooperation with supervisory authorities

The parties agree to deposit a copy of this contract with the supervisory authority if it so requests or if such deposit its required under national law.

Clause 9

Termination of the Clauses

The parties agree that the termination of the Clauses at any time, in any circumstances and for whatever reason does not exempt them from the obligations and/or conditions under the Clauses as regards the processing of the data transferred.

Clause 10

Governing Law

The Clauses shall be governed by the law of the Member State in wich the Data Exporter is established, namely . . . .

Clause 11

Variation of the contract

The parties undertake not to vary or modify the terms of the clauses.

On behalf of the data exporter:

Name (written out in full): . . . .

Position: . . . .

Address: . . . .

Other information necessary in order for the contract to be binding (if any): . . . .

. . . .

. . . .
(signature)

(stamp of organisation)

On behalf of the data importer:

Name (written out in full): . . . .

15

Position: ....

Address: ....

Other information necessary in order for the contract to be binding (if any): ....
....
....

....
(signature)

(stamp of organisation)

Appendix 1
to the standard contractual clauses

This Appendix forms part of the Clauses and must be completed and signed by the parties.

(The Member States may complete or specify, according to their national procedures, any additional necessary information to be contained in this Appendix.)

Data exporter

The data exporter is (please specify briefly your activities relevant to the transfer):
....
....

Data importer

The data importer is (please specify briefly your activities relevant to the transfer):
....
....

Data subjects

The personal data transferred concern the following categories of data subjects (please specify):
....
....

Purposes of the transfer

The transfer is necessary for the following purposes (please specify):

....

....

....

Categories of data

The personal data transferred fall within the following categories of data (please specify):

....

....

....

Sensitive data (if appropriate)

The personal data transferred fall within the following categories of sensitive data (please specify):

....

....

....

Recipients

The personal data transferred may be disclosed only to the following recipients or categories of recipients (please specify):

....

....

....

Storage limit

The personal data transferred may be stored for no more than (please indicate): ....
(months/years)

Data exporter	Date importer
Name:	Name: ....
....	....
(Authorised signature)	(Authorised signature)

15

194

Appendix 2
to the standard contractual clauses

Mandatory data protection principles referred to in the first paragraph of Clause 5(b)

These data protection principles should be read and interpreted in the light of the provisions (principles and relevant exceptions) of Directive 95/46/EC.

They shall apply subject to the mandatory requirements of the national legislation applicable to the data importer which do not go beyond what is necessary in a democratic society on the basis of one of the interests listed in Article 13(1) of Directive 95/46/EC, that is, if they constitute a necessary measure to safeguard national security, defence, public security, the prevention, investigation, detection and prosecution of criminal offences or of breaches of ethics for the regulated professions, an important economic or financial interest of the State or the protection of the data subject or the rights and freedoms of others.

1. *Purpose limitation:* data must be processed and subsequently used or further communicated only for the specific purposes in Appendix I to the Clauses. Data must not be kept longer than necessary for the purposes for which they are transferred.

2. *Data quality and proportionality:* data must be accurate and, where necessary, kept up to date. The data must be adequate, relevant and not excessive in relation to the purposes for which they are transferred and further processed.

3. *Transparency:* data subjects must be provided with information as to the purposes of the processing and the identity of the data controller in the third country, and other information

insofar as this is necessary to ensure fair processing, unless such information has already been given by the data exporter.

4. *Security and confidentiality:* technical and organisational security measures must be taken by the data controller that are appropriate to the risks, such as unauthorised access, presented by the processing. Any person acting under the authority of the data controller, including a processor, must not process the data except on instructions from the controller.

5. *Rights of access, rectification, erasure and blocking of data:* as provided for in Article 12 of Directive 95/46/EC, the data subject must have a right of access to all data relating to him that are processed and, as appropriate, the right to the rectification, erasure or blocking of data the processing of which does not comply with the principles set out in this Appendix, in particular because the data are incomplete or inaccurate. He should also be able to object to the processing of the data relating to him on compelling legitimate grounds relating to his particular situation.

6. *Restrictions on onwards transfers:* further transfers of personal data from the data importer to another controller established in a third country not providing adequate protection or not covered by a decision adopted by the Commission pursuant to Article 25(6) of Directive 95/46/EC (onward transfer) may take place only if either:

(a) data subjects have, in the case of special categories of data, given their unambiguous consent to the onward transfer or, in other cases, have been given the opportunity to object.

The minimum information to be provided to data subjects must contain in a language understandable to them:

– the purposes of the onward transfer,

15

– the identification of the data exporter established in the Community,

– the categories of further recipients of the data and the countries of destination, and

– an explanation that, after the onward transfer, the data may be processed by a controller established in a country where there is not an adequate level of protection of the privacy of individuals; or

(b) the data exporter and the data importer agree to the adherence to the Clauses of another controller which thereby becomes a party to the Clauses and assumes the same obligations as the data importer.

7. *Special categories of data:* where data revealing racial or ehtnic origin, political opinions, religious or philosophical beliefs or trade union memberships and data concerning health or sex life and data relating to offences, criminal convictions or security measures are processed, additional safeguards should be in place within the meaning of Directive 95/46/EC, in particular, appropriate security measures such as strong encryption for transmission or such as keeping a record of access to sensitive data.

8. *Direct marketing:* where data are processed for the purposes of direct marketing, effective procedures should exist allowing the data subject at any time to "opt-out" from having his data used for such purposes.

9. *Automated individual decisions:* data subjects are entitled not to be subject to a decision which is based soley on automated processing of data, unless other measures are taken to safeguard the individual's legitimate interests as provided for in Article 15(2) of Directive 95/46/EC. Where the purpose of the transfer is the taking of an automated decision as referred to in Article 15 of Directive 95/46/EC, which produces legal effects concerning the individual or significantly affects him and which is based solely on automated processing of data intended to evaluate certain personal aspects relating to him, such as his performance at work, creditworthiness, reliability, conduct, etc., the individual should have the right to know the reasoning for this decision.

Appendix 3
to the standard contractual clauses

Mandatory data protection principles referred to in the second paragraph of Clause 5(b)

1. *Purpose limitation:* data must be processed and subsequently used or further communicated only for the specific purposes in Appendix I to the Clauses. Data must not be kept longer than necessary for the purposes for which they are transferred.

2. *Rights of access, rectification, erasure and blocking of data:* as provided for in Article 12 of Directive 95/46/EC, the data subject must have a right of access to all data relating to him that are processed and, as appropriate, the right to the rectification, erasure or blocking of data the processing of which does not comply with the principles set out in this Appendix, in particular because the data is incomplete or inaccurate. He should also be able to object to the processing of the data relating to him on compelling legitimate grounds relating to his particular situation.

3. *Restrictions on onward transfers:* further transfers of personal data from the data importer to another controller established in a third country not providing adequate protection or not covered by a decision adopted by the Commission pursuant to Article 25(6)

15

of Directive 95/46/EC (onward transfer) may take place only if either:

(a) data subjects have, in the case of special categories of data, given their unambiguous consent to the onward transfer, or, in other cases, have been given the opportunity to object.

The minimum information to be provided to data subjects must contain in a language understandable to them:
– the purposes of the onward transfer,
– the identification of the data exporter established in the Community,
– the categories of further recipients of the data and the countries of destination, and
– an explanation that, after the onward transfer, the data may be processed by a controller established in a country where there is not an adequate level of protection of the privacy of individuals; or

(b) the data exporter and the data importer agree to the adherence to the Clauses of another controller which thereby becomes a party to the Clauses and assumes the same obligations as the data importer.

SET II

Standard contractual clauses for the transfer of personal data from the Community to third countries (controller to controller transfers)

Data transfer agreement

between

. . . .
(name)

. . . .
(address and country of establishment)
hereinafter 'data exporter')

197

and

. . . .
(name)

. . . .
(address and country of establishment)
hereinafter 'data importer'
each a 'party'; together 'the parties'".

Definitions

For the purposes of the clauses:

(a) 'personal data', 'special categories of data/sensitive data', 'process/processing', 'controller', 'processor', 'data subject' and 'supervisory authority/authority' shall have the same meaning as in Directive 95/46/EC of 24 October 1995 (whereby 'the authority' shall mean the competent data protection authority in the territory in which the data exporter is established);

(b) 'the data exporter' shall mean the controller who transfers the personal data;

(c) 'the data importer' shall mean the controller who agrees to receive from the data exporter personal data for further processing in accordance with the terms of these clauses and who is not subject to a third country's system ensuring adequate protection;

(d) 'clauses' shall mean these contractual clauses, which are a free-standing document that does not incorporate commercial business terms established by the parties under separate commercial arrangements.

The details of the transfer (as well as the personal data covered) are specified in Annex B, which forms an integral part of the clauses.

I. Obligations of the data exporter

The data exporter warrants and undertakes that:

15

(a) The personal data have been collected, processed and transferred in accordance with the laws applicable to the data exporter.

(b) It has used reasonable efforts to determine that the data importer is able to satisfy its legal obligations under these clauses.

(c) It will provide the data importer, when so requested, with copies of relevant data protection laws or references to them (where relevant, and not including legal advice) of the country in which the data exporter is established.

(d) It will respond to enquiries from data subjects and the authority concerning processing of the personal data by the data importer, unless the parties have agreed that the data importer will so respond, in which case the data exporter will still respond to the extent reasonably possible and with the information reasonably available to it if the data importer is unwilling or unable to respond. Responses will be made within a reasonable time.

(e) It will make available, upon request, a copy of the clauses to data subjects who are third party beneficiaries under clause III, unless the clauses contain confidential information, in which case it may remove such information. Where information is removed, the data exporter shall inform data subjects in writing of the reason for removal and of their right to draw the removal to the attention of the authority. However, the data exporter shall abide by a decision of the authority regarding access to the full text of the clauses by data subjects, as long as data subjects have agreed to respect the confidentiality of the confidential information removed. The data exporter shall also provide a copy of the clauses to the authority where required.

II. Obligations of the data importer

The data importer warrants and undertakes that:

(a) It will have in place appropriate technical and organisational measures to protect the personal data against accidental or unlawful destruction or accidental loss, alteration, unauthorised disclosure or access, and which provide a level of security appropriate to the risk represented by the processing and the nature of the data to be protected.

(b) It will have in place procedures so that any third party it authorises to have access to the personal data, including processors, will respect and maintain the confidentiality and security of the personal data. Any person acting under the authority of the data importer, including a data processor, shall be obligated to process the personal data only on instructions from the data importer. This provision does not apply to persons authorised or required by law or regulation to have access to the personal data.

(c) It has no reason to believe, at the time of entering into these clauses, in the existence of any local laws that would have a substantial adverse effect on the guarantees provided for under these clauses, and it will inform the data exporter (which will pass such notification on to the authority where required) if it becomes aware of any such laws.

(d) It will process the personal data for purposes described in Annex B, and has the legal authority to give the warranties and fulfil the undertakings set out in these clauses.

(e) It will identify to the data exporter a contact point within its organisation authorised to respond to enquiries concerning processing of the personal data, and will cooperate in good faith with the data exporter, the data subject and the authority concerning all such enquiries within a reasonable time. In case of legal dissolution of the data exporter, or if the parties have so agreed, the data importer will assume responsibility for compliance with the provisions of clause I(e).

(f) At the request of the data exporter, it will provide the data exporter with evidence of financial resources sufficient to fulfil its responsibilities under clause III (which may include insurance coverage).

(g) Upon reasonable request of the data exporter, it will submit its data processing facilities, data files and documentation needed for processing to reviewing, auditing and/or certifying by the data exporter (or any independent or impartial inspection agents or auditors, selected by the data exporter and not reasonably objected to by the data importer) to ascertain compliance with the warranties and undertakings in these clauses, with reasonable notice and during regular business hours. The request will be subject to any necessary consent or approval from a regulatory or supervisory authority within the country of the data importer, which consent or approval the data importer will attempt to obtain in a timely fashion.

(h) It will process the personal data, at its option, in accordance with:

(i) the data protection laws of the country in which the data exporter is established, or

(ii) the relevant provisions[5] of any Commission decision pursuant to

Article 25(6) of Directive 95/46/EC, where the data importer complies with the relevant provisions of such an authorisation or decision and is based in a country to which such an authorisation or decision pertains, but is not covered by such authorisation or decision for the purposes of the transfer(s) of the personal data[6]), or

(iii) the data processing principles set forth in Annex A.

Data importer to indicate which option it selects: ....
....
....

Initials of data importer: ....
....
....

(i) It will not disclose or transfer the personal data to a third party data controller located outside the European Economic Area (EEA) unless it notifies the data exporter about the transfer and

(i) the third party data controller processes the personal data in accordance with a Commission decision finding that a third country provides adequate protection, or

(ii) the third party data controller becomes a signatory to these clauses or another data transfer agreement approved by a competent authority in the EU, or

(iii) data subjects have been given the opportunity to object, after having been informed of the purposes of the transfer, the categories of recipients and the fact that the countries to which

---

[5] 'Relevant provisions' means those provisions of any authorisation or decision except for the enforcement provisions of any authorisation or decision (which shall be governed by these clauses).

[6] However, the provisions of Annex A.5 concerning rights of access, rectification, deletion and objection must be applied when this option is chosen and take precedence over any comparable provisions of the Commission Decision selected.

15

data is exported may have different data protection standards, or

(iv) with regard to onward transfers of sensitive data, data subjects have given their unambiguous consent to the onward transfer

III. Liability and third party rights

(a) Each party shall be liable to the other parties for damages it causes by any breach of these clauses. Liability as between the parties is limited to actual damage suffered. Punitive damages (i.e. damages intended to punish a party for its outrageous conduct) are specifically excluded. Each party shall be liable to data subjects for damages it causes by any breach of third party rights under these clauses. This does not affect the liability of the data exporter under its data protection law.

(b) The parties agree that a data subject shall have the right to enforce as a third party beneficiary this clause and clauses I(b), I(d), I(e), II(a), II(c), II(d), II(e), II(h), II(i), III(a), V, VI(d) and VII against the data importer or the data exporter, for their respective breach of their contractual obligations, with regard to his personal data, and accept jurisdiction for this purpose in the data exporter's country of establishment. In cases involving allegations of breach by the data importer, the data subject must first request the data exporter to take appropriate action to enforce his rights against the data importer; if the data exporter does not take such action within a reasonable period (which under normal circumstances would be one month), the data subject may then enforce his rights against the data importer directly. A data subject is entitled to proceed directly against a data exporter that has failed to use reasonable efforts to deter-

mine that the data importer is able to satisfy its legal obligations under these clauses (the data exporter shall have the burden to prove that it took reasonable efforts).

IV. Law applicable to the clauses

These clauses shall be governed by the law of the country in which the data exporter is established, with the exception of the laws and regulations relating to processing of the personal data by the data importer under clause II(h), which shall apply only if so selected by the data importer under that clause.

V. Resolution of disputes with data subjects or the authority

(a) In the event of a dispute or claim brought by a data subject or the authority concerning the processing of the personal data against either or both of the parties, the parties will inform each other about any such disputes or claims, and will cooperate with a view to settling them amicably in a timely fashion.

(b) The parties agree to respond to any generally available non-binding mediation procedure initiated by a data subject or by the authority. If they do participate in the proceedings, the parties may elect to do so remotely (such as by telephone or other electronic means). The parties also agree to consider participating in any other arbitration, mediation or other dispute resolution proceedings developed for data protection disputes.

(c) Each party shall abide by a decision of a competent court of the data exporter's country of establishment or of the authority which is final and against which no further appeal is possible.

15

VI. Termination

(a) In the event that the data importer is in breach of its obligations under these clauses, then the data exporter may temporarily suspend the transfer of personal data to the data importer until the breach is repaired or the contract is terminated.

(b) In the event that:

(i) the transfer of personal data to the data importer has been temporarily suspended by the data exporter for longer than one month pursuant to paragraph (a);

(ii) compliance by the data importer with these clauses would put it in breach of its legal or regulatory obligations in the country of import;

(iii) the data importer is in substantial or persistent breach of any warranties or undertakings given by it under these clauses;

(iv) a final decision against which no further appeal is possible of a competent court of the data exporter's country of establishment or of the authority rules that there has been a breach of the clauses by the data importer or the data exporter; or

(v) a petition is presented for the administration or winding up of the data importer, whether in its personal or business capacity, which petition is not dismissed within the applicable period for such dismissal under applicable law; a winding up order is made; a receiver is appointed over any of its assets; a trustee in bankruptcy is appointed, if the data importer is an individual; a company voluntary arrangement is commenced by it; or any equivalent event in any jurisdiction occurs

then the data exporter, without prejudice to any other rights which it may have against the data importer, shall be entitled to terminate these clauses, in which case the authority shall be informed where required. In cases covered by (i), (ii), or (iv) above the data importer may also terminate these clauses.

(c) Either party may terminate these clauses if

(i) any Commission positive adequacy decision under Article 25(6) of Directive 95/46/EC (or any superseding text) is issued in relation to the country (or a sector thereof) to which the data is transferred and processed by the data importer, or

(ii) Directive 95/46/EC (or any superseding text) becomes directly applicable in such country.

(d) The parties agree that the termination of these clauses at any time, in any circumstances and for whatever reason (except for termination under clause VI(c)) does not exempt them from the obligations and/or conditions under the clauses as regards the processing of the personal data transferred.

VII. Variation of these clauses

The parties may not modify these clauses except to update any information in Annex B, in which case they will inform the authority where required. This does not preclude the parties from adding additional commercial clauses where required.

VIII. Description of the Transfer

The details of the transfer and of the personal data are specified in Annex B. The parties agree that Annex B may contain confidential business information which they will not disclose to third parties, except as required by law or in response to a competent regulatory or government agency, or as required under clause I(e). The parties may execute additional annexes to

15

cover additional transfers, which will be submitted to the authority where required. Annex B may, in the alternative, be drafted to cover multiple transfers.

Dated: . . . .

. . . .

FOR DATA IMPORTER

. . . .

. . . .

. . . .

FOR DATA EXPORTER

. . . .

. . . .

. . . .

ANNEX A
DATA PROCESSING PRINCIPLES

1. Purpose limitation: Personal data may be processed and subsequently used or further communicated only for purposes described in Annex B or subsequently authorised by the data subject.

2. Data quality and proportionality: Personal data must be accurate and, where necessary, kept up to date. The personal data must be adequate, relevant and not excessive in relation to the purposes for which they are transferred and further processed.

3. Transparency: Data subjects must be provided with information necessary to ensure fair processing (such as information about the purposes of processing and about the transfer), unless such information has already been given by the data exporter.

4. Security and confidentiality: Technical and organisational security measures must be taken by the data controller that are appropriate to the risks, such as against accidental or unlawful destruction or accidental loss, alteration, unauthorised disclosure or access, presented by the processing. Any person acting under the authority of the data controller, including a processor, must not process the data except on instructions from the data controller.

5. Rights of access, rectification, deletion and objection: As provided in Article 12 of Directive 95/46/EC, data subjects must, whether directly or via a third party, be provided with the personal information about them that an organisation holds, except for requests which are manifestly abusive, based on unreasonable intervals or their number or repetitive or systematic nature, or for which access need not be granted under the law of the country of the data exporter. Provided that the authority has given its prior approval, access need also not be granted when doing so would be likely to seriously harm the interests of the data importer or other organisations dealing with the data importer and such interests are not overridden by the interests for fundamental rights and freedoms of the data subject. The sources of the personal data need not be identified when this is not possible by reasonable efforts, or where the rights of persons other than the individual would be violated. Data subjects must be able to have the personal information about them rectified, amended, or deleted where it is inaccurate or processed against these principles. If there are compelling grounds to doubt the legitimacy of the request, the organisation may require further justifications before proceeding to rectifi-

cation, amendment or deletion. Notification of any rectification, amendment or deletion to third parties to whom the data have been disclosed need not be made when this involves a disproportionate effort. A data subject must also be able to object to the processing of the personal data relating to him if there are compelling legitimate grounds relating to his particular situation. The burden of proof for any refusal rests on the data importer, and the data subject may always challenge a refusal before the authority.

6. Sensitive data: The data importer shall take such additional measures (e.g. relating to security) as are necessary to protect such sensitive data in accordance with its obligations under clause II.

7. Data used for marketing purposes: Where data are processed for the purposes of direct marketing, effective procedures should exist allowing the data subject at any time to "opt-out" from having his data used for such purposes.

8. Automated decisions: For purposes hereof "automated decision" shall mean a decision by the data exporter or the data importer which produces legal effects concerning a data subject or significantly affects a data subject and which is based solely on automated processing of personal data intended to evaluate certain personal aspects relating to him, such as his performance at work, creditworthiness, reliability, conduct, etc. The data importer shall not make any automated decisions concerning data subjects, except when:

(a) (i) such decisions are made by the data importer in entering into or performing a contract with the data subject, and

(ii) (the data subject is given an opportunity to discuss the results of a relevant automated decision with a representative of the parties making such decision or otherwise to make representations to that parties.

or

(b) where otherwise provided by the law of the data exporter.

ANNEX B
DESCRIPTION OF THE TRANSFER

(To be completed by the parties)

Data subjects

The personal data transferred concern the following categories of data subjects:

....

....

....

....

Purposes of the transfer(s)

The transfer is made for the following purposes:

....

....

....

....

Categories of data

The personal data transferred concern the following categories of data:

....

....

....

....

Recipients

The personal data transferred may be disclosed only to the following recipients or categories of recipients:

. . . .

. . . .

. . . .

Sensitive data (if appropriate)

The personal data transferred concern the following categories of sensitive data:

. . . .

. . . .

. . . .

. . . .

Data protection registration information of data exporter (where applicable)

. . . .

. . . .

Additional useful information (storage limits and other relevant information)

. . . .

. . . .

Contact points for data protection enquiries

Data importer

. . . .

. . . .

. . . .

Data exporter

. . . .

. . . .

. . . .

ILLUSTRATIVE COMMERCIAL CLAUSES (OPTIONAL)

Indemnification between the data exporter and data importer:

"The parties will indemnify each other and hold each other harmless from any cost, charge, damages, expense or loss which they cause each other as a result of their breach of any of the provisions of these clauses. Indemnification hereunder is contingent upon (a) the party(ies) to be indemnified (the 'indemnified party(ies)') promptly notifying the other party(ies) (the 'indemnifying party(ies)') of a claim, (b) the indemnifying party(ies) having sole control of the defence and settlement of any such claim, and (c) the indemnified party(ies) providing reasonable cooperation and assistance to the indemnifying party(ies) in defence of such claim.".

Dispute resolution between the data exporter and data importer (the parties may of course substitute any other alternative dispute resolution or jurisdictional clause):

'In the event of a dispute between the data importer and the data exporter concerning any alleged breach of any provision of these clauses, such dispute shall be finally settled under the rules of arbitration of the International Chamber of Commerce by one or more arbitrators appointed in accordance with the said rules. The place of arbi-

15

tration shall be [ ]. The number of arbitrators shall be [ ].'

Allocation of costs:

'Each party shall perform its obligations under these clauses at its own cost.'

Extra termination clause:

'In the event of termination of these clauses, the data importer must return all personal data and all copies of the personal data subject to these clauses to the data exporter forthwith or, at the data exporter's choice, will destroy all copies of the same and certify to the data exporter that it has done so, unless the data importer is prevented by its national law or local regulator from destroying or returning all or part of such data, in which event the data will be kept confidential and will not be actively processed for any purpose. The data importer agrees that, if so requested by the data exporter, it will allow the data exporter, or an inspection agent selected by the data exporter and not reasonably objected to by the data importer, access to its establishment to verify that this has been done, with reasonable notice and during business hours.'

16

Standard Contractual Clauses for the Transfer of Personal Data to Processors Established in Non-EU Member States Commission Decision 2002/16/EC of 27 December 2001 on standard contractual clauses for the transfer of personal data to processors established in third countries, under Directive 95/46/EC

OJ L 6, 10. 1. 2002, p. 52

THE COMMISSION OF THE EURO-PEAN COMMUNITIES,

Having regard to the Treaty establishing the European Community,

Having regard to Directive 95/46/EC of the European Parliament and of the Council of 24 October 1995 on the protection of individuals with regard to the processing of personal data and on the free movement of such data[1]), and in particular Article 26(4) thereof,

Whereas:

(1) Pursuant to Directive 95/46/EC Member States are required to provide that a transfer of personal data to a third country may only take place if the third country in question ensures an adequate level of data protection and the Member States' laws, which comply with the other provisions of the Directive, are respected prior to the transfer.

(2) However, Article 26(2) of Directive 95/46/EC provides that Member States may authorise, subject to certain safeguards, a transfer or a set of transfers of personal data to third countries which do not ensure an adequate level of protection. Such safeguards may in

particular result from appropriate contractual clauses.

(3) Pursuant to Directive 95/46/EC the level of data protection should be assessed in the light of all the circumstances surrounding the data transfer operation or set of data transfer operations. The Working Party on the Protection of Individuals with regard to the Processing of Personal Data established under that Directive[2]) has issued guidelines to aid with the assessment[3]).

---

[2]) The web address of the Working Party is: http://europa.eu.int/comm/internal_market/en/dataprot/wpdocs/index.htm.

[3]) WP 4 (5020/97): 'First orientations on Transfers of Personal Data to Third Countries – Possible Ways Forward in Assessing Adequacy', a discussion document adopted by the Working Party on 26 June 1997.

WP 7 (5057/97): Working document: 'Judging industry self-regulation: when does it make a meaningful contribution to the level of data protection in a third country?', adopted by the Working Party on 14 January 1998.

WP 9 (5005/98): Working Document: 'Preliminary views on the use of contractual provisions in the context of transfers of personal data to third countries', adopted by the Working Party on 22 April 1998.

WP 12: Transfers of personal data to third countries: Applying Articles 25 and 26 of the EU data protection directive,

---

[1]) OJ L 281, 23. 11. 1995, p. 31.

16

(4) The standard contractual clauses relate only to data protection. The data exporter and the data importer are free to include any other clauses on business related issues which they consider as being pertinent for the contract as long as they do not contradict the standard contractual clauses.

(5) This Decision should be without prejudice to national authorisations Member States may grant in accordance with national provisions implementing Article 26(2) of Directive 95/46/EC. This Decision only has the effect of requiring the Member States not to refuse to recognise as providing adequate safeguards the contractual clauses set out in it and does not therefore have any effect on other contractual clauses.

(6) The scope of this Decision is limited to establishing that the clauses which it sets out may be used by a data controller established in the Community in order to adduce adequate safeguards within the meaning of Article 26(2) of Directive 95/46/EC for the transfer of personal data to a processor established in a third country.

(7) This Decision should implement the obligation provided for in Article 17(3) of Directive 95/46/EC and does not prejudice the content of the contracts or legal acts established pursuant to that provision. However, some of the standard contractual clauses, in particular as regards the data exporter's obligations, should be included in order to increase clarity as to the provisions which may be contained in a contract between a controller and a processor.

(8) Supervisory authorities of the Member States play a key role in this contractual mechanism in ensuring that personal data are adequately protected after the transfer. In exceptional cases where data exporters refuse or are unable to instruct the data importer properly, with an imminent risk of grave harm to the data subjects, the standard contractual clauses should allow the supervisory authorities to audit data importers and, where appropriate, take decisions which are binding on data importers. The supervisory authorities should have the power to prohibit or suspend a data transfer or a set of transfers based on the standard contractual clauses in those exceptional cases where it is established that a transfer on contractual basis is likely to have a substantial adverse effect on the warranties and obligations providing adequate protection for the data subject.

(9) The Commission may also consider in the future whether standard contractual clauses for the transfer of personal data to data processors established in third countries not offering an adequate level of data protection, submitted by business organisations or other interested parties, offer adequate safeguards in accordance with Article 26(2) of Directive 95/46/EC.

(10) A disclosure of personal data to a data processor established outside the Community is an international transfer protected under Chapter IV of Directive 95/46/EC. Consequently, this Decision does not cover the transfer of personal data by controllers established in the Community to controllers established outside the Community who fall within the scope of Commission Decision 2001/497/EC of 15 June 2001 on

---

adopted by the Working Party on 24 July 1998, available on the website 'http://europa.eu.int/comm/internal_market/en/dataprot/wpdocs/wp12en.htm' hosted by the European Commission.

standard contractual clauses for the transfer of personal data to third countries, under Directive 95/46/EC[4]).

(11) The standard contractual clauses should provide for the technical and organisational security measures ensuring a level of security appropriate to the risks represented by the processing and the nature of the data to be protected that a data processor established in a third country not providing adequate protection must apply. Parties should make provision in the contract for those technical and organisational measures which, having regard to applicable data protection law, the state of the art and the cost of their implementation, are necessary in order to protect personal data against accidental or unlawful destruction or accidental loss, alteration, unauthorised disclosure or access or any other unlawful forms of processing.

(12) In order to facilitate data flows from the Community, it is desirable that processors providing data processing services to several data controllers in the Community be allowed to apply the same technical and organisational security measures irrespective of the Member State from which the data transfer originates, in particular in those cases where the data importer receives data for further processing from different establishments of the data exporter in the Community, in which case the law of the designated Member State of establishment should apply.

(13) It is appropriate to lay down the minimum information that the parties must specify in the contract dealing with the transfer. Member States should retain the power to particularise the information the parties

[4]) OJ L 181, 4. 7. 2001, p. 19.

are required to provide. The operation of this Decision should be reviewed in the light of experience.

(14) The data importer should process the transferred personal data only on behalf of the data exporter and in accordance with his instructions and the obligations contained in the clauses. In particular the data importer should not disclose the personal data to a third party unless in accordance with certain conditions. The data exporter should instruct the data importer throughout the duration of the data processing Services to process the data in accordance with his instructions, the applicable data protection laws and the obligations contained in the clauses. The transfer of personal data to processors established outside the Community does not prejudice the fact that the processing activities should be governed in any case by the applicable data protection law.

(15) The standard contractual clauses should be enforceable not only by the organisations which are parties to the contract, but also by the data subjects, in particular where the data subjects suffer damage as a consequence of a breach of the contract.

(16) The data subject should be entitled to take action and, where appropriate, receive compensation from the data exporter who is the data controller of the personal data transferred. Exceptionally, the data subject should also be entitled to take action, and, where appropriate, receive compensation from the data importer in those cases, arising out of a breach by the data importer of any of his obligations referred to in the second paragraph of clause 3, where the data exporter has factually disappeared or has ceased to exist in law or has become insolvent.

(17) In the event of a dispute between a data subject, who invokes the third-party beneficiary clause and the data importer, which is not amicably resolved, the data importer should agree to provide the data subject with the choice between mediation, arbitration or litigation. The extent to which the data subject will have an effective choice should depend on the availability of reliable and recognised systems of mediation and arbitration. Mediation by the data protection supervisory authorities of the Member State in which the data exporter is established should be an option where they provide such a service.

(18) The contract should be governed by the law of the Member State in which the data exporter is established enabling a third-party beneficiary to enforce a contract. Data subjects should be allowed to be represented by associations or other bodies if they so wish and if authorised by national law.

(19) The Working Party on the Protection of Individuals with regard to the processing of Personal Data established under Article 29 of Directive 95/46/EC has delivered an opinion on the level of protection provided under the standard contractual clauses annexed to this Decision, which has been taken into account in the preparation of this Decision[5]).

(20) The measures provided for in this Decision are in accordance with the opinion of the Committee established under Article 31 of Directive 95/46/EC,

HAS ADOPTED THIS DECISION:

---

[5]) Opinion No 7/2001 adopted by the Working Party on 13 September 2001 (DG MARKT....), available on the website 'Europa' hosted by the European Commission.

Article 1

The standard contractual clauses set out in the Annex are considered as offering adequate safeguards with respect to the protection of the privacy and fundamental rights and freedoms of individuals and as regards the exercise of the corresponding rights as required by Article 26(2) of Directive 95/46/EC.

Article 2

This Decision concerns only the adequacy of protection provided by the standard contractual clauses set out in the Annex for the transfer of personal data to processors. It does not affect the application of other national provisions implementing Directive 95/46/EC that pertain to the processing of personal data within the Member States.

This Decision shall apply to the transfer of personal data by controllers established in the Community to recipients established outside the territory of the Community who act only as processors.

Article 3

For the purposes of this Decision:

(a) the definitions in Directive 95/46/EC shall apply;

(b) 'special categories of data' means the data referred to in Article 8 of that Directive;

(c) 'supervisory authority' means the authority referred to in Article 28 of that Directive;

(d) 'data exporter' means the controller who transfers the personal data;

(e) 'data importer' means the processor established in a third country who agrees to receive from the data exporter personal data intended for processing on the data exporter's behalf after the transfer in accordance with his instructions and the terms of this Decision and who is not subject to a third country's system ensuring adequate protection;

(f) 'applicable data protection law' means the legislation protecting the fundamental rights and freedoms of natural persons and, in particular, their right to privacy with respect to the processing of personal data applicable to a data controller in the Member State in which the data exporter is established;

(g) 'technical and organisational security measures' means those measures aimed at protecting personal data against accidental or unlawful destruction or accidental loss, alteration, unauthorised disclosure or access, in particular where the processing involves the transmission of data over a network, and against all other unlawful forms of processing.

Article 4

1. Without prejudice to their powers to take action to ensure compliance with national provisions adopted pursuant to Chapters II, III, V and VI of Directive 95/46/EC, the competent authorities in the Member States may exercise their existing powers to prohibit or suspend data flows to third countries in order to protect individuals with regard to the processing of their personal data in cases where:

(a) it is established that the law to which the data importer is subject imposes upon him requirements to derogate from the applicable data protection law which go beyond the restrictions necessary in a democratic society as provided for in Article 13 of Directive 95/46/EC where those requirements are likely to have a substantial adverse effect on the guarantees provided by the ap-

plicable data protection law and the standard contractual clauses; or

(b) a competent authority has established that the data importer has not respected the contractual clauses in the Annex; or

(c) there is a substantial likelihood that the standard contractual clauses in the Annex are not being or will not be complied with and the continuing transfer would create an imminent risk of grave harm to the data subjects.

2. The prohibition or suspension pursuant to paragraph 1 shall be lifted as soon as the reasons for the suspension or prohibition no longer exist.

3. When Member States adopt measures pursuant to paragraphs 1 and 2, they shall, without delay, inform the Commission which will forward the information to the other Member States.

Article 5

The Commission shall evaluate the operation of this Decision on the basis of available information three years after its notification to the Member States. It shall submit a report on the findings to the Committee established under Article 31 of Directive 95/46/EC. It shall include any evidence that could affect the evaluation concerning the adequacy of the standard contractual clauses in the Annex and any evidence that this Decision is being applied in a discriminatory way.

Article 6

This Decision shall apply from 3 April 2002.

Article 7

This Decision is addressed to the Member States.

ANNEX

Standard Contractual Clauses (processors)

For the purposes of Article 26(2) of Directive 95/46/EC for the transfer of personal data to processors established in third countries wich do not ensure an adequate level of data protection

Name of the data exporting organisation: ....

address: ....

....

tel.: ....;   fax: ....;   e-mail: ....

Other information needed to identify the organisation:

....

(the data exporter)

and

Name of the data importing organisation: ....

address: ....

....

tel.: ....;   fax: ....;   e-mail: ....

Other information needed to identify the organisation:

....

('the data importer')

HAVE AGREED on the following Contractual Clauses (the Clauses) in order to adduce adequate safeguards with respect to the protection of privacy and fundamental rights and freedoms of individuals for the transfer by the data exporter to the data importer of the personal data specified in Appendix 1.

Clause 1

Definitions

For the purposes of the Clauses:
(a) 'personal data', 'special categories of data', 'process/processing', 'controller', 'processor', 'data subject' and 'supervisory authority' shall have the same meaning as in Directive 95/46/EC of the European Parliament and of the Council of 24 October 1995 on the protection of individuals with regard to the processing of personal data and on the free movement of such data (the Directive) ([1]);
(b) the 'data exporter' shall mean the controller who transfers the personal data;
(c) the 'data importer' shall mean the processor who agrees to receive from the data exporter personal data intended for processing on his behalf after the transfer in accordance with his instructions and the terms of these Clauses and who is not subject to a third country's system ensuring to adequate protection;
(d) 'the applicable data protection law' shall mean the legislation protecting the fundamental rights and freedoms of natural persons and, in particular, their right to privacy with

---

([1]) Parties may reproduce definitions and meanings contained in Directive 95/46/EC within this Clause if they considered it better for the contract to stand alone.

   16

respect to the processing of personal data applicable to a data controller in the Member State in wich the data exporter is established;

(e) 'technical and organisational security measures' shall mean those measures aimed at protecting personal data against accidental or unlawful destruction or accidental loss, alteration , unauthorised disclosure or access, in particular where the processing involves the transmission of data over a network, and against all other unlawful forms of processing.

Clause 2

Details of the transfer

The details of the transfer and in particular the categories of personal data where applicable are specified in Appendix 1 wich forms an integral part of the Clauses.

Clause 3

Third-party beneficiary clause

The data subjects can enforce the data exporter this Clause, Clause 4(b) to (h), Clause 5(a) to (e) and (g), Clause 6(1) and (2), Clause 7, Clause 8(2), and Clauses 9, 10 and 11, as third-party beneficaries.

The data subjects can enforce the data importer this Clause, Clause 5(a) to (e) and (g), Clause 6(1) and (2), Clause 7, Clause 8(2), and Clauses 9, 10 and 11, in cases where the data exporter has factually disappeared or has ceased to exist in law.

The parties do not object to the data subjects being represented by an association or other bodies if they so wish and if permitted by national law.

Clause 4

Obligations of the data exporter

The data exporter agrees and warrants:

(a) that the processing, including the transfer itself, of the personal data by him has been and will continue to be carried out in accordance with the relevant provisions of the applicable data protection law (and where applicable has been notified to the relevant authorities of the Member State where the data exporter is established) and does not violate the relevant provisions of that State;

(b) that he has instructed and troughout the duration of the personal data processing services will instruct the data importer to process the personal data transferred only on the data exporter's behalf and in accordance with the applicable data protection law and these clauses;

(c) that the data importer shall provide sufficient guarantees in respect of the technical and organisational security measures specified in Appendix 2 to this contract;

(d) that after assessment of the requirements of the applicable data protection law, the security measures are appropriate to protect personal data against accidental or unlawful destruction or accidental loss, alteration, unauthorised disclosure or access, in particular where the processing involves the transmission of data over a network, and against all other unlawful forms of processing, and that these measures ensure a level of security appropriate to the risk presented by the processing and the nature of the data to be protected having regard to the state of the art and the cost of their implementation;

(e) that will ensure compliance with the security measures;

(f) that, if the transfer involves special categories of data, the data subject has been informed or will be informed before, or as soon as possible after, the transfer that his data could be transmitted to a third country not providing adequate protection;

(g) that he agrees to forward the notification received from the data importer pursuant to Clause 5(b) to the data protection supervisory authority if he decides to continue the transfer or to lift his suspension;

(h) to make available to the data subjects upon request a copy of the Clauses set out in this Annex, with the exception of Appendix 2 wich shall be replaced by a summary description of the security measures.

Clause 5
Obligations of the data importer ([1])

The data importer agrees and warrants:

(a) to process the personal data only on behalf of the data exporter and in compliance with his instructions and the clauses; if he cannot provide such compliance for whatever reasons, he agrees to inform promptly the data exporter of his inybility to comply, in wich case the data exporter is entitled to suspend the transfer of data and/or terminate the contract;

(b) that he has no reason to believe that the legislation applicable to him prevents him from fulfilling the instructions received from the data exporter and his obligations under the contract and that in the event of a change in this legislation wich is likely to have a substantial adverse effect on the warranties and obligations provided by the Clauses, he will promptly notify the change to the data exporter as soon as he is aware, in wich case the data exporter is entitled to suspend the transfer of data and/or terminate the contract;

(c) that he has implemented the technical and organisational security measures specified in Appendix 2 before processing the personal data transferred;

(d) that he shall promptly notify the data exporter about:
 (i) any legally binding request for disclosure of the personal data by law enforcement authority unless otherwise prohibited, such as a prohibition under criminal law to preserve the confidentiality of a law enforcement investigation;
 (ii) any accidental or unauthorised access; and
 (iii) any request received derictly from the data subjects without responding to that request, unless he has been otherwise authorised to do so;

(e) to deal promptly and proberly with all inquires from the data exporter relating to his processing of the personal data subject to the transfer and to abide by the advice of the supervisory authority with regard to the processing of the data transferred;

(f) at the request of the data exporter to submit his data processing facilities for audit of the processing activities covered by the clauses wich shall be carried out by the data exporter or an inspection body composed of independent members and in possession of the required professional qualifications bound by a duty of confidentiality, selected by the data exporter, where applicable, in agreement with the supervisory authority;

(g) to make available to the data subject upon request a copy of the Clauses set out in this Annex, with the exception of Appendix 2 wich shall be replaced by a summary description of the security measures in those cases where the data subject is unable to obtain a copy from the data exporter.

Clause 6
Liability

1. The parties agree that a data subject who has suffered damage as a result of any violation of the provisions referred to in Clause 3 is entitled to receive compensation from the data exporter for the damage suffered.

([1]) Mandatory requirements of the data importer wich do not go beyond what is necessary in a democratic society on the basis of one of the interests listed in Article 13(1) of Directive 95/46/EC, that is, if they constitute a necessary measure to safeguard national security defence, public security, the prevention, investigation, detection and prosecution of criminal offences or of breaches of ethics for the regulated professions, an important economic or financial interest of the State or the protection of the data subject or the rights and freedoms of other, are not in contradiction with the standard contractual clauses. Some examples of such mandatory requirements wich do not beyond what is necessary in a democratic society are, inter alia, internationally recognised sanctions, tax-reporting requirements or anti-money-laundering reporting requirements.

16

2002 Standard Contractual Privacy Clauses for Non-EU Member States

2. If a data subject is not able to bring the action referred to in paragraph 1 arising out of a breach by the data importer of any of his obligations referred to in Clause 3 against the data exporter because the data exporter has disappeared factually or has ceased to exist in law or became insolvent, the data importer agrees that the data subject may issue a claim against the data importer as if he were the data exporter.

3. The parties agree that if one party is held liable for a violation of the clauses committed by the other party, the latter will, to the extent to wich it is liable, indemnify the first party for any cost, charge, damages, expenses or loss it has incurred.

Indemnifaction is contingent upon:

(a) the data exporterpromptly notifying the data importer of claim; and

(b) the data importer being given the possibility to cooperate with the data exporter in the defence and settlement of the claim (¹).

Clause 7
Mediation und jurisdiction

1. The data importer agrees that if the data subject invokes the third-party beneficiary rights and/or claims compensation for damages under the clauses, the data importer will accept the decision of the data subject:

(a) to refer the dispute to mediation by an independent person or, where applicable, by the supervisory authority;

(b) to refer the dispute to the courts in the Member State in wich the data exporter is established.

2. The data importer agrees that, by agreement with the data subject, the resolution of a specific dispute can be referred to an arbitration body if the data importer is established in a country which has ratified the New York Convention on enforcement of arbitration awards.

3. The parties agree that the choice made by the data subject will not prejudice his substantitve or procedural rights to seek remedies in accordance with other provisions of national or international law.

Clause 8
Cooperation with supervisory authorities

1. The data exporter agrees to deposit a copy of this contract with the supervisory authority if it so requests or if such deposit its required under the applicable data protection law.

2. The parties agree that the supervisory authority has the right to conduct an audit of the data importer which has the same scope and is subject to the same conditions as would apply to an audit of the data exporter under the applicable data protection law.

Clause 9
Governing Law

The Clauses shall be governed by the law of the Member State in wich the data exporter is established, namely . . . .

Clause 10
Variation of the contract

The parties undertake not to vary or modify the terms of the clauses.

(¹) Paragraph 3 is optional.

Clause 11

Obligation after the termination of personal data processing services

1. The parties agree that on the termination of the provision of data processing services, the data importer shall, at the choice of the data exporter, return al the personal data transferred and the choices thereof to the data exporter or shall destroy all the personal data and certify to the data exporter that he has done so, unless legislation imposed upon the data importer prevents him from returning or destroying all or part of the personal data transferred. In that case, the data importer warrants that he will guarantee the confidentiality of the personal data transferred and will not actively process the personal data transferred anymore.

2. The data importer warrants that upon request of the data exporter and/or of the supervisory authority, he will submit his data processing facilities for an audit of the measures referred to in paragraph 1.

On behalf of the data exporter:

Name (written out in full): . . . .

Position: . . . .

Address: . . . .

Other information necessary in order for the contract to be binding (if any): . . . .

. . . .

Signature . . . .

(stamp of organisation)

On behalf of the data importer:

Name (written out in full): . . . .

Position: . . . .

Address: . . . .

Other information necessary in order for the contract to be binding (if any): . . . .

Signature . . . .

(stamp of organisation)

16

Appendix 1
to the standard contractual clauses

This Appendix forms part of the Clauses and must be completed and signed by the parties.

(*) The Member States may complete or specify, according to their national procedures, any additional necessary information to be contained in this Appendix.)

Data exporter

The data exporter is (please specify briefly your activities relevant to the transfer):

. . . .

. . . .

. . . .

Data importer

The data importer is (please specify briefly your activities relevant to the transfer):

. . . .

. . . .

. . . .

Data subjects

The personal data transferred concern the following categories of data subjects (please specify):

. . . .

. . . .

. . . .

Categories of data

The personal data transferred fall within the following categories of data (please specify):

. . . .

. . . .

. . . .

Special categories of data (if appropriate)

The personal data transferred concern the following special categories of data (please specify):

. . . .

. . . .

. . . .

Processing operations

The personal data transferred will be subject to the following basic processing activities (please specify):

....

....

....

DATA EXPORTER

Name: ....

Authorised signature

....

DATA IMPORTER

Name: ....

Authorised signature

....

Appendix 2
to the standard contractual clauses

This Appendix forms part of the Clauses and must be completed and signed by the parties.

Description of the technical and organisational security measures implemented by the data importer in accordance with Clauses 4(d) and 5(c) (or document/legislation attached):

....

....

....

16

17

Rome Convention on the Law Applicable to Contractual Obligations

consolidated version, OJ C 334, 30. 12. 2005, p. 1

PRELIMINARY NOTE

[. . .] The text printed in this edition was drawn up by the General Secretariat of the Council, in whose archives the originals of the instruments concerned are deposited. It should be noted, however, that this text has no binding force. The official texts of the instruments consolidated are to be found in the following Official Journals.

German ǀ L 266, 9. 10. 1980, p. 1 ǀ L 146, 31. 5. 1984, p. 1 ǀ L 48, 20. 2. 1989, p. 1 ǀ L 48, 20. 2. 1989, p. 17 ǀ L 333, 18. 11. 1992, p. 1 ǀ C 15, 15. 1. 1997, p. 10 ǀ C 169, 8. 7. 2005, p. 1 ǀ

English ǀ L 266, 9. 10. 1980, p. 1 ǀ L 146, 31. 5. 1984, p. 1 ǀ L 48, 20. 2. 1989, p. 1 ǀ L 48, 20. 2. 1989, p. 17 ǀ L 333, 18. 11. 1992, p. 1 ǀ C 15, 15. 1. 1997, p. 10 ǀ C 169, 8. 7. 2005, p. 1 ǀ

Danish ǀ L 266, 9. 10. 1980, p. 1 ǀ L 146, 31. 5. 1984, p. 1 ǀ L 48, 20. 2. 1989, p. 1 ǀ L 48, 20. 2. 1989, p. 17 ǀ L 333, 18. 11. 1992, p. 1 ǀ C 15, 15. 1. 1997, p. 10 ǀ C 169, 8. 7. 2005, p. 1 ǀ

French ǀ L 266, 9. 10. 1980, p. 1 ǀ L 146, 31. 5. 1984, p. 1 ǀ L 48, 20. 2. 1989, p. 1 ǀ L 48, 20. 2. 1989, p. 17 ǀ L 333, 18. 11. 1992, p. 1 ǀ C 15, 15. 1. 1997, p. 10 ǀ C 169, 8. 7. 2005, p. 1 ǀ

Greek ǀ L 146, 31. 5. 1984, p. 7 ǀ L 146, 31. 5. 1984, p. 1 ǀ L 48, 20. 2. 1989, p. 1 ǀ L 48, 20. 2. 1989, p. 17 ǀ L 333, 18. 11. 1992, p. 1 ǀ C 15, 15. 1. 1997, p. 10 ǀ C 169, 8. 7. 2005, p. 1 ǀ

Irish ǀ Special Edition (L 266) ǀ Special Edition (L 146) ǀ Special Edition (L 48) ǀ Special Edition (L 48) ǀ Special Edition (L 333) ǀ Special Edition (C 15) ǀ Special Edition (C 169) ǀ

Italian ǀ L 266, 9. 10. 1980, p. 1 ǀ L 146, 31. 5. 1984, p. 1 ǀ L 48, 20. 2. 1989, p. 1 ǀ L 48, 20. 2. 1989, p. 17 ǀ L 333, 18. 11. 1992, p. 1 ǀ C 15, 15. 1. 1997, p. 10 ǀ C 169, 8. 7. 2005, p. 1 ǀ

Dutch ǀ L 266, 9. 10. 1980, p. 1 ǀ L 146, 31. 5. 1984, p. 1 ǀ L 48, 20. 2. 1989, p. 1 ǀ L 48, 20. 2. 1989, p. 17 ǀ L 333, 18. 11. 1992, p. 1 ǀ C 15, 15. 1. 1997, p. 10 ǀ C 169, 8. 7. 2005, p. 1 ǀ

Spanish ǀ Special Edition, Chapter 1, Volume 3, p. 36 (see also OJ L 333, p. 17) ǀ Special Edition, Chapter 1, Volume 4, p. 36 (see also OJ L 333, p. 72) ǀ L 48, 20. 2. 1989, p. 1 ǀ L 48, 20. 2. 1989, p. 17 ǀ L 333, 18. 11. 1992, p. 1 ǀ C 15, 15. 1. 1997, p. 10 ǀ C 169, 8. 7. 2005, p. 1 ǀ

Portuguese ǀ Special Edition, Chapter 1, Volume 3, p. 36 (see also OJ L 333, p. 7) ǀ Special Edition, Chapter 1, Volume 4, p. 72 (see also OJ L 333, p. 7) ǀ L 48, 20. 2. 1989, p. 1 ǀ L 48, 20. 2. 1989, p. 17 ǀ L 333, 18. 11. 1992, p. 1 ǀ C 15, 15. 1. 1997, p. 10 ǀ C 169, 8. 7. 2005, p. 1 ǀ

Finnish ǀ C 15, 15. 1. 1997, p. 70 ǀ C 15, 15. 1. 1997, p. 66 ǀ C 15, 15. 1. 1997, p. 60 ǀ C 15, 15. 1. 1997, p. 64 ǀ C 15, 15. 1. 1997, p. 68 ǀ C 15, 15. 1. 1997, p. 53 ǀ C 169, 8. 7. 2005, p. 1 ǀ

17

Swedish | C 15, 15. 1. 1997, p. 70 |
C 15, 15. 1. 1997, p. 66 | C 15, 15. 1.
1997, p. 60 | C 15, 15. 1. 1997, p. 64 |
C 15, 15. 1. 1997, p. 68 | C 15, 15. 1.
1997, p. 53 | C 169, 8. 7. 2005, p. 1 |

Czech | C 169, 8. 7. 2005, p. 10 |
C 169, 8. 7. 2005, p. 23 | C 169, 8. 7.
2005, p. 10 | C 169, 8. 7. 2005, p. 10 |
C 169, 8. 7. 2005, p. 26 | C 169, 8. 7.
2005, p. 28 | C 169, 8. 7. 2005, p. 1 |

Estonian | C 169, 8. 7. 2005, p. 10 |
C 169, 8. 7. 2005, p. 23 | C 169, 8. 7.
2005, p. 10 | C 169, 8. 7. 2005, p. 10 |
C 169, 8. 7. 2005, p. 26 | C 169, 8. 7.
2005, p. 28 | C 169, 8. 7. 2005, p. 1 |

Latvian | C 169, 8. 7. 2005, p. 10 |
C 169, 8. 7. 2005, p. 23 | C 169, 8. 7.
2005, p. 10 | C 169, 8. 7. 2005, p. 10 |
C 169, 8. 7. 2005, p. 26 | C 169, 8. 7.
2005, p. 28 | C 169, 8. 7. 2005, p. 1 |

Lithuanian | C 169, 8. 7. 2005, p. 10 |
C 169, 8. 7. 2005, p. 23 | C 169, 8. 7.
2005, p. 10 | C 169, 8. 7. 2005, p. 10 |
C 169, 8. 7. 2005, p. 26 | C 169, 8. 7.
2005, p. 28 | C 169, 8. 7. 2005, p. 1 |

Hungarian | C 169, 8. 7. 2005, p. 10 |
C 169, 8. 7. 2005, p. 23 | C 169, 8. 7.
2005, p. 10 | C 169, 8. 7. 2005, p. 10 |
C 169, 8. 7. 2005, p. 26 | C 169, 8. 7.
2005, p. 28 | C 169, 8. 7. 2005, p. 1 |

Maltese | C 169, 8. 7. 2005, p. 10 |
C 169, 8. 7. 2005, p. 23 | C 169, 8. 7.
2005, p. 10 | C 169, 8. 7. 2005, p. 10 |
C 169, 8. 7. 2005, p. 26 | C 169, 8. 7.
2005, p. 28 | C 169, 8. 7. 2005, p. 1 |

Polish | C 169, 8. 7. 2005, p. 10 |
C 169, 8. 7. 2005, p. 23 | C 169, 8. 7.
2005, p. 10 | C 169, 8. 7. 2005, p. 10 |
C 169, 8. 7. 2005, p. 26 | C 169, 8. 7.
2005, p. 28 | C 169, 8. 7. 2005, p. 1 |

Slovak | C 169, 8. 7. 2005, p. 10 |
C 169, 8. 7. 2005, p. 23 | C 169, 8. 7.
2005, p. 10 | C 169, 8. 7. 2005, p. 10 |
C 169, 8. 7. 2005, p. 26 | C 169, 8. 7.
2005, p. 28 | C 169, 8. 7. 2005, p. 1 |

Slovene | C 169, 8. 7. 2005, p. 10 |
C 169, 8. 7. 2005, p. 23 | C 169, 8. 7.
2005, p. 10 | C 169, 8. 7. 2005, p. 10 |
C 169, 8. 7. 2005, p. 26 | C 169, 8. 7.
2005, p. 28 | C 169, 8. 7. 2005, p. 1 |

CONVENTION[1]) ON THE LAW APPLICABLE TO CONTRACTUAL OBLIGATIONS OPENED FOR SIGNATURE IN ROME ON 19 JUNE 1980

PREAMBLE

THE HIGH CONTRACTING PARTIES to the Treaty establishing the European Economic Community,

ANXIOUS to continue in the field of private international law the work of unification of law which has already been done within the Community, in particular in the field of jurisdiction and enforcement of judgments,

WISHING to establish uniform rules concerning the law applicable to contractual obligations, HAVE AGREED AS FOLLOWS:

---

[1]) Text as amended by the Convention of 10 April 1984 on the accession of the Hellenic Republic – hereafter referred to as the '1984 Accession Convention' –, by the Convention of 18 May 1992 on the accession of the Kingdom of Spain and the Portuguese Republic – hereafter referred to as the '1992 Accession Convention' –, by the Convention of 29 November 1996 on the accession of the Republic of Austria, the Republic of Finland and the Kingdom of Sweden – hereafter referred to as the '1996 Accession Convention' – and by the Convention of 14 April 2005 on the accession of the Czech Republic, the Republic of Estonia, the Republic of Cyprus, the Republic of Latvia, the Republic of Lithuania, the Republic of Hungary, the Republic of Malta, the Republic of Poland, the Republic of Slovenia and the Slovak Republic – hereafter referred to as the '2005 Accession Convention.'

17

TITLE I
SCOPE OF THE CONVENTION

Article 1
Scope of the Convention

1. The rules of this Convention shall apply to contractual obligations in any situation involving a choice between the laws of different countries.

2. They shall not apply to:

(a) questions involving the status or legal capacity of natural persons, without prejudice to Article 11;

(b) contractual obligations relating to:

– wills and succession,

– rights in property arising out of a matrimonial relationship,

– rights and duties arising out of a family relationship, parentage, marriage or affinity, including maintenance obligations in respect of children who are not legitimate;

(c) obligations arising under bills of exchange, cheques and promissory notes and other negotiable instruments to the extent that the obligations under such other negotiable instruments arise out of their negotiable character;

(d) arbitration agreements and agreements on the choice of court;

(e) questions governed by the law of companies and other bodies corporate or unincorporate such as the creation, by registration or otherwise, legal capacity, internal organisation or winding up of companies and other bodies corporate or unincorporate and the personal liability of officers and members as such for the obligations of the company or body;

(f) the question whether an agent is able to bind a principal, or an organ to bind a company or body corporate or unincorporate, to a third party;

(g) the constitution of trusts and the relationship between settlors, trustees and beneficiaries;

(h) evidence and procedure, without prejudice to Article 14.

3. The rules of this Convention do not apply to contracts of insurance which cover risks situated in the territories of the Member States of the European Economic Community. In order to determine whether a risk is situated in those territories the court shall apply its internal law.

4. The preceding paragraph does not apply to contracts of re-insurance.

Article 2
Application of law of non-contracting States

Any law specified by this Convention shall be applied whether or not it is the law of a Contracting State.

TITLE II
UNIFORM RULES

Article 3
Freedom of choice

1. A contract shall be governed by the law chosen by the parties. The choice must be expressed or demonstrated with reasonable certainty by the terms of the contract or the circumstances of the case. By their choice the parties can select the law applicable to the whole or a part only of the contract.

2. The parties may at any time agree to subject the contract to a law other than that which previously governed it, whether as a result of an earlier choice under this Article or of other provisions of this Convention. Any variation by the parties of the law to be applied made after the conclusion of the contract shall not prejudice its formal

validity under Article 9 or adversely affect the rights of third parties.

3. The fact that the parties have chosen a foreign law, whether or not accompanied by the choice of a foreign tribunal, shall not, where all the other elements relevant to the situation at the time of the choice are connected with one country only, prejudice the application of rules of the law at the country which cannot be derogated from by contract, hereinafter called 'mandatory rules'.

4. The existence and validity of the consent of the parties as to the choice of the applicable law shall be determined in accordance with the provisions of Articles 8, 9 and 11.

Article 4
Applicable law in the absence of choice

1. To the extent that the law applicable to the contract has not been chosen in accordance with Article 3, the contract shall be governed by the law of the country with which it is most closely connected. Nevertheless, a separable part of the contract which has a closer connection with another country may by way of exception be governed by the law of that other country.

2. Subject to the provisions of paragraph 5 of this Article, it shall be presumed that the contract is most closely connected with the country where the party who is to effect the performance which is characteristic of the contract has, at the time of conclusion of the contract, his habitual residence, or, in the case of a body corporate or unincorporate, its central administration. However, if the contract is entered into in the course of that party's trade or profession, that country shall be the country in which the principal place of business is situated or, where under the terms of the contract the performance is to be effected through a place of business other than the principal place of business, the country in which that other place of business is situated.

3. Notwithstanding the provisions of paragraph 2 of this Article, to the extent that the subject matter of the contract is a right in immovable property or a right to use immovable property it shall be presumed that the contract is most closely connected with the country where the immovable property is situated.

4. A contract for the carriage of goods shall not be subject to the presumption in paragraph 2. In such a contract if the country in which, at the time the contract is concluded, the carrier has his principal place of business is also the country in which the place of loading or the place of discharge or the principal place of business of the consignor is situated, it shall be presumed that the contract is most closely connected with that country. In applying this paragraph single voyage charterparties and other contracts the main purpose of which is the carriage of goods shall be treated as contracts for the carriage of goods.

5. Paragraph 2 shall not apply if the characteristic performance cannot be determined, and the presumptions in paragraphs 2, 3 and 4 shall be disregarded if it appears from the circumstances as a whole that the contract is more closely connected with another country.

Article 5
Certain consumer contracts

1. This Article applies to a contract the object of which is the supply of goods or services to a person ('the con-

sumer') for a purpose which can be regarded as being outside his trade or profession, or a contract for the provision of credit for that object.

2. Notwithstanding the provisions of Article 3, a choice of law made by the parties shall not have the result of depriving the consumer of the protection afforded to him by the mandatory rules of the law of the country in which he has his habitual residence:

– if in that country the conclusion of the contract was preceded by a specific invitation addressed to him or by advertising, and he had taken in that country all the steps necessary on his part for the conclusion of the contract, or

– if the other party or his agent received the consumer's order in that country, or

– if the contract is for the sale of goods and the consumer travelled from that country to another country and there gave his order, provided that the consumer's journey was arranged by the seller for the purpose of inducing the consumer to buy.

3. Notwithstanding the provisions of Article 4, a contract to which this Article applies shall, in the absence of choice in accordance with Article 3, be governed by the law of the country in which the consumer has his habitual residence if it is entered into in the circumstances described in paragraph 2 of this Article.

4. This Article shall not apply to:

(a) a contract of carriage;

(b) a contract for the supply of services where the services are to be supplied to the consumer exclusively in a country other than that in which he has his habitual residence.

5. Notwithstanding the provisions of paragraph 4, this Article shall apply to a contract which, for an inclusive price, provides for a combination of travel and accommodation.

Article 6
Individual employment contracts

1. Notwithstanding the provisions of Article 3, in a contract of employment a choice of law made by the parties shall not have the result of depriving the employee of the protection afforded to him by the mandatory rules of the law which would be applicable under paragraph 2 in the absence of choice.

2. Notwithstanding the provisions of Article 4, a contract of employment shall, in the absence of choice in accordance with Article 3, be governed:

(a) by the law of the country in which the employee habitually carries out his work in performance of the contract, even if he is temporarily employed in another country; or

(b) if the employee does not habitually carry out his work in any one country, by the law of the country in which the place of business through which he was engaged is situated; unless it appears from the circumstances as a whole that the contract is more closely connected with another country, in which case the contract shall be governed by the law of that country.

Article 7
Mandatory rules

1. When applying under this Convention the law of a country, effect may be given to the mandatory rules of the law of another country with which the situation has a close connection, if and in so far as, under the law of the latter country, those rules must be applied whatever the law applicable to the con-

tract. In considering whether to give effect to these mandatory rules, regard shall be had to their nature and purpose and to the consequences of their application or non-application.

2. Nothing in this Convention shall restrict the application of the rules of the law of the forum in a situation where they are mandatory irrespective of the law otherwise applicable to the contract.

Article 8
Material validity

1. The existence and validity of a contract, or of any term of a contract, shall be determined by the law which would govern it under this Convention if the contract or term were valid.

2. Nevertheless a party may rely upon the law of the country in which he has his habitual residence to establish that he did not consent if it appears from the circumstances that it would not be reasonable to determine the effect of his conduct in accordance with the law specified in the preceding paragraph.

Article 9
Formal validity

1. A contract concluded between persons who are in the same country is formally valid if it satisfies the formal requirements of the law which governs it under this Convention or of the law of the country where it is concluded.

2. A contract concluded between persons who are in different countries is formally valid if it satisfies the formal requirements of the law which governs it under this Convention or of the law of one of those countries.

3. Where a contract is concluded by an agent, the country in which the agent acts is the relevant country for the purposes of paragraphs 1 and 2.

4. An act intended to have legal effect relating to an existing or contemplated contract is formally valid if it satisfies the formal requirements of the law which under this Convention governs or would govern the contract or of the law of the country where the act was done.

5. The provisions of the preceding paragraphs shall not apply to a contract to which Article 5 applies, concluded in the circumstances described in paragraph 2 of Article 5. The formal validity of such a contract is governed by the law of the country in which the consumer has his habitual residence.

6. Notwithstanding paragraphs 1 to 4 of this Article, a contract the subject matter of which is a right in immovable property or a right to use immovable property shall be subject to the mandatory requirements of form of the law of the country where the property is situated if by that law those requirements are imposed irrespective of the country where the contract is concluded and irrespective of the law governing the contract.

Article 10
Scope of applicable law

1. The law applicable to a contract by virtue of Articles 3 to 6 and 12 of this Convention shall govern in particular:

(a) interpretation;

(b) performance;

(c) within the limits of the powers conferred on the court by its procedural law, the consequences of breach, including the assessment of damages in so far as it is governed by rules of law;

(d) the various ways of extinguishing obligations, and prescription and limitation of actions;

(e) the consequences of nullity of the contract.

2. In relation to the manner of performance and the steps to be taken in the event of defective performance regard shall be had to the law of the country in which performance takes place.

Article 11
Incapacity

In a contract concluded between persons who are in the same country, a natural person who would have capacity under the law of that country may invoke his incapacity resulting from another law only if the other party to the contract was aware of this incapacity at the time of the conclusion of the contract or was not aware thereof as a result of negligence.

Article 12
Voluntary assignment

1. The mutual obligations of assignor and assignee under a voluntary assignment of a right against another person ('the debtor') shall be governed by the law which under this Convention applies to the contract between the assignor and assignee.

2. The law governing the right to which the assignment relates shall determine its assignability, the relationship between the assignee and the debtor, the conditions under which the assignment can be invoked against the debtor and any question whether the debtor's obligations have been discharged.

Article 13
Subrogation

1. Where a person ('the creditor') has a contractual claim upon another

('the debtor'), and a third person has a duty to satisfy the creditor, or has in fact satisfied the creditor in discharge of that duty, the law which governs the third person's duty to satisfy the creditor shall determine whether the third person is entitled to exercise against the debtor the rights which the creditor had against the debtor under the law governing their relationship and, if so, whether he may do so in full or only to a limited extent.

2. The same rule applies where several persons are subject to the same contractual claim and one of them has satisfied the creditor.

Article 14
Burden of proof, etc.

1. The law governing the contract under this Convention applies to the extent that it contains, in the law of contract, rules which raise presumptions of law or determine the burden of proof.

2. A contract or an act intended to have legal effect may be proved by any mode of proof recognised by the law of the forum or by any of the laws referred to in Article 9 under which that contract or act is formally valid, provided that such mode of proof can be administered by the forum.

Article 15
Exclusion of convoi

The application of the law of any country specified by this Convention means the application of the rules of law in force in that country other than its rules of private international law.

Article 16
'Ordre public'

The application of a rule of the law of any country specified by this Convention may be refused only if such application is manifestly incompatible with the public policy ('ordre public') of the forum.

Article 17
No retrospective effect

This Convention shall apply in a Contracting State to contracts made after the date on which this Convention has entered into force with respect to that State.

Article 18
Uniform interpretation

In the interpretation and application of the preceding uniform rules, regard shall be had to their international character and to the desirability of achieving uniformity in their interpretation and application.

Article 19
States with more than one legal system

1. Where a State comprises several territorial units each of which has its own rules of law in respect of contractual obligations, each territorial unit shall be considered as a country for the purposes of identifying the law applicable under this Convention.

2. A State within which different territorial units have their own rules of law in respect of contractual obligations shall not be bound to apply this Convention to conflicts solely between the laws of such units.

Article 20
Precedence of Community law

This Convention shall not affect the application of provisions which, in relation to particular matters, lay down choice of law rules relating to contractual obligations and which are or will be contained in acts of the institutions of the European Communities or in national laws harmonised in implementation of such acts.

Article 21
Relationship with other conventions

This Convention shall not prejudice the application of international conventions to which a Contracting State is, or becomes, a party.

Article 22
Reservations

1. Any Contracting State may, at the time of signature, ratification, acceptance or approval, reserve the right not to apply:

(a) the provisions of Article 7(1);

(b) the provisions of Article 10(1)(e).

2.[2])

3. Any Contracting State may at any time withdraw a reservation which it has made; the reservation shall cease to have effect on the first day of the third calendar month after notification of the withdrawal.

TITLE III
FINAL PROVISIONS
Article 23

1. If, after the date on which this Convention has entered into force for a Contracting State, that State wishes to adopt any new choice of law rule in regard to any particular category of contract within the scope of this Conven-

---

[2]) Paragraph deleted by Article 2(1) of the 1992 Accession Convention.

17

tion, it shall communicate its intention to the other signatory States through the Secretary-General of the Council of the European Communities.

2. Any signatory State may, within six months from the date of the communication made to the Secretary-General, request him to arrange consultations between signatory States in order to reach agreement. (. . .) [3].

3. If no signatory State has requested consultations within this period or if within two years following the communication made to the Secretary-General no agreement is reached in the course of consultations, the Contracting State concerned may amend its law in the manner indicated. The measures taken by that State shall be brought to the knowledge of the other signatory States through the Secretary-General of the Council of the European Communities.

Article 24

1. If, after the date on which this Convention has entered into force with respect to a Contracting State, that State wishes to become a party to a multilateral convention whose principal aim or one of whose principal aims is to lay down rules of private international law concerning any of the matters governed by this Convention, the procedure set out in Article 23 shall apply. However, the period of two years, referred to in paragraph 3 of that Article, shall be reduced to one year.

2. The procedure referred to in the preceding paragraph need not be followed if a Contracting State or one of the European Communities is already a party to the multilateral convention, or

---

[3] Phrase deleted by the 1992 Accession Convention.

if its object is to revise a convention to which the State concerned is already a party, or if it is a convention concluded within the framework of the Treaties establishing the European Communities.

Article 25

If a Contracting State considers that the unification achieved by this Convention is prejudiced by the conclusion of agreements not covered by Article 24(1), that State may request the Secretary-General of the Council of the European Communities to arrange consultations between the signatory States of this Convention.

Article 26

Any Contracting State may request the revision of this Convention. In this event a revision conference shall be convened by the President of the Council of the European Communities.

Article 27[4]

Article 28

1. This Convention shall be open from 19 June 1980 for signature by the States party to the Treaty establishing the European Economic Community.

2. This Convention shall be subject to ratification, acceptance or approval by the signatory States. The instruments of ratification, acceptance or approval shall be deposited with the Secretary-General of the Council of the European Communities[5].

---

[4] Article deleted by Article 2(1) of the 1992 Accession Convention.

[5] Ratification of the Accession Conventions is governed by the following provisions of those Conventions:

− as regards the 1984 Accession Convention, by Article 3 of that Convention, which reads as follows:

17

Article 29[6])

1. This Convention shall enter into force on the first day of the third month

_____

'Article 3

This Convention shall be ratified by signatory States. The instruments of ratification shall be deposited with the Secretary-General of the Council of the European Communities.',

– as regards the 1992 Accession Convention, by Article 4 of that Convention, which reads as follows:

'Article 4

This Convention shall be ratified by signatory States. The instruments of ratification shall be deposited with the Secretary-General of the Council of the European Communities.',

– as regards the 1996 Accession Convention, by Article 5 of that Convention, which reads as follows:

'Article 5

This Convention shall be ratified by signatory States. The instruments of ratification shall be deposited with the Secretary-General of the Council of the European Union.',

– as regards the 2005 Accession Convention, by Article 4 of the Convention, which reads as follows:

'Article 4

This Convention shall be ratified by signatory States. The instruments of ratification shall be deposited with the Secretary-General of the Council of the European Union.'.

6) The entry into force of the Accession Conventions is governed by the following provisions of those Conventions:

– as regards the 1984 Accession Convention, by Article 4 of that Convention, which reads as follows:

'Article 4

This Convention shall enter into force, as between the States which have ratified it, on the first day of the third month following the deposit of the last instrument of ratification by the Hellenic Republic and seven States which have ratified the Convention on the law applicable to contractual obligations.

This Convention shall enter into force for each Contracting State which subsequently ratifies it on the first day of the third month following the deposit of its instrument of ratification.',

following the deposit of the seventh instrument of ratification, acceptance or approval.

2. This Convention shall enter into force for each signatory State ratifying, accepting or approving at a later date on the first day of the third month following the deposit of its instrument of ratification, acceptance or approval.

_____

– as regards the 1992 Accession Convention, by Article 5 of that Convention, which reads as follows:

'Article 5

This Convention shall enter into force, as between the States which have ratified it, on the first day of the third month following the deposit of the last instrument of ratification by the Kingdom of Spain or the Portuguese Republic and by one State which has ratified the Convention on the law applicable to contractual obligations.

This Convention shall enter into force for each Contracting State which subsequently ratifies it on the first day of the third month following the deposit of its instrument of ratification.',

– as regards the 1996 Accession Convention, by Article 6 of that Convention, which reads as follows:

'Article 6

1. This Convention shall enter into force, as between the States which have ratified it, on the first day of the third month following the deposit of the last instrument of ratification by the Republic of Austria, the Republic of Finland or the Kingdom of Sweden and by one Contracting State which has ratified the Convention on the law applicable to contractual obligations.

2. This Convention shall enter into force for each Contracting State which subsequently ratifies it on the first day of the third month following the deposit of its instrument of ratification.',

– as regards the 2005 Accession Convention, by Article 5 of the Convention, which reads as follows:

'Article 5

1. This Convention shall enter into force between the States which have ratified it, on the first day of the third month following the

Article 30

1. This Convention shall remain in force for 10 years from the date of its entry into force in accordance with Article 29(1), even for States for which it enters into force at a later date.

2. If there has been no denunciation it shall be renewed tacitly every five years.

3. A Contracting State which wishes to denounce shall, not less than six months before the expiration of the period of 10 or five years, as the case may be, give notice to the Secretary-General of the Council of the European Communities.[7]).

4. The denunciation shall have effect only in relation to the State which has notified it. The Convention will remain in force as between all other Contracting States.

Article 31[8])

The Secretary-General of the Council of the European Communities shall

_____

deposit of the second instrument of ratification.'

2. Thereafter, this Convention shall enter into force, for each signatory State which subsequently ratifies it, on the first day of the third month following the deposit of its instrument of ratification.

[7]) Phrase deleted by the 1992 Accession Convention.

[8]) Notification concerning the Accession Conventions is governed by the following provisions of those Conventions:

– as regards the 1984 Accession Convention, by Article 5 of that Convention, which reads as follows:

'Article 5

The Secretary-General of the Council of the European Communities shall notify the signatory States of:

(a) the deposit of each instrument of ratification;

(b) the dates of entry into force of this Convention for the Contracting States.',

notify the States party to the Treaty establishing the European Economic Community of:

(a) the signatures;

(b) deposit of each instrument of ratification, acceptance or approval;

(c) the date of entry into force of this Convention;

(d) communications made in pursuance of Articles 23, 24, 25, 26 and 30[9]);

(e) the reservations and withdrawals of reservations referred to in Article 22.

_____

– as regards the 1992 Accession Convention, by Article 6 of that Convention, which reads as follows:

'Article 6

The Secretary-General of the Council of the European Communities shall notify the signatory States of:

(a) the deposit of each instrument of ratification;

(b) the dates of entry into force of this Convention for the Contracting States.',

– as regards the 1996 Accession Convention, by Article 7 of that Convention, which reads as follows:

'Article 7

The Secretary-General of the Council of the European Union shall notify the signatory States of:

(a) the deposit of each instrument of ratification;

(b) the dates of entry into force of this Convention for the Contracting States.',

– as regards the 2005 Accession Convention, by Article 6 of the Convention, which reads as follows:

'Article 6

The Secretary-General of the Council of the European Communities shall notify the signatory States of:

(a) the deposit of each instrument of ratification;

(b) the dates of entry into force of this Convention for the Contracting States.'

[9]) point (d) as amended by the 1992 Accession Convention.

Article 32

The Protocol annexed to this Convention shall form an integral part thereof.

Article 33[10])

This Convention, drawn up in a single original in the Danish, Dutch,

---

[10]) An indication of the authentic texts of the Accession Convention is to be found in the following provisions:
– as regards the 1984 Accession Convention, in Articles 2 and 6 of that Convention, which reads as follows:
'Article 2
The Secretary-General of the Council of the European Communities shall transmit a certified copy of the Convention on the law applicable to contractual obligations in the Danish, Dutch, English, French, German, Irish and Italian languages to the Government of the Hellenic Republic.
The text of the Convention on the law applicable to contractual obligations in the Greek language is annexed hereto. The text in the Greek language shall be authentic under the same conditions as the other texts of the Convention on the law applicable to contractual obligations.'
'Article 6
This Convention, drawn up in a single original in the Danish, Dutch, English, French, German, Greek, Irish and Italian languages, all eight texts being equally authentic, shall be deposited in the archives of the General Secretariat of the Council of the European Communities. The Secretary-General shall transmit a certified copy to the government of each Signatory State.'
– as regards the 1992 Accession Convention, in Articles 3 and 7 of that Convention, which reads as follows:
'Article 3
1. The Secretary-General of the Council of the European Communities shall transmit a certified copy of the Convention on the law applicable to contractual obligations in the Danish, Dutch, English, French, German, Greek, Irish and Italian languages to the Governments of the Kingdom of Spain and the Portuguese Republic.

English, French, German, Irish and Italian languages, these texts being equally

---

2. The text of the Convention on the law applicable to contractual obligations in the Portuguese and Spanish languages is set out in Annexes I and II to this Convention. The texts drawn up in the Portuguese and Spanish languages shall be authentic under the same conditions as the other texts of the Convention on the law applicable to contractual obligations.'
'Article 7
This Convention, drawn up in a single original in the Danish, Dutch, English, French, German, Greek, Irish, Italian, Portuguese and Spanish languages, all ten texts being equally authentic, shall be deposited in the archives of the General Secretariat of the Council of the European Communities. The Secretary-General shall transmit a certified copy to the government of each Signatory State.'
– as regards the 1996 Accession Convention, in Articles 4 and 8 of that Convention, which read as follows:
'Article 4
1. The Secretary-General of the Council of the European Union shall transmit a certified copy of the Convention of 1980, the Convention of 1984, the First Protocol of 1988, the Second Protocol of 1988 and the Convention of 1992 in the Danish, Dutch, English, French, German, Greek, Irish, Italian, Spanish and Portuguese languages to the Governments of the Republic of Austria, the Republic of Finland and the Kingdom of Sweden.
2. The text of the Convention of 1980, the Convention of 1984, the First Protocol of 1988, the Second Protocol of 1988 and the Convention of 1992 in the Finnish and Swedish languages shall be authentic under the same conditions as the other texts of the Convention of 1980, the Convention of 1984, the First Protocol of 1988, the Second Protocol of 1988 and the Convention of 1992.'
'Article 8
This Convention, drawn up in a single original in the Danish, Dutch, English, Finnish, French, German, Greek, Irish, Italian, Portuguese, Spanish and Swedish languages, all twelve texts being equally authentic, shall

17

authentic, shall be deposited in the archives of the Secretariat of the Council of the European Communities. The

---

be deposited in the archives of the General Secretariat of the Council of the European Union. The Secretary-General shall transmit a certified copy to the government of each Signatory State.'

2. The text of the Convention of 1980, the Convention of 1984, the First Protocol of 1988, the Second Protocol of 1988, the Convention of 1992 and the Convention of 1996 in the Czech, Estonian, Hungarian, Latvian, Lithuanian, Maltese, Polish, Slovakian and Slovenian languages shall be authentic under the same conditions as the other texts of the Convention of 1980, the Convention of 1984, the First Protocol of 1988, the Second Protocol of 1988, the Convention of 1992 and the Convention of 1996.'

'Article 7

This Convention, drawn up in a single original in the Czech, Danish, Dutch, English, Estonian, Finnish, French, German, Greek, Hungarian, Irish, Italian, Latvian, Lithuanian, Maltese, Polish, Portuguese, Slovakian, Slovenian, Spanish and Swedish languages, all twenty-one texts being equally authentic, shall be deposited in the archives of the General Secretariat of the Council of the European Union. The Secretary-General shall transmit a certified copy to the Government of each signatory state.'

– as regards the 2005 Accession Convention, in Articles 3 and 7 of that Convention, which reads as follows:

'Article 3

1. The Secretary-General of the Council of the European Union shall transmit a certified copy of the Convention of 1980, the Convention of 1984, the FirstProtocol of 1988, the Second Protocol of 1988, the Convention of 1992 and the Convention of 1996 in the Danish, Dutch, English, Finnish, French, German, Greek, Irish, Italian, Portuguese, Spanish and Swedish languages to the Governments of the Czech Republic, the Republic of Estonia, the Republic of Cyprus, the Republic of Latvia, the Republic of Lithuania, the Republic of Hungary, the Republic of Malta, the Republic of Poland, the Republic of Slovenia and the Slovak Republic.

Secretary-General shall transmit a certified copy thereof to the Government of each signatory State.

PROTOCOL[11])

The High Contracting Parties have agreed upon the following provision which shall be annexed to the Convention:

'Notwithstanding the provisions of the Convention, Denmark, Sweden and Finland may retain national provisions concerning the law applicable to questions relating to the carriage of goods by sea and may amend such provisions without following the procedure provided for in Article 23 of the Convention of Rome. The national provisions applicable in this respect are the following:

– in Denmark, paragraphs 252 and 321 (3) and (4) of the "Sølov" (maritime law),

---

2. The text of the Convention of 1980, the Convention of 1984, the First Protocol of 1988, the Second Protocol of 1988, the Convention of 1992 and the Convention of 1996 in the Czech, Estonian, Hungarian, Latvian, Lithuanian, Maltese, Polish, Slovakian and Slovenian languages shall be authentic under the same conditions as the other texts of the Convention of 1980, the Convention of 1984, the First Protocol of 1988, the Second Protocol of 1988, the Convention of 1992 and the Convention of 1996.'

'Article 7

This Convention, drawn up in a single original in the Czech, Danish, Dutch, English, Estonian, Finnish, French, German, Greek, Hungarian, Irish, Italian, Latvian, Lithuanian, Maltese, Polish, Portuguese, Slovakian, Slovenian, Spanish and Swedish languages, all twenty-one texts being equally authentic, shall be deposited in the archives of the General Secretariat of the Council of the European Union. The Secretary-General shall transmit a certified copy to the Government of each signatory state.'

[11]) Text as amended by the 1996 Accession Convention.

17

– in Sweden, Chapter 13, Article 2(1) and (2), and Chapter 14, Article 1(3), of "sjölagen" (maritime law),

– in Finland, Chapter 13, Article 2(1) and (2), and Chapter 14, Article 1(3), of "merilaki"/"sjölagen" (maritime law).'

17

18

Jurisdiction and Enforcement Regulation
Council Regulation (EC) No 44/2001 of 22 December 2000 on jurisdiction and the recognition and enforcement of judgments in civil and commercial matters

OJ L 12, 16. 1. 2001, p. 1, amended by OJ L 225, 22. 8. 2002, p. 13, OJ L 236, 23. 9. 2003, p. 33, OJ L 334, 10. 11. 2004, p. 3, OJ L 381, 28. 12. 2004, p. 10, OJ L 363, 20. 12. 2006, p. 1, and corrected by OJ L 307, 24. 11. 2001, p. 28

THE COUNCIL OF THE EUROPEAN UNION,

Having regard to the Treaty establishing the European Community, and in particular Article 61(c) and Article 67(1) thereof,

Having regard to the proposal from the Commission[1]),

Having regard to the opinion of the European Parliament[2]),

Having regard to the opinion of the Economic and Social Committee[3]),

Whereas:

(1) The Community has set itself the objective of maintaining and developing an area of freedom, security and justice, in which the free movement of persons is ensured. In order to establish progressively such an area, the Community should adopt, amongst other things, the measures relating to judicial cooperation in civil matters which are necessary for the sound operation of the internal market.

(2) Certain differences between national rules governing jurisdiction and recognition of judgments hamper the sound operation of the internal market. provisions to unify the rules of conflict of jurisdiction in civil and commercial matters and to simplify the formalities with a view to rapid and simple recognition and enforcement of judgments from Member States bound by this Regulation are essential.

(3) This area is within the field of judicial cooperation in civil matters within the meaning of Article 65 of the Treaty.

(4) In accordance with the principles of subsidiarity and proportionality as set out in Article 5 of the Treaty, the objectives of this Regulation cannot be sufficiently achieved by the Member States and can therefore be better achieved by the Community. This Regulation confines itself to the minimum required in order to achieve those objectives and does not go beyond what is necessary for that purpose.

(5) On 27 September 1968 the Member States, acting under Article 293, fourth indent, of the Treaty, concluded the Brussels Convention on Jurisdiction and the Enforcement of Judgments in Civil and Commercial

---

[1]) OJ C 376, 28. 12. 1999, p. 1.
[2]) Opinion delivered on 21 September 2000 (not yet published in the Official Journal).
[3]) OJ C 117, 26. 4. 2000, p. 6.

18

Matters, as amended by Conventions on the Accession of the New Member States to that Convention (hereinafter referred to as the 'Brussels Convention')[4]. On 16 September 1988 Member States and EFTA States concluded the Lugano Convention on Jurisdiction and the Enforcement of Judgments in Civil and Commercial Matters, which is a parallel Convention to the 1968 Brussels Convention. Work has been undertaken for the revision of those Conventions, and the Council has approved the content of the revised texts. Continuity in the results achieved in that revision should be ensured.

(6) In order to attain the objective of free movement of judgments in civil and commercial matters, it is necessary and appropriate that the rules governing jurisdiction and the recognition and enforcement of judgments be governed by a Community legal instrument which is binding and directly applicable.

(7) The scope of this Regulation must cover all the main civil and commercial matters apart from certain well-defined matters.

(8) There must be a link between proceedings to which this Regulation applies and the territory of the Member States bound by this Regulation. Accordingly common rules on jurisdiction should, in principle, apply when the defendant is domiciled in one of those Member States.

(9) A defendant not domiciled in a Member State is in general subject to national rules of jurisdiction applicable in the territory of the Member State of the court seised, and a defendant domiciled in a Member State not bound by this Regulation must remain subject to the Brussels Convention.

(10) For the purposes of the free movement of judgments, judgments given in a Member State bound by this Regulation should be recognised and enforced in another Member State bound by this Regulation, even if the judgment debtor is domiciled in a third State.

(11) The rules of jurisdiction must be highly predictable and founded on the principle that jurisdiction is generally based on the defendant's domicile and jurisdiction must always be available on this ground save in a few well-defined situations in which the subject-matter of the litigation or the autonomy of the parties warrants a different linking factor. The domicile of a legal person must be defined autonomously so as to make the common rules more transparent and avoid conflicts of jurisdiction.

(12) In addition to the defendant's domicile, there should be alternative grounds of jurisdiction based on a close link between the court and the action or in order to facilitate the sound administration of justice.

(13) In relation to insurance, consumer contracts and employment, the weaker party should be protected by rules of jurisdiction more favourable to his interests than the general rules provide for.

(14) The autonomy of the parties to a contract, other than an insurance, consumer or employment contract, where only limited autonomy to determine the courts having jurisdiction is allowed, must be respected subject to the exclusive grounds of jurisdiction laid down in this Regulation.

---

[4] OJ L 299, 31. 12. 1972, p. 32.
OJ L 304, 30. 10. 1978, p. 1.
OJ L 388, 31. 12. 1982, p. 1.
OJ L 285, 3. 10. 1989, p. 1.
OJ C 15, 15. 1. 1997, p. 1.
For a consolidated text, see OJ C 27, 26. 1. 1998, p. 1.

(15) In the interests of the harmonious administration of justice it is necessary to minimise the possibility of concurrent proceedings and to ensure that irreconcilable judgments will not be given in two Member States. There must be a clear and effective mechanism for resolving cases of *lis pendens* and related actions and for obviating problems flowing from national differences as to the determination of the time when a case is regarded as pending. For the purposes of this Regulation that time should be defined autonomously.

(16) Mutual trust in the administration of justice in the Community justifies judgments given in a Member State being recognised automatically without the need for any procedure except in cases of dispute.

(17) By virtue of the same principle of mutual trust, the procedure for making enforceable in one Member State a judgment given in another must be efficient and rapid. To that end, the declaration that a judgment is enforceable should be issued virtually automatically after purely formal checks of the documents supplied, without there being any possibility for the court to raise of its own motion any of the grounds for non-enforcement provided for by this Regulation.

(18) However, respect for the rights of the defence means that the defendant should be able to appeal in an adversarial procedure, against the declaration of enforceability, if he considers one of the grounds for non-enforcement to be present. Redress procedures should also be available to the claimant where his application for a declaration of enforceability has been rejected.

(19) Continuity between the Brussels Convention and this Regulation should be ensured, and transitional provisions should be laid down to that end. The same need for continuity applies as regards the interpretation of the Brussels Convention by the Court of Justice of the European Communities and the 1971 Protocol[5]) should remain applicable also to cases already pending when this Regulation enters into force.

(20) The United Kingdom and Ireland, in accordance with Article 3 of the Protocol on the position of the United Kingdom and Ireland annexed to the Treaty on European Union and to the Treaty establishing the European Community, have given notice of their wish to take part in the adoption and application of this Regulation.

(21) Denmark, in accordance with Articles 1 and 2 of the Protocol on the position of Denmark annexed to the Treaty on European Union and to the Treaty establishing the European Community, is not participating in the adoption of this Regulation, and is therefore not bound by it nor subject to its application.

(22) Since the Brussels Convention remains in force in relations between Denmark and the Member States that are bound by this Regulation, both the Convention and the 1971 Protocol continue to apply between Denmark and the Member States bound by this Regulation.

(23) The Brussels Convention also continues to apply to the territories of the Member States which fall within the territorial scope of that Convention

---

[5]) OJ L 204, 2. 8. 1975, p. 28.
OJ L 304, 30. 10. 1978, p. 1.
OJ L 388, 31. 12. 1982, p. 1.
OJ L 285, 3. 10. 1989, p. 1.
OJ C 15, 15. 1. 1997, p. 1.
For a consolidated text see OJ C 27, 26. 1. 1998, p. 28.

and which are excluded from this Regulation pursuant to Article 299 of the Treaty.

(24) Likewise for the sake of consistency, this Regulation should not affect rules governing jurisdiction and the recognition of judgments contained in specific Community instruments.

(25) Respect for international commitments entered into by the Member States means that this Regulation should not affect conventions relating to specific matters to which the Member States are parties.

(26) The necessary flexibility should be provided for in the basic rules of this Regulation in order to take account of the specific procedural rules of certain Member States. Certain provisions of the Protocol annexed to the Brussels Convention should accordingly be incorporated in this Regulation.

(27) In order to allow a harmonious transition in certain areas which were the subject of special provisions in the Protocol annexed to the Brussels Convention, this Regulation lays down, for a transitional period, provisions taking into consideration the specific situation in certain Member States.

(28) No later than five years after entry into force of this Regulation the Commission will present a report on its application and, if need be, submit proposals for adaptations.

(29) The Commission will have to adjust Annexes I to IV on the rules of national jurisdiction, the courts or competent authorities and redress procedures available on the basis of the amendments forwarded by the Member State concerned; amendments made to Annexes V and VI should be adopted in accordance with Council Decision 1999/468/EC of 28 June 1999

laying down the procedures for the exercise of implementing powers conferred on the Commission[6]),

HAS ADOPTED THIS REGULATION:

CHAPTER I
SCOPE

Article 1

1. This Regulation shall apply in civil and commercial matters whatever the nature of the court or tribunal. It shall not extend, in particular, to revenue, customs or administrative matters.

2. The Regulation shall not apply to:

(a) the status or legal capacity of natural persons, rights in property arising out of a matrimonial relationship, wills and succession;

(b) bankruptcy, proceedings relating to the winding-up of insolvent companies or other legal persons, judicial arrangements, compositions and analogous proceedings;

(c) social security;

(d) arbitration.

3. In this Regulation, the term 'Member State' shall mean Member States with the exception of Denmark.

CHAPTER II
JURISDICTION

Section 1
General provisions

Article 2

1. Subject to this Regulation, persons domiciled in a Member State shall, whatever their nationality, be sued in the courts of that Member State.

---

[6]) OJ L 184, 17. 7. 1999, p. 23.

2. Persons who are not nationals of the Member State in which they are domiciled shall be governed by the rules of jurisdiction applicable to nationals of that State.

Article 3

1. Persons domiciled in a Member State may be sued in the courts of another Member State only by virtue of the rules set out in Sections 2 to 7 of this Chapter.

2. In particular the rules of national jurisdiction set out in Annex I shall not be applicable as against them.

Article 4

1. If the defendant is not domiciled in a Member State, the jurisdiction of the courts of each Member State shall, subject to Articles 22 and 23, be determined by the law of that Member State.

2. As against such a defendant, any person domiciled in a Member State may, whatever his nationality, avail himself in that State of the rules of jurisdiction there in force, and in particular those specified in Annex I, in the same way as the nationals of that State.

Section 2
Special jurisdiction

Article 5

A person domiciled in a Member State may, in another Member State, be sued:

1. (a) in matters relating to a contract, in the courts for the place of performance of the obligation in question;

(b) for the purpose of this provision and unless otherwise agreed, the place of performance of the obligation in question shall be:

– in the case of the sale of goods, the place in a Member State where, under the contract, the goods were delivered or should have been delivered,

– in the case of the provision of services, the place in a Member State where, under the contract, the services were provided or should have been provided,

(c) if subparagraph (b) does not apply then subparagraph (a) applies;

2. in matters relating to maintenance, in the courts for the place where the maintenance creditor is domiciled or habitually resident or, if the matter is ancillary to proceedings concerning the status of a person, in the court which, according to its own law, has jurisdiction to entertain those proceedings, unless that jurisdiction is based solely on the nationality of one of the parties;

3. in matters relating to tort, *delict* or *quasi-delict*, in the courts for the place where the harmful event occurred or may occur;

4. as regards a civil claim for damages or restitution which is based on an act giving rise to criminal proceedings, in the court seised of those proceedings, to the extent that that court has jurisdiction under its own law to entertain civil proceedings;

5. as regards a dispute arising out of the operations of a branch, agency or other establishment, in the courts for the place in which the branch, agency or other establishment is situated;

6. as settlor, trustee or beneficiary of a trust created by the operation of a statute, or by a written instrument, or created orally and evidenced in writing, in the courts of the Member State in which the trust is domiciled;

7. as regards a dispute concerning the payment of remuneration claimed in respect of the salvage of a cargo or freight, in the court under the authority

of which the cargo or freight in question:

(a) has been arrested to secure such payment, or

(b) could have been so arrested, but bail or other security has been given;

provided that this provision shall apply only if it is claimed that the defendant has an interest in the cargo or freight or had such an interest at the time of salvage.

Article 6

A person domiciled in a Member State may also be sued:

1. where he is one of a number of defendants, in the courts for the place where any one of them is domiciled, provided the claims are so closely connected that it is expedient to hear and determine them together to avoid the risk of irreconcilable judgments resulting from separate proceedings;

2. as a third party in an action on a warranty or guarantee or in any other third party proceedings, in the court seised of the original proceedings, unless these were instituted solely with the object of removing him from the jurisdiction of the court which would be competent in his case;

3. on a counter-claim arising from the same contract or facts on which the original claim was based, in the court in which the original claim is pending;

4. in matters relating to a contract, if the action may be combined with an action against the same defendant in matters relating to rights *in rem* in immovable property, in the court of the Member State in which the property is situated.

Article 7

Where by virtue of this Regulation a court of a Member State has jurisdiction in actions relating to liability from the use or operation of a ship, that court, or any other court substituted for this purpose by the internal law of that Member State, shall also have jurisdiction over claims for limitation of such liability.

Section 3
Jurisdiction in matters relating to insurance

Article 8

In matters relating to insurance, jurisdiction shall be determined by this Section, without prejudice to Article 4 and point 5 of Article 5.

Article 9

1. An insurer domiciled in a Member State may be sued:

(a) in the courts of the Member State where he is domiciled, or

(b) in another Member State, in the case of actions brought by the policyholder, the insured or a beneficiary, in the courts for the place where the plaintiff is domiciled,

(c) if he is a co-insurer, in the courts of a Member State in which proceedings are brought against the leading insurer.

2. An insurer who is not domiciled in a Member State but has a branch, agency or other establishment in one of the Member States shall, in disputes arising out of the operations of the branch, agency or establishment, be deemed to be domiciled in that Member State.

Article 10

In respect of liability insurance or insurance of immovable property, the insurer may in addition be sued in the

18

courts for the place where the harmful event occurred. The same applies if movable and immovable property are covered by the same insurance policy and both are adversely affected by the same contingency.

Article 11

1. In respect of liability insurance, the insurer may also, if the law of the court permits it, be joined in proceedings which the injured party has brought against the insured.

2. Articles 8, 9 and 10 shall apply to actions brought by the injured party directly against the insurer, where such direct actions are permitted.

3. If the law governing such direct actions provides that the policyholder or the insured may be joined as a party to the action, the same court shall have jurisdiction over them.

Article 12

1. Without prejudice to Article 11(3), an insurer may bring proceedings only in the courts of the Member State in which the defendant is domiciled, irrespective of whether he is the policyholder, the insured or a beneficiary.

2. The provisions of this Section shall not affect the right to bring a counter-claim in the court in which, in accordance with this Section, the original claim is pending.

Article 13

The provisions of this Section may be departed from only by an agreement:

1. which is entered into after the dispute has arisen, or

2. which allows the policyholder, the insured or a beneficiary to bring

proceedings in courts other than those indicated in this Section, or

3. which is concluded between a policyholder and an insurer, both of whom are at the time of conclusion of the contract domiciled or habitually resident in the same Member State, and which has the effect of conferring jurisdiction on the courts of that State even if the harmful event were to occur abroad, provided that such an agreement is not contrary to the law of that State, or

4. which is concluded with a policyholder who is not domiciled in a Member State, except in so far as the insurance is compulsory or relates to immovable property in a Member State, or

5. which relates to a contract of insurance in so far as it covers one or more of the risks set out in Article 14.

Article 14

The following are the risks referred to in Article 13(5):

1. any loss of or damage to:

(a) seagoing ships, installations situated offshore or on the high seas, or aircraft, arising from perils which relate to their use for commercial purposes;

(b) goods in transit other than passengers' baggage where the transit consists of or includes carriage by such ships or aircraft;

2. any liability, other than for bodily injury to passengers or loss of or damage to their baggage:

(a) arising out of the use or operation of ships, installations or aircraft as referred to in point 1(a) in so far as, in respect of the latter, the law of the Member State in which such aircraft are registered does not prohibit agreements on jurisdiction regarding insurance of such risks;

(b) for loss or damage caused by goods in transit as described in point 1(b);

3. any financial loss connected with the use or operation of ships, installations or aircraft as referred to in point 1(a), in particular loss of freight or charter-hire;

4. any risk or interest connected with any of those referred to in points 1 to 3;

5. notwithstanding points 1 to 4, all 'large risks' as defined in Council Directive 73/239/EEC[7]), as amended by Council Directives 88/357/EEC[8]) and 90/618/EEC[9]), as they may be amended.

Section 4
Jurisdiction over consumer contracts

Article 15

1. In matters relating to a contract concluded by a person, the consumer, for a purpose which can be regarded as being outside his trade or profession, jurisdiction shall be determined by this Section, without prejudice to Article 4 and point 5 of Article 5, if:

(a) it is a contract for the sale of goods on instalment credit terms; or

(b) it is a contract for a loan repayable by instalments, or for any other form of credit, made to finance the sale of goods; or

(c) in all other cases, the contract has been concluded with a person who pursues commercial or professional ac-

tivities in the Member State of the consumer's domicile or, by any means, directs such activities to that Member State or to several States including that Member State, and the contract falls within the scope of such activities.

2. Where a consumer enters into a contract with a party who is not domiciled in the Member State but has a branch, agency or other establishment in one of the Member States, that party shall, in disputes arising out of the operations of the branch, agency or establishment, be deemed to be domiciled in that State.

3. This Section shall not apply to a contract of transport other than a contract which, for an inclusive price, provides for a combination of travel and accommodation.

Article 16

1. A consumer may bring proceedings against the other party to a contract either in the courts of the Member State in which that party is domiciled or in the courts for the place where the consumer is domiciled.

2. Proceedings may be brought against a consumer by the other party to the contract only in the courts of the Member State in which the consumer is domiciled.

3. This Article shall not affect the right to bring a counter-claim in the court in which, in accordance with this Section, the original claim is pending.

Article 17

The provisions of this Section may be departed from only by an agreement:

1. which is entered into after the dispute has arisen; or

---

[7]) OJ L 228, 16. 8. 1973, p. 3. Directive as last amended by Directive 2000/26/EC of the European Parliament and of the Council (OJ L 181, 20. 7. 2000, p. 65).

[8]) OJ L 172, 4. 7. 1988, p. 1. Directive as last amended by Directive 2000/26/EC.

[9]) OJ L 330, 29. 11. 1990, p. 44.

2. which allows the consumer to bring proceedings in courts other than those indicated in this Section; or

3. which is entered into by the consumer and the other party to the contract, both of whom are at the time of conclusion of the contract domiciled or habitually resident in the same Member State, and which confers jurisdiction on the courts of that Member State, provided that such an agreement is not contrary to the law of that Member State.

Section 5
Jurisdiction over individual contracts of employment

Article 18

1. In matters relating to individual contracts of employment, jurisdiction shall be determined by this Section, without prejudice to Article 4 and point 5 of Article 5.

2. Where an employee enters into an individual contract of employment with an employer who is not domiciled in a Member State but has a branch, agency or other establishment in one of the Member States, the employer shall, in disputes arising out of the operations of the branch, agency or establishment, be deemed to be domiciled in that Member State.

Article 19

An employer domiciled in a Member State may be sued:

1. in the courts of the Member State where he is domiciled; or

2. in another Member State:

(a) in the courts for the place where the employee habitually carries out his work or in the courts for the last place where he did so, or

(b) if the employee does not or did not habitually carry out his work in any one country, in the courts for the place where the business which engaged the employee is or was situated.

Article 20

1. An employer may bring proceedings only in the courts of the Member State in which the employee is domiciled.

2. The provisions of this Section shall not affect the right to bring a counter-claim in the court in which, in accordance with this Section, the original claim is pending.

Article 21

The provisions of this Section may be departed from only by an agreement on jurisdiction:

1. which is entered into after the dispute has arisen; or

2. which allows the employee to bring proceedings in courts other than those indicated in this Section.

Section 6
Exclusive jurisdiction

Article 22

The following courts shall have exclusive jurisdiction, regardless of domicile:

1. in proceedings which have as their object rights *in rem* in immovable property or tenancies of immovable property, the courts of the Member State in which the property is situated.

However, in proceedings which have as their object tenancies of immovable property concluded for temporary private use for a maximum period of six consecutive months, the courts of the Member State in which the defendant is domiciled shall also have jurisdiction, provided that the tenant is a natural person and that the landlord and the tenant are domiciled in the same Member State;

2. in proceedings which have as their object the validity of the constitution, the nullity or the dissolution of companies or other legal persons or associations of natural or legal persons, or of the validity of the decisions of their organs, the courts of the Member State in which the company, legal person or association has its seat. In order to determine that seat, the court shall apply its rules of private international law;

3. in proceedings which have as their object the validity of entries in public registers, the courts of the Member State in which the register is kept;

4. in proceedings concerned with the registration or validity of patents, trade marks, designs, or other similar rights required to be deposited or registered, the courts of the Member State in which the deposit or registration has been applied for, has taken place or is under the terms of a Community instrument or an international convention deemed to have taken place.

Without prejudice to the jurisdiction of the European Patent Office under the Convention on the Grant of European Patents, signed at Munich on 5 October 1973, the courts of each Member State shall have exclusive jurisdiction, regardless of domicile, in proceedings concerned with the registration or validity of any European patent granted for that State;

5. in proceedings concerned with the enforcement of judgments, the courts of the Member State in which the judgment has been or is to be enforced.

Section 7
Prorogation of jurisdiction
Article 23

1. If the parties, one or more of whom is domiciled in a Member State, have agreed that a court or the courts of a Member State are to have jurisdiction to settle any disputes which have arisen or which may arise in connection with a particular legal relationship, that court or those courts shall have jurisdiction. Such jurisdiction shall be exclusive unless the parties have agreed otherwise. Such an agreement conferring jurisdiction shall be either:

(a) in writing or evidenced in writing; or

(b) in a form which accords with practices which the parties have established between themselves; or

(c) in international trade or commerce, in a form which accords with a usage of which the parties are or ought to have been aware and which in such trade or commerce is widely known to, and regularly observed by, parties to contracts of the type involved in the particular trade or commerce concerned.

2. Any communication by electronic means which provides a durable record of the agreement shall be equivalent to 'writing'.

3. Where such an agreement is concluded by parties, none of whom is domiciled in a Member State, the courts of other Member States shall have no jurisdiction over their disputes unless the court or courts chosen have declined jurisdiction.

4. The court or courts of a Member State on which a trust instrument has conferred jurisdiction shall have exclusive jurisdiction in any proceedings brought against a settlor, trustee or beneficiary, if relations between these

18

persons or their rights or obligations under the trust are involved.

5. Agreements or provisions of a trust instrument conferring jurisdiction shall have no legal force if they are contrary to Articles 13, 17 or 21, or if the courts whose jurisdiction they purport to exclude have exclusive jurisdiction by virtue of Article 22.

Article 24

Apart from jurisdiction derived from other provisions of this Regulation, a court of a Member State before which a defendant enters an appearance shall have jurisdiction. This rule shall not apply where appearance was entered to contest the jurisdiction, or where another court has exclusive jurisdiction by virtue of Article 22.

Section 8
Examination as to jurisdiction and admissibility
Article 25

Where a court of a Member State is seised of a claim which is principally concerned with a matter over which the courts of another Member State have exclusive jurisdiction by virtue of Article 22, it shall declare of its own motion that it has no jurisdiction.

Article 26

1. Where a defendant domiciled in one Member State is sued in a court of another Member State and does not enter an appearance, the court shall declare of its own motion that it has no jurisdiction unless its jurisdiction is derived from the provisions of this Regulation.

2. The court shall stay the proceedings so long as it is not shown that the defendant has been able to receive the document instituting the proceedings or an equivalent document in sufficient time to enable him to arrange for his defence, or that all necessary steps have been taken to this end.

3. Article 19 of Council Regulation (EC) No 1348/2000 of 29 May 2000 on the service in the Member States of judicial and extrajudicial documents in civil or commercial matters[10]) shall apply instead of the provisions of paragraph 2 if the document instituting the proceedings or an equivalent document had to be transmitted from one Member State to another pursuant to this Regulation.

4. Where the provisions of Regulation (EC) No 1348/2000 are not applicable, Article 15 of the Hague Convention of 15 November 1965 on the Service Abroad of Judicial and Extrajudicial Documents in Civil or Commercial Matters shall apply if the document instituting the proceedings or an equivalent document had to be transmitted pursuant to that Convention.

Section 9
Lis pendens – related actions
Article 27

1. Where proceedings involving the same cause of action and between the same parties are brought in the courts of different Member States, any court other than the court first seised shall of its own motion stay its proceedings until such time as the jurisdiction of the court first seised is established.

2. Where the jurisdiction of the court first seised is established, any court other than the court first seised shall decline jurisdiction in favour of that court.

---

[10]) OJ L 160, 30. 6. 2000, p. 37.

Article 28

1. Where related actions are pending in the courts of different Member States, any court other than the court first seised may stay its proceedings.

2. Where these actions are pending at first instance, any court other than the court first seised may also, on the application of one of the parties, decline jurisdiction if the court first seised has jurisdiction over the actions in question and its law permits the consolidation thereof.

3. For the purposes of this Article, actions are deemed to be related where they are so closely connected that it is expedient to hear and determine them together to avoid the risk of irreconcilable judgments resulting from separate proceedings.

Article 29

Where actions come within the exclusive jurisdiction of several courts, any court other than the court first seised shall decline jurisdiction in favour of that court.

Article 30

For the purposes of this Section, a court shall be deemed to be seised:

1. at the time when the document instituting the proceedings or an equivalent document is lodged with the court, provided that the plaintiff has not subsequently failed to take the steps he was required to take to have service effected on the defendant, or

2. if the document has to be served before being lodged with the court, at the time when it is received by the authority responsible for service, provided that the plaintiff has not subsequently failed to take the steps he was required to take to have the document lodged with the court.

Section 10
provisional, including protective, measures

Article 31

Application may be made to the courts of a Member State for such provisional, including protective, measures as may be available under the law of that State, even if, under this Regulation, the courts of another Member State have jurisdiction as to the substance of the matter.

CHAPTER III
RECOGNITION
AND ENFORCEMENT

Article 32

For the purposes of this Regulation, 'judgment' means any judgment given by a court or tribunal of a Member State, whatever the judgment may be called, including a decree, order, decision or writ of execution, as well as the determination of costs or expenses by an officer of the court.

Section 1
Recognition

Article 33

1. A judgment given in a Member State shall be recognised in the other Member States without any special procedure being required.

2. Any interested party who raises the recognition of a judgment as the principal issue in a dispute may, in accordance with the procedures provided for in Sections 2 and 3 of this Chapter, apply for a decision that the judgment be recognised.

3. If the outcome of proceedings in a court of a Member State depends on the determination of an incidental question of recognition that court shall have jurisdiction over that question.

Article 34

A judgment shall not be recognised:

1. if such recognition is manifestly contrary to public policy in the Member State in which recognition is sought;

2. where it was given in default of appearance, if the defendant was not served with the document which instituted the proceedings or with an equivalent document in sufficient time and in such a way as to enable him to arrange for his defence, unless the defendant failed to commence proceedings to challenge the judgment when it was possible for him to do so;

3. if it is irreconcilable with a judgment given in a dispute between the same parties in the Member State in which recognition is sought;

4. if it is irreconcilable with an earlier judgment given in another Member State or in a third State involving the same cause of action and between the same parties, provided that the earlier judgment fulfils the conditions necessary for its recognition in the Member State addressed.

Article 35

1. Moreover, a judgment shall not be recognised if it conflicts with Sections 3, 4 or 6 of Chapter II, or in a case provided for in Article 72.

2. In its examination of the grounds of jurisdiction referred to in the foregoing paragraph, the court or authority applied to shall be bound by the findings of fact on which the court of the Member State of origin based its jurisdiction.

3. Subject to the paragraph 1, the jurisdiction of the court of the Member State of origin may not be reviewed. The test of public policy referred to in point 1 of Article 34 may not be applied to the rules relating to jurisdiction.

Article 36

Under no circumstances may a foreign judgment be reviewed as to its substance.

Article 37

1. A court of a Member State in which recognition is sought of a judgment given in another Member State may stay the proceedings if an ordinary appeal against the judgment has been lodged.

2. A court of a Member State in which recognition is sought of a judgment given in Ireland or the United Kingdom may stay the proceedings if enforcement is suspended in the State of origin, by reason of an appeal.

Section 2
Enforcement
Article 38

1. A judgment given in a Member State and enforceable in that State shall be enforced in another Member State when, on the application of any interested party, it has been declared enforceable there.

2. However, in the United Kingdom, such a judgment shall be enforced in England and Wales, in Scotland, or in Northern Ireland when, on the application of any interested party, it has been registered for enforcement in that part of the United Kingdom.

Article 39

1. The application shall be submitted to the court or competent authority indicated in the list in Annex II.

2. The local jurisdiction shall be determined by reference to the place of domicile of the party against whom enforcement is sought, or to the place of enforcement.

Article 40

1. The procedure for making the application shall be governed by the law of the Member State in which enforcement is sought.

2. The applicant must give an address for service of process within the area of jurisdiction of the court applied to. However, if the law of the Member State in which enforcement is sought does not provide for the furnishing of such an address, the applicant shall appoint a representative *ad litem*.

3. The documents referred to in Article 53 shall be attached to the application.

Article 41

The judgment shall be declared enforceable immediately on completion of the formalities in Article 53 without any review under Articles 34 and 35. The party against whom enforcement is sought shall not at this stage of the proceedings be entitled to make any submissions on the application.

Article 42

1. The decision on the application for a declaration of enforceability shall forthwith be brought to the notice of the applicant in accordance with the procedure laid down by the law of the Member State in which enforcement is sought.

2. The declaration of enforceability shall be served on the party against whom enforcement is sought, accompanied by the judgment, if not already served on that party.

Article 43

1. The decision on the application for a declaration of enforceability may be appealed against by either party.

2. The appeal is to be lodged with the court indicated in the list in Annex III.

3. The appeal shall be dealt with in accordance with the rules governing procedure in contradictory matters.

4. If the party against whom enforcement is sought fails to appear before the appellate court in proceedings concerning an appeal brought by the applicant, Article 26(2) to (4) shall apply even where the party against whom enforcement is sought is not domiciled in any of the Member States.

5. An appeal against the declaration of enforceability is to be lodged within one month of service thereof. If the party against whom enforcement is sought is domiciled in a Member State other than that in which the declaration of enforceability was given, the time for appealing shall be two months and shall run from the date of service, either on him in person or at his residence. No extension of time may be granted on account of distance.

Article 44

The judgment given on the appeal may be contested only by the appeal referred to in Annex IV.

Article 45

1. The court with which an appeal is lodged under Article 43 or Article 44

shall refuse or revoke a declaration of enforceability only on one of the grounds specified in Articles 34 and 35. It shall give its decision without delay.

2. Under no circumstances may the foreign judgment be reviewed as to its substance.

Article 46

1. The court with which an appeal is lodged under Article 43 or Article 44 may, on the application of the party against whom enforcement is sought, stay the proceedings if an ordinary appeal has been lodged against the judgment in the Member State of origin or if the time for such an appeal has not yet expired; in the latter case, the court may specify the time within which such an appeal is to be lodged.

2. Where the judgment was given in Ireland or the United Kingdom, any form of appeal available in the Member State of origin shall be treated as an ordinary appeal for the purposes of paragraph 1.

3. The court may also make enforcement conditional on the provision of such security as it shall determine.

Article 47

1. When a judgment must be recognised in accordance with this Regulation, nothing shall prevent the applicant from availing himself of provisional, including protective, measures in accordance with the law of the Member State requested without a declaration of enforceability under Article 41 being required.

2. The declaration of enforceability shall carry with it the power to proceed to any protective measures.

3. During the time specified for an appeal pursuant to Article 43(5)

against the declaration of enforceability and until any such appeal has been determined, no measures of enforcement may be taken other than protective measures against the property of the party against whom enforcement is sought.

Article 48

1. Where a foreign judgment has been given in respect of several matters and the declaration of enforceability cannot be given for all of them, the court or competent authority shall give it for one or more of them.

2. An applicant may request a declaration of enforceability limited to parts of a judgment.

Article 49

A foreign judgment which orders a periodic payment by way of a penalty shall be enforceable in the Member State in which enforcement is sought only if the amount of the payment has been finally determined by the courts of the Member State of origin.

Article 50

An applicant who, in the Member State of origin has benefited from complete or partial legal aid or exemption from costs or expenses, shall be entitled, in the procedure provided for in this Section, to benefit from the most favourable legal aid or the most extensive exemption from costs or expenses provided for by the law of the Member State addressed.

Article 51

No security, bond or deposit, however described, shall be required of a party who in one Member State applies for enforcement of a judgment given in another Member State on the ground that he is a foreign national or that he is not domiciled or resident in the State in which enforcement is sought.

Article 52

In proceedings for the issue of a declaration of enforceability, no charge, duty or fee calculated by reference to the value of the matter at issue may be levied in the Member State in which enforcement is sought.

Section 3
Common provisions
Article 53

1. A party seeking recognition or applying for a declaration of enforceability shall produce a copy of the judgment which satisfies the conditions necessary to establish its authenticity.

2. A party applying for a declaration of enforceability shall also produce the certificate referred to in Article 54, without prejudice to Article 55.

Article 54

The court or competent authority of a Member State where a judgment was given shall issue, at the request of any interested party, a certificate using the standard form in Annex V to this Regulation.

Article 55

1. If the certificate referred to in Article 54 is not produced, the court or competent authority may specify a time for its production or accept an equivalent document or, if it considers that it has sufficient information before it, dispense with its production.

2. If the court or competent authority so requires, a translation of the documents shall be produced. The translation shall be certified by a person qualified to do so in one of the Member States.

Article 56

No legalisation or other similar formality shall be required in respect of the documents referred to in Article 53 or Article 55(2), or in respect of a document appointing a representative *ad litem*.

CHAPTER IV
AUTHENTIC INSTRUMENTS AND COURT SETTLEMENTS
Article 57

1. A document which has been formally drawn up or registered as an authentic instrument and is enforceable in one Member State shall, in another Member State, be declared enforceable there, on application made in accordance with the procedures provided for in Articles 38, *et seq.* The court with which an appeal is lodged under Article 43 or Article 44 shall refuse or revoke a declaration of enforceability only if enforcement of the instrument is manifestly contrary to public policy in the Member State addressed.

2. Arrangements relating to maintenance obligations concluded with administrative authorities or authenticated by them shall also be regarded as authentic instruments within the meaning of paragraph 1.

3. The instrument produced must satisfy the conditions necessary to establish its authenticity in the Member State of origin.

18

4. Section 3 of Chapter III shall apply as appropriate. The competent authority of a Member State where an authentic instrument was drawn up or registered shall issue, at the request of any interested party, a certificate using the standard form in Annex VI to this Regulation.

Article 58

A settlement which has been approved by a court in the course of proceedings and is enforceable in the Member State in which it was concluded shall be enforceable in the State addressed under the same conditions as authentic instruments. The court or competent authority of a Member State where a court settlement was approved shall issue, at the request of any interested party, a certificate using the standard form in Annex V to this Regulation.

CHAPTER V
GENERAL PROVISIONS

Article 59

1. In order to determine whether a party is domiciled in the Member State whose courts are seised of a matter, the court shall apply its internal law.

2. If a party is not domiciled in the Member State whose courts are seised of the matter, then, in order to determine whether the party is domiciled in another Member State, the court shall apply the law of that Member State.

Article 60

1. For the purposes of this Regulation, a company or other legal person or association of natural or legal persons is domiciled at the place where it has its:

(a) statutory seat, or

(b) central administration, or

(c) principal place of business.

2. For the purposes of the United Kingdom and Ireland 'statutory seat' means the registered office or, where there is no such office anywhere, the place of incorporation or, where there is no such place anywhere, the place under the law of which the formation took place.

3. In order to determine whether a trust is domiciled in the Member State whose courts are seised of the matter, the court shall apply its rules of private international law.

Article 61

Without prejudice to any more favourable provisions of national laws, persons domiciled in a Member State who are being prosecuted in the criminal courts of another Member State of which they are not nationals for an offence which was not intentionally committed may be defended by persons qualified to do so, even if they do not appear in person. However, the court seised of the matter may order appearance in person; in the case of failure to appear, a judgment given in the civil action without the person concerned having had the opportunity to arrange for his defence need not be recognised or enforced in the other Member States.

Article 62

In Sweden, in summary proceedings concerning orders to pay (betalningsföreläggande) and assistance (handräckning), the expression 'court' includes the 'Swedish enforcement service' (kronofogdemyndighet).

Article 63

1. A person domiciled in the territory of the Grand Duchy of Luxembourg and sued in the court of another Member State pursuant to Article 5(1) may refuse to submit to the jurisdiction of that court if the final place of delivery of the goods or provision of the services is in Luxembourg.

2. Where, under paragraph 1, the final place of delivery of the goods or provision of the services is in Luxembourg, any agreement conferring jurisdiction must, in order to be valid, be accepted in writing or evidenced in writing within the meaning of Article 23(1)(a).

3. The provisions of this Article shall not apply to contracts for the provision of financial services.

4. The provisions of this Article shall apply for a period of six years from entry into force of this Regulation.

Article 64

1. In proceedings involving a dispute between the master and a member of the crew of a seagoing ship registered in Greece or in Portugal, concerning remuneration or other conditions of service, a court in a Member State shall establish whether the diplomatic or consular officer responsible for the ship has been notified of the dispute. It may act as soon as that officer has been notified.

2. The provisions of this Article shall apply for a period of six years from entry into force of this Regulation.

Article 65

1. The jurisdiction specified in Article 6(2) and Article 11 in actions on a warranty of guarantee or in any other third party proceedings may not be resorted to in Germany, Austria and Hungary. Any person domiciled in another Member State may be sued in the courts:

(a) of Germany, pursuant to Articles 68 and 72 to 74 of the Code of Civil Procedure (Zivilprozessordnung) concerning third-party notices;

(b) of Austria, pursuant to Article 21 of the Code of Civil Procedure (Zivilprozessordnung) concerning third-party notices;

(c) of Hungary, pursuant to Articles 58 to 60 of the Code of Civil Procedure (Polgári perrendtartás) concerning third-party notices.

2. Judgments given in other Member States by virtue of Article 6 (2), or Article 11 shall be recognised and enforced in Germany, Austria and Hungary in accordance with Chapter III. Any effects which judgments given in these States may have on third parties by application of the provisions in paragraph 1 shall also be recognised in the other Member States.

CHAPTER VI
TRANSITIONAL PROVISIONS

Article 66

1. This Regulation shall apply only to legal proceedings instituted and to documents formally drawn up or registered as authentic instruments after the entry into force thereof.

2. However, if the proceedings in the Member State of origin were instituted before the entry into force of this Regulation, judgments given after that date shall be recognised and enforced in accordance with Chapter III,

(a) if the proceedings in the Member State of origin were instituted after the entry into force of the Brussels or the Lugano Convention both in the

Member State or origin and in the Member State addressed;

(b) in all other cases, if jurisdiction was founded upon rules which accorded with those provided for either in Chapter II or in a convention concluded between the Member State of origin and the Member State addressed which was in force when the proceedings were instituted.

CHAPTER VII
RELATIONS WITH OTHER INSTRUMENTS

Article 67

This Regulation shall not prejudice the application of provisions governing jurisdiction and the recognition and enforcement of judgments in specific matters which are contained in Community instruments or in national legislation harmonised pursuant to such instruments.

Article 68

1. This Regulation shall, as between the Member States, supersede the Brussels Convention, except as regards the territories of the Member States which fall within the territorial scope of that Convention and which are excluded from this Regulation pursuant to Article 299 of the Treaty.

2. In so far as this Regulation replaces the provisions of the Brussels Convention between Member States, any reference to the Convention shall be understood as a reference to this Regulation.

Article 69

Subject to Article 66(2) and Article 70, this Regulation shall, as between Member States, supersede the

following conventions and treaty concluded between two or more of them:

– the Convention between Belgium and France on Jurisdiction and the Validity and Enforcement of Judgments, Arbitration Awards and Authentic Instruments, signed at Paris on 8 July 1899,

– the Convention between Belgium and the Netherlands on Jurisdiction, Bankruptcy, and the Validity and Enforcement of Judgments, Arbitration Awards and Authentic Instruments, signed at Brussels on 28 March 1925,

– the Convention between France and Italy on the Enforcement of Judgments in Civil and Commercial Matters, signed at Rome on 3 June 1930,

– the Convention between the United Kingdom and the French Republic providing for the reciprocal enforcement of judgments in civil and commercial matters, with Protocol, signed at Paris on 18 January 1934,

– the Convention between the United Kingdom and the Kingdom of Belgium providing for the reciprocal enforcement of judgments in civil and commercial matters, with Protocol, signed at Brussels on 2 May 1934,

– the Convention between Germany and Italy on the Recognition and Enforcement of Judgments in Civil and Commercial Matters, signed at Rome on 9 March 1936,

– the Convention between Belgium and Austria on the Reciprocal Recognition and Enforcement of Judgments and Authentic Instruments relating to Maintenance Obligations, signed at Vienna on 25 October 1957,

– the Convention between Germany and Belgium on the Mutual Recognition and Enforcement of Judgments, Arbitration Awards and Authentic Instruments in Civil and Commercial Matters, signed at Bonn on 30 June 1958,

– the Convention between the Netherlands and Italy on the Recognition and Enforcement of Judgments in Civil and Commercial Matters, signed at Rome on 17 April 1959,

– the Convention between Germany and Austria on the Reciprocal Recognition and Enforcement of Judgments, Settlements and Authentic Instruments in Civil and Commercial Matters, signed at Vienna on 6 June 1959,

– the Convention between Belgium and Austria on the Reciprocal Recognition and Enforcement of Judgments, Arbitral Awards and Authentic Instruments in Civil and Commercial Matters, signed at Vienna on 16 June 1959,

– the Convention between the United Kingdom and the Federal Republic of Germany for the reciprocal recognition and enforcement of judgments in civil and commercial matters, signed at Bonn on 14 July 1960,

– the Convention between the United Kingdom and Austria providing for the reciprocal recognition and enforcement of judgments in civil and commercial matters, signed at Vienna on 14 July 1961, with amending Protocol signed at London on 6 March 1970,

– the Convention between Greece and Germany for the Reciprocal Recognition and Enforcement of Judgments, Settlements and Authentic Instruments in Civil and Commercial Matters, signed in Athens on 4 November 1961,

– the Convention between Belgium and Italy on the Recognition and Enforcement of Judgments and other Enforceable Instruments in Civil and Commercial Matters, signed at Rome on 6 April 1962,

– the Convention between the Netherlands and Germany on the Mutual Recognition and Enforcement of Judgments and Other Enforceable Instruments in Civil and Commercial Matters, signed at The Hague on 30 August 1962,

– the Convention between the Netherlands and Austria on the Reciprocal Recognition and Enforcement of Judgments and Authentic Instruments in Civil and Commercial Matters, signed at The Hague on 6 February 1963,

– the Convention between the United Kingdom and the Republic of Italy for the reciprocal recognition and enforcement of judgments in civil and commercial matters, signed at Rome on 7 February 1964, with amending Protocol signed at Rome on 14 July 1970,

– the Convention between France and Austria on the Recognition and Enforcement of Judgments and Authentic Instruments in Civil and Commercial Matters, signed at Vienna on 15 July 1966,

– the Convention between the United Kingdom and the Kingdom of the Netherlands providing for the reciprocal recognition and enforcement of judgments in civil matters, signed at The Hague on 17 November 1967,

– the Convention between Spain and France on the Recognition and Enforcement of Judgment Arbitration Awards in Civil and Commercial Matters, signed at Paris on 28 May 1969,

– the Convention between Luxembourg and Austria on the Recognition and Enforcement of Judgments and Authentic Instruments in Civil and Commercial Matters, signed at Luxembourg on 29 July 1971,

– the Convention between Italy and Austria on the Recognition and En-

18

forcement of Judgments in Civil and Commercial Matters, of Judicial Settlements and of Authentic Instruments, signed at Rome on 16 November 1971,

– the Convention between Spain and Italy regarding Legal Aid and the Recognition and Enforcement of Judgments in Civil and Commercial Matters, signed at Madrid on 22 May 1973,

– the Convention between Finland, Iceland, Norway, Sweden and Denmark on the Recognition and Enforcement of Judgments in Civil Matters, signed at Copenhagen on 11 October 1977,

– the Convention between Austria and Sweden on the Recognition and Enforcement of Judgments in Civil Matters, signed at Stockholm on 16 September 1982,

– the Convention between Spain and the Federal Republic of Germany on the Recognition and Enforcement of Judgments, Settlements and Enforceable Authentic Instruments in Civil and Commercial Matters, signed at Bonn on 14 November 1983,

– the Convention between Austria and Spain on the Recognition and Enforcement of Judgments, Settlements and Enforceable Authentic Instruments in Civil and Commercial Matters, signed at Vienna on 17 February 1984,

– the Convention between Finland and Austria on the Recognition and Enforcement of Judgments in Civil Matters, signed at Vienna on 17 November 1986,

– the Treaty between Belgium, the Netherlands and Luxembourg in Jurisdiction, Bankruptcy, and the Validity and Enforcement of Judgments, Arbitration Awards and Authentic Instruments, signed at Brussels on 24 November 1961, in so far as it is in force,

– the Convention between the Czechoslovak Republic and Portugal on the Recognition and Enforcement of Court Decisions, signed at Lisbon on 23 November 1927, still in force between the Czech Republic and Portugal,

– the Convention between the Federative People's Republic of Yugoslavia and the Republic of Austria on Mutual Judicial Cooperation, signed at Vienna on 16 December 1954,

– the Convention between the Polish People's Republic and the Hungarian People's Republic on the Legal Assistance in Civil, Family and Criminal Matters, signed at Budapest on 6 March 1959,

– the Convention between the Federative People's Republic of Yugoslavia and the Kingdom of Greece on the Mutual Recognition and Enforcement of Judgments, signed at Athens on 18 June 1959,

– the Convention between the Polish People's Republic and the Federative People's Republic of Yugoslavia on the Legal Assistance in Civil and Criminal Matters, signed at Warsaw on 6 February 1960, now in force between Poland and Slovenia,

– the Agreement between the Federative People's Republic of Yugoslavia and the Republic of Austria on the Mutual Recognition and Enforcement of Arbitral Awards and Arbitral Settlements in Commercial Matters, signed at Belgrade on 18 March 1960,

– the Agreement between the Federative People's Republic of Yugoslavia and the Republic of Austria on the Mutual Recognition and Enforcement of Decisions in Alimony Matters, signed at Vienna on 10 October 1961,

– the Convention between Poland and Austria on Mutual Relations in

18

Civil Matters and on Documents, signed at Vienna on 11 December 1963,
- the Treaty between the Czechoslovak Socialist Republic and the Socialist Federative Republic of Yugoslavia on Settlement of Legal Relations in Civil, Family and Criminal Matters, signed at Belgrade on 20 January 1964, still in force between the Czech Republic, Slovakia and Slovenia,
- the Convention between Poland and France on Applicable Law, Jurisdiction and the Enforcement of Judgments in the Field of Personal and Family Law, concluded in Warsaw on 5 April 1967,
- the Convention between the Governments of Yugoslavia and France on the Recognition and Enforcement of Judgments in Civil and Commercial Matters, signed at Paris on 18 May 1971,
- the Convention between the Federative Socialist Republic of Yugoslavia and the Kingdom of Belgium on the Recognition and Enforcement of Court Decisions in Alimony Matters, signed at Belgrade on 12 December 1973,
- the Convention between Hungary and Greece on Legal Assistance in Civil and Criminal Matters, signed at Budapest on 8 October 1979,
- the Convention between Poland and Greece on Legal Assistance in Civil and Criminal Matters, signed at Athens on 24 October 1979,
- the Convention between Hungary and France on Legal Assistance in Civil and Family Law, on the Recognition and Enforcement of Decisions and on Legal Assistance in Criminal Matters and on Extradition, signed at Budapest on 31 July 1980,
- the Treaty between the Czechoslovak Socialist Republic and the Hellenic Republic on Legal Aid in Civil and Criminal Matters, signed at Athens on 22 October 1980, still in force between the Czech Republic, Slovakia and Greece,
- the Convention between the Republic of Cyprus and the Hungarian People's Republic on Legal Assistance in Civil and Criminal Matters, signed at Nicosia on 30 November 1981,
- the Treaty between the Czechoslovak Socialistic Republic and the Republic of Cyprus on Legal Aid in Civil and Criminal Matters, signed at Nicosia on 23 April 1982, still in force between the Czech Republic, Slovakia and Cyprus,
- the Agreement between the Republic of Cyprus and the Republic of Greece on Legal Cooperation in Matters of Civil, Family, Commercial and Criminal Law, signed at Nicosia on 5 March 1984,
- the Treaty between the Government of the Czechoslovak Socialist Republic and the Government of the Republic of France on Legal Aid and the Recognition and Enforcement of Judgments in Civil, Family and Commercial Matters, signed at Paris on 10 May 1984, still in force between the Czech Republic, Slovakia and France,
- the Agreement between the Republic of Cyprus and the Socialist Federal Republic of Yugoslavia on Legal Assistance in Civil and Criminal Matters, signed at Nicosia on 19 September 1984, now in force between Cyprus and Slovenia,
- the Treaty between the Czechoslovak Socialist Republic and the Italian Republic on Legal Aid in Civil and Criminal Matters, signed at Prague on 6 December 1985, still in force between the Czech Republic, Slovakia and Italy,
- the Treaty between the Czechoslovak Socialist Republic and the Kingdom of Spain on Legal Aid, Recognition and Enforcement of Court Deci-

18

sions in Civil Matters, signed at Madrid on 4 May 1987, still in force between the Czech Republic, Slovakia and Spain,

– the Treaty between the Czechoslovak Socialist Republic and the Polish People's Republic on Legal Aid and Settlement of Legal Relations in Civil, Family, Labour and Criminal Matters, signed at Warsaw on 21 December 1987, still in force between the Czech Republic, Slovakia and Poland,

– the Treaty between the Czechoslovak Socialist Republic and the Hungarian People's Republic on Legal Aid and Settlement of Legal Relations in Civil, Family and Criminal Matters, signed at Bratislava on 28 March 1989, still in force between the Czech Republic, Slovakia and Hungary,

– the Convention between Poland and Italy on Judicial Assistance and the Recognition and Enforcement of Judgments in Civil Matters, signed at Warsaw on 28 April 1989,

– the Treaty between the Czech Republic and the Slovak Republic on Legal Aid provided by Judicial Bodies and on Settlements of Certain Legal Relations in Civil and Criminal Matters, signed at Prague on 29 October 1992,

– the Agreement between the Republic of Latvia, the Republic of Estonia and the Republic of Lithuania on Legal Assistance and Legal Relationships, signed at Tallinn on 11 November 1992,

– the Agreement between the Republic of Poland and the Republic of Lithuania on Legal Assistance and Legal Relations in Civil, Family, Labour and Criminal Matters, signed in Warsaw on 26 January 1993,

– the Agreement between the Republic of Latvia and the Republic of Poland on Legal Assistance and Legal Relationships in Civil, Family, Labour and

Criminal Matters, signed at Riga on 23 February 1994,

– the Agreement between the Republic of Cyprus and the Republic of Poland on Legal Cooperation in Civil and Criminal Matters, signed at Nicosia on 14 November 1996, and

– the Agreement between Estonia and Poland on Granting Legal Assistance and Legal Relations on Civil, Labour and Criminal Matters, signed at Tallinn on 27 November 1998,

– the Convention between Bulgaria and Belgium on certain Judicial Matters, signed at Sofia on 2 July 1930,

– the Agreement between the People's Republic of Bulgaria and the Federative People's Republic of Yugoslavia on Mutual Legal Assistance, signed at Sofia on 23 March 1956, still in force between Bulgaria and Slovenia,

– the Treaty between the People's Republic of Romania and the People's Republic of Hungary on Legal Assistance in Civil, Family and Criminal Matters, signed at Bucharest on 7 October 1958,

– the Treaty between the People's Republic of Romania and the Czechoslovak Republic on Legal Assistance in Civil, Family and Criminal Matters, signed at Prague on 25 October 1958, still in force between Romania and Slovakia,

– the Agreement between the People's Republic of Bulgaria and the Romanian People's Republic on Legal Assistance in Civil, Family and Criminal Matters, signed at Sofia on 3 December 1958,

– the Treaty between the People's Republic of Romania and the Federal People's Republic of Yugoslavia on Legal Assistance, signed at Belgrade on 18 October 1960 and its Protocol, still in force between Romania and Slovenia,

18

– the Agreement between the People's Republic of Bulgaria and the Polish People's Republic on Legal Assistance and Legal Relations in Civil, Family and Criminal Matters, signed at Warsaw on 4 December 1961,

– the Convention between the Socialist Republic of Romania and the Republic of Austria on Legal Assistance in Civil and Family law and the Validity and Service of Documents and its annexed Protocol, signed at Vienna on 17 November 1965,

– the Agreement between the People's Republic of Bulgaria and the Hungarian People's Republic on Legal Assistance in Civil, Family and Criminal Matters, signed at Sofia on 16 May 1966,

– the Convention between the Socialist Republic of Romania and the Hellenic Republic on Legal Assistance in Civil and Criminal Matters and its Protocol, signed at Bucharest on 19 October 1972,

– the Convention between the Socialist Republic of Romania and the Italian Republic on Judicial Assistance in Civil and Criminal Matters, signed at Bucharest on 11 November 1972,

– the Convention between the Socialist Republic of Romania and the French Republic on Legal Assistance in Civil and Commercial Matters, signed at Paris on 5 November 1974,

– the Convention between the Socialist Republic of Romania and the Kingdom of Belgium on Legal Assistance in Civil and Commercial Matters, signed at Bucharest on 30 October 1975,

– the Agreement between the People's Republic of Bulgaria and the Hellenic Republic on Legal Assistance in Civil and Criminal Matters, signed at Athens on 10 April 1976,

– the Agreement between the People's Republic of Bulgaria and the Czechoslovak Socialist Republic on Legal Assistance and Settlement of Relations in Civil, Family and Criminal Matters, signed at Sofia on 25 November 1976,

– the Convention between the Socialist Republic of Romania and the United Kingdom of Great Britain and Northern Ireland on Legal Assistance in Civil and Commercial Matters, signed at London on 15 June 1978,

– the Additional Protocol to the Convention between the Socialist Republic of Romania and the Kingdom of Belgium on Legal Assistance Civil and Commercial Matters, signed at Bucharest on 30 October 1979,

– the Convention between the Socialist Republic of Romania and the Kingdom of Belgium on Recognition and Enforcement of Decisions in Alimony Obligations, signed at Bucharest on 30 October 1979,

– the Convention between the Socialist Republic of Romania and the Kingdom of Belgium on Recognition and Enforcement of Divorce Decisions, signed at Bucharest on 6 November 1980,

– the Agreement between the People's Republic of Bulgaria and the Republic of Cyprus on Legal Assistance in Civil and Criminal Matters, signed at Nicosia on 29 April 1983,

– the Agreement between the Government of the People's Republic of Bulgaria and the Government of the French Republic on Mutual Legal Assistance in Civil Matters, signed at Sofia on 18 January 1989,

– the Agreement between the People's Republic of Bulgaria and the Italian Republic on Legal Assistance and Enforcement of Decisions in Civil

18

Matters, signed at Rome on 18 May 1990,

– the Agreement between the Republic of Bulgaria and the Kingdom of Spain on Mutual Legal Assistance in Civil Matters, signed at Sofia on 23 May 1993,

– the Treaty between Romania and the Czech Republic on Judicial Assistance in Civil Matters, signed at Bucharest on 11 July 1994,

– the Convention between Romania and the Kingdom of Spain on Jurisdiction, Recognition and Enforcement of Decisions in Civil and Commercial Matters, signed at Bucharest on 17 November 1997,

– the Convention between Romania and the Kingdom of Spain — complementary to the Hague Convention relating to civil procedure law (Hague, 1 March 1954), signed at Bucharest on 17 November 1997,

– the Treaty between Romania and the Republic of Poland on Legal Assistance and Legal Relations in Civil Cases, signed at Bucharest on 15 May 1999.

Article 70

1. The Treaty and the Conventions referred to in Article 69 shall continue to have effect in relation to matters to which this Regulation does not apply.

2. They shall continue to have effect in respect of judgments given and documents formally drawn up or registered as authentic instruments before the entry into force of this Regulation.

Article 71

1. This Regulation shall not affect any conventions to which the Member States are parties and which in relation to particular matters, govern jurisdiction or the recognition or enforcement of judgments.

2. With a view to its uniform interpretation, paragraph 1 shall be applied in the following manner:

(a) this Regulation shall not prevent a court of a Member State, which is a party to a convention on a particular matter, from assuming jurisdiction in accordance with that convention, even where the defendant is domiciled in another Member State which is not a party to that convention. The court hearing the action shall, in any event, apply Article 26 of this Regulation;

(b) judgments given in a Member State by a court in the exercise of jurisdiction provided for in a convention on a particular matter shall be recognised and enforced in the other Member States in accordance with this Regulation.

Where a convention on a particular matter to which both the Member State of origin and the Member State addressed are parties lays down conditions for the recognition or enforcement of judgments, those conditions shall apply. In any event, the provisions of this Regulation which concern the procedure for recognition and enforcement of judgments may be applied.

Article 72

This Regulation shall not affect agreements by which Member States undertook, prior to the entry into force of this Regulation pursuant to Article 59 of the Brussels Convention, not to recognise judgments given, in particular in other Contracting States to that Convention, against defendants domiciled or habitually resident in a third country where, in cases provided for in Article 4 of that Convention, the judgment could only be founded on a ground of jurisdiction specified in the second paragraph of Article 3 of that Convention.

CHAPTER VIII
FINAL PROVISIONS
Article 73

No later than five years after the entry into force of this Regulation, the Commission shall present to the European Parliament, the Council and the Economic and Social Committee a report on the application of this Regulation. The report shall be accompanied, if need be, by proposals for adaptations to this Regulation.

Article 74

1. The Member States shall notify the Commission of the texts amending the lists set out in Annexes I to IV. The Commission shall adapt the Annexes concerned accordingly.

2. The updating or technical adjustment of the forms, specimens of which appear in Annexes V and VI, shall be adopted in accordance with the advisory procedure referred to in Article 75(2).

Article 75

1. The Commission shall be assisted by a committee.

2. Where reference is made to this paragraph, Articles 3 and 7 of Decision 1999/468/EC shall apply.

3. The Committee shall adopt its rules of procedure.

Article 76

This Regulation shall enter into force on 1 March 2002.

This Regulation is binding in its entirety and directly applicable in the Member States in accordance with the Treaty establishing the European Community.

ANNEX I
Rules of jurisdiction referred to in Article 3(2) and Article 4(2)

The rules of jurisdiction referred to in Article 3(2) and Article 4(2) are the following:

– in Belgium: Article 15 of the Civil Code (Code civil/Burgerlijk Wetboek) and Article 638 of the Judicial Code (Code judiciaire/Gerechtelijk Wetboek);

– in Bulgaria: Article 4(1), of the International Private Law Code,

– in the Czech Republic: Article 86 of Act No 99/1963 Coll., the Code of Civil Procedure (občanský soudní řád), as amended,

– in Germany: Article 23 of the Code of Civil Procedure (Zivilprozessordnung),

– in Estonia: Article 139, paragraph 2 of the Code of Civil Procedure (tsiviilkohtumenetluse seadustik),

– in Greece, Article 40 of the Code of Civil Procedure (Κώδικας Πολιτικής Δικονομίας);

– in France: Articles 14 and 15 of the Civil Code (Code civil),

– in Ireland: the rules which enable jurisdiction to be founded on the document instituting the proceedings having been served on the defendant during his temporary presence in Ireland,

– in Italy: Articles 3 and 4 of Act 218 of 31 May 1995,

– in Cyprus: Section 21(2) of the Courts of Justice Law No 14 of 1960, as amended,

– in Latvia: Section 27 and paragraphs 3, 5, 6 and 9 of Section 28 of the Civil Procedure Law (Civilprocesa likums),

– in Lithuania: Article 31 of the Code of Civil Procedure (Civilinio proceso kodeksas),

– in Luxembourg: Articles 14 and 15 of the Civil Code (Code civil),

– in Hungary: Article 57 of Law Decree No. 13 of 1979 on International Private Law (a nemzetközi magánjogról szóló 1979. évi 13. törvényerejű rendelet),

– in Malta: Articles 742, 743 and 744 of the Code of Organisation and Civil Procedure – Cap. 12 (Kodiċi ta' Organizzazzjoni u Proċedura Ċivili – Kap. 12) and Article 549 of the Commercial Code – Cap. 13 (Kodiċi talkummerċ – Kap. 13),

– in Austria: Article 99 of the Court Jurisdiction Act (Jurisdiktionsnorm),

– in Poland: Articles 1103 and 1110 of the Code of Civil Procedure (Kodeks postępowania cywilnego),

– in Portugal: Articles 65 and 65 A of the Code of Civil Procedure (Código de Processo Civil) and Article 11 of the Code of Labour Procedure (Código de Processo de Trabalho),

– in Romania: Articles 148–157 of Law No. 105/1992 on Private International Law Relations,

– in Slovenia: Article 48(2) of the Private International Law and Procedure Act (Zakon o medarodnem zasebnem pravu in postopku) in relation to Article 47 (2) of Civil Procedure Act (Zakon o pravdnem postopku) and Article 58(1) of the Private International Law and Procedure Act (Zakon o medarodnem zasebnem pravu in postopku) in relation to Article 57(1) and 47(2) of Civil Procedure Act (Zakon o pravdnem postopku),

– in Slovakia: Articles 37 to 37 e of Act No 97/1963 on Private International Law and the Rules of Procedure relating thereto,

– in Finland: the second, third and fourth sentences of the first paragraph of Section 1 of Chapter 10 of the Code

of Judicial Procedure (oikeudenkäymiskaari/rättegångsbalken),

– in Sweden: the first sentence of the first paragraph of Section 3 of Chapter 10 of the Code of Judicial Procedure (rättegångsbalken),

– in the United Kingdom: rules which enable jurisdiction to be founded on:

(a) the document instituting the proceedings having been served on the defendant during his temporary presence in the United Kingdom; or

(b) the presence within the United Kingdom of property belonging to the defendant; or

(c) the seizure by the plaintiff of property situated in the United Kingdom.

ANNEX II

The courts or competent authorities to which the application referred to in Article 39 may be submitted are the following:

– in Belgium, the 'tribunal de première instance' or 'rechtbank van eerste aanleg' or 'erstinstanzliches Gericht',

– in Bulgaria, the 'Софийски градски съд',

– in the Czech Republic, the 'okresní soud' or 'soudní exekutor',

– in Germany:

(a) the presiding Judge of a chamber of the 'Landgericht';

(b) a notary ('...') in a procedure of declaration of enforceability of an authentic instrument,

– in Estonia, the 'maakohus' or the 'linnakohus',

– in Greece, the 'Μονομελές Πρωτοδικείο',

– in Spain, the 'Juzgado de Primera Instancia',

- in France:
  (a) the 'greffier en chef du tribunal de grande instance',
  (b) the 'président de la chambre départementale des notaires' in the case of application for a declaration of enforceability of a notarial authentic instrument,
- in Ireland, the High Court,
- in Italy, the 'Corte d'appello',
- in Cyprus, the 'Επαρχιακό Δικαστήριο' or in the case of a maintenance judgment the 'Οικογενειακό Δικαστήριο',
- in Latvia, the 'rajona (pilsētas) tiesa',
- in Lithuania, the 'Lietuvos apeliacinis teismas',
- in Luxembourg, the presiding judge of the 'tribunal d'arrondissement',
- in Hungary, the 'megyei bíróság székhelyén működő helyi bíróság', and in Budapest the 'Budai Központi Kerületi Bíróság',
- in Malta, the 'Prim' Awla tal-Qorti Ċivili' or 'Qorti tal-Maġistrati ta' Għawdex fil-ġurisdizzjoni superjuri tagħha', or, in the case of a maintenance judgment, the 'Reġistratur tal-Qorti' on transmission by the 'Ministru responsabbli għall-Ġustizzja',
- in the Netherlands, the 'voorzieningenrechter van de rechtbank',
- in Austria, the 'Bezirksgericht',
- in Poland, the 'Sąd Okręgowy',
- in Portugal, the 'Tribunal de Comarca',
- in Romania, the 'Tribunal',
- in Slovenia, the 'okrožno sodišče',
- in Slovakia, the 'okresný súd',
- in Finland, the 'käräjäoikeus/tingsrätt',
- in Sweden, the 'Svea hovrätt',
- in the United Kingdom:
  (a) in England and Wales, the High Court of Justice, or in the case of a

maintenance judgment, the Magistrate's Court on transmission by the Secretary of State;
  (b) in Scotland, the Court of Session, or in the case of a maintenance judgment, the Sheriff Court on transmission by the Secretary of State;
  (c) in Northern Ireland, the High Court of Justice, or in the case of a maintenance judgment, the Magistrate's Court on transmission by the Secretary of State;
  (d) in Gibraltar, the Supreme Court of Gibraltar, or in the case of a maintenance judgment, the Magistrates' Court on transmission by the Attorney General of Gibraltar.

ANNEX III

The courts with which appeals referred to in Article 43(2) may be lodged are the following:
- in Belgium,
  (a) as regards appeal by the defendant: the 'tribunal de première instance' or 'rechtbank van eerste aanleg' or 'erstinstanzliches Gericht',
  (b) as regards appeal by the applicant: the 'Cour d'appel' or 'hof van beroep',
- in Bulgaria, the 'Апелативен съд — София',
- in the Czech Republic, the 'okresní soud',
- in the Federal Republic of Germany, the 'Oberlandesgericht',
- in Estonia, the 'ringkonnakohus',
- in Greece, the 'Εφετείο',
- in Spain, the 'Audiencia Provincial',
- in France:
  (a) the 'cour d'appel' on decisions allowing the application,
  (b) the presiding judge of the 'tribunal de grande instance', on decisions rejecting the application,

18

- in Ireland, the High Court,
- in Italy, the 'corte d'appello',
- in Cyprus, the 'Επαρχιακό Δικαστήριο' or in the case of a maintenance judgment the 'Οικογενειακό Δικαστήριο',
- in Latvia, the 'Apgabaltiesa',
- in Lithuania, the 'Lietuvos apeliacinis teismas',
- in Luxembourg, the 'Cour supérieure de Justice' sitting as a court of civil appeal,
- in Hungary, the 'megyei bíróság'; in Budapest, the 'Fővárosi Bíróság',
- in Malta, the 'Qorti ta' l-Appell' in accordance with the procedure laid down for appeals in the Kodiċi ta' Organizzazzjoni u Proċedura Ċivili – Kap.12 or in the case of a maintenance judgment by 'ċitazzjoni' before the 'Prim' Awla tal-Qorti ivili jew il-Qorti tal-Maġistrati ta' Għawdex fil-ġurisdizzjoni superjuri tagħha",
- in the Netherlands:
  (a) for the defendant: the 'arrondissementsrechtbank',
  (b) for the applicant: the 'gerechtshof',
- in Austria, the 'Bezirksgericht',
- in Poland, the 'Sąd Apelacyjny',
- in Portugal, the 'Tribunal de Relação',
- in Romania, the 'Curte de Apel',
- in Slovenia, the 'okrožno sodišče',
- in Slovakia, the 'okresný súd',
- in Finland, the 'hovioikeus/hovrätt',
- in Sweden, the 'Svea hovrätt',
- in the United Kingdom:
  (a) in England and Wales, the High Court of Justice, or in the case of a maintenance judgment, the Magistrate's Court;
  (b) in Scotland, the Court of Session, or in the case of a maintenance judgment, the Sheriff Court;

(c) in Northern Ireland, the High Court of Justice, or in the case of a maintenance judgment, the Magistrate's Court;
(d) in Gibraltar, the Supreme Court of Gibraltar, or in the case of a maintenance judgment, the Magistrates' Court.

ANNEX IV

The appeals which may be lodged pursuant to Article 44 are the following
- in Belgium, Greece, Spain, France, Italy, Luxembourg and the Netherlands, an appeal in cassation,
- in Bulgaria, 'обжалване пред Върховния касационен съд',
- in the Czech Republic, a 'dovolání' and a 'žaloba pro zmatečnost',
- in Germany, a 'Rechtsbeschwerde',
- in Estonia, a 'kassatsioonkaebus',
- in Ireland, an appeal on a point of law to the Supreme Court,
- in Cyprus, an appeal to the Supreme Court,
- in Latvia, an appeal to the 'Augstākā tiesa',
- in Lithuania, an appeal to the 'Lietuvos Aukščiausiasis Teismas',
- in Hungary, 'felülvizsgálati kérelem',
- in Malta, no further appeal lies to any other court; in the case of a maintenance judgment the 'Qorti ta' l-Appell' in accordance with the procedure laid down for appeal in the 'kodiċi ta' Organizzazzjoni u Procedura Ċivili – Kap. 12',
- in Austria, a 'Revisionsrekurs',
- in Poland, by an appeal in cassation to the 'Sąd Najwyższy',
- in Portugal, an appeal on a point of law,
- in Romania, a 'contestatie in anulare' or a 'revizuire',

- in Slovenia, an appeal to the 'Vrhovno sodišče Republike Slovenije',
- in Slovakia, the 'dovolanie',
- in Finland, an appeal to the 'korkein oikeus/högsta domstolen',
- in Sweden, an appeal to the 'Högsta domstolen',
- in the United Kingdom, a single further appeal on a point of law.

5. Names of parties to whom legal aid has been granted

The judgment/court settlement[15]) is enforceable in the Member State of origin (Articles 38 and 58 of the Regulation) against:

Name:

Done at . . . , date . . .

Signature and/or stamp . . .

ANNEX V
Certificate referred to in Articles 54 and 58 of the Regulation on judgments and court settlements

(English, inglés, anglais, inglese, . . .)

1. Member State of origin
2. Court or competent authority issuing the certificate
   2.1. Name
   2.2. Address
   2.3. Tel./fax/e-mail
3. Court which delivered the judgment/approved the court settlement[11])
   3.1. Type of court
   3.2. Place of court
4. Judgment/court settlement[12])
   4.1. Date
   4.2. Reference number
   4.3. The parties to the judgment/court settlement[13])
      4.3.1. Name(s) of plaintiff(s)
      4.3.2. Name(s) of defendant(s)
      4.3.3. Name(s) of other party(ies), if any
   4.4. Date of service of the document instituting the proceedings where judgment was given in default of appearance
   4.5. Text of the judgment/court settlement[14]) as annexed to this certificate

---

11) Delete as appropriate.
12) Delete as appropriate.
13) Delete as appropriate.
14) Delete as appropriate.

ANNEX VI
Certificate referred to in Article 57(4) of the Regulation on authentic instruments

(English, inglés, anglais, inglese . . . .)

1. Member State of origin
2. Competent authority issuing the certificate
   2.1. Name
   2.2. Address
   2.3. Tel./fax/e-mail
3. Authority which has given authenticity to the instrument
   3.1. Authority involved in the drawing up of the authentic instrument (if applicable)
      3.1.1. Name and designation of authority
      3.1.2. Place of authority
   3.2. Authority which has registered the authentic instrument (if applicable)
      3.2.1. Type of authority
      3.2.2. Place of authority
4. Authentic instrument
   4.1. Description of the instrument
   4.2. Date
      4.2.1. on which the instrument was drawn up
      4.2.2. if different: on which the instrument was registered

---

15) Delete as appropriate.

18

4.3. Reference number
4.4. Parties to the instrument
4.4.1. Name of the creditor
4.4.2. Name of the debtor
5. Text of the enforceable obligation as annexed to this certificate

The authentic instrument is enforceable against the debtor in the Member State of origin (Article 57(1) of the Regulation)

Done at . . ., date . . .

Signature and/or stamp . . .